FINANCIAL INSTITUTIONS AND SERVICES

THE LEHMAN BROTHERS BANKRUPTCY

ANALYSES

FINANCIAL INSTITUTIONS AND SERVICES

Additional books in this series can be found on Nova's website
under the Series tab.

Additional E-books in this series can be found on Nova's website
under the E-book tab.

BANKING AND BANKING DEVELOPMENTS

Additional books in this series can be found on Nova's website
under the Series tab.

Additional E-books in this series can be found on Nova's website
under the E-book tab.

FINANCIAL INSTITUTIONS AND SERVICES

THE LEHMAN BROTHERS BANKRUPTCY

ANALYSES

GARY E. WALKER
AND
LINDEL D. CLARKE
EDITORS

Nova Science Publishers, Inc.
New York

For permission to use material from this book please contact us:
Telephone 631-231-7269; Fax 631-231-8175
Web Site: http://www.novapublishers.com

Library of Congress Cataloging-in-Publication Data

ISBN: 978-1-62081-730-8

Published by Nova Science Publishers, Inc. + New York

CONTENTS

PREFACE

The bankruptcy filing of Lehman Brothers Holdings Inc. (LBHI) on September 15, 2008, was one of the signal events of the financial crisis. The disorderly and costly nature of the LBHI bankruptcy - the largest, and still ongoing, financial bankruptcy in U.S. history - contributed to the massive financial disruption of late 2008. This book examines how the government could have structured a resolution of Lehman under the orderly liquidation authority of Title II of the Dodd-Frank Wall Street Reform and Consumer Protection Act (Dodd-Frank) and how the outcome could have differed from the outcome under bankruptcy. Key figures surrounding this important financial event also provide their analysis.

Chapter 1 - In the United States, the insolvencies of depository institutions are not handled according to the procedures of the U.S. Bankruptcy Code. Instead, they and their subsidiaries are subject to a separate regime prescribed in federal law, called a conservatorship or receivership. Under this regime, the conservator or receiver, which generally is the Federal Deposit Insurance Corporation (FDIC), is provided substantial authority to deal with virtually every aspect of the insolvency. The failure of most other financial institutions within bank, thrift, and financial holding company umbrellas (including the holding companies themselves) generally are dealt with under the Bankruptcy Code.

Two clear lessons of the 2008 recession are that no financial institution, regardless of its size, complexity, or diversification, is invincible, and the failure of large or highly interconnected financial firms can negatively impact other companies and the financial system as a whole. Congress, as a result, is left with the question of how best to handle the failure of these so-called "systemically significant financial companies" (SSFCs). Some have proposed legislation that would impose a conservatorship/receivership regime, much like that for depository institutions, on insolvent financial institutions that are deemed systemically significant. Others have proposed resolving these institutions through a new chapter of the Bankruptcy Code.

In order to make a policy assessment concerning the appropriateness and likely effectiveness of these proposals, it is important to understand both the similarities and differences between insured depositories and other financial institutions large enough or interconnected enough to pose systemic risk to the U.S. economy upon failure, as well as the differences between the Bankruptcy Code and the FDIC's conservatorship/receivership authority.

To address these questions, other CRS reports analyze the FDIC's conservatorship and receivership powers over failed banks and thrifts and compare the FDIC's resolution regime with the Bankruptcy Code. This report seeks to build on those reports by examining the specific failures of two large financial institutions: IndyMac Bancorp, Inc. and Lehman Brothers Holdings Inc. (LBHI).

Chapter 2 - The bankruptcy filing of Lehman Brothers Holdings Inc. (Lehman or LBHI) on September 15, 2008, was one of the signal events of the financial crisis. The disorderly and costly nature of the LBHI bankruptcy—the largest, and still ongoing, financial bankruptcy in U.S. history—contributed to the massive financial disruption of late 2008. This paper examines how the government could have structured a resolution of Lehman under the orderly liquidation authority of Title II of the Dodd-Frank Wall Street Reform and Consumer Protection Act (Dodd-Frank Act) and how the outcome could have differed from the outcome under bankruptcy.

Chapter 3 – This is Statement of Thomas C. Baxter Jr. Hearing on "Too Big To Fail: Expectations and Impact of Extraordinary Government Intervention and the Role of Systemic Risk in the Financial Crisis".

Chapter 4 - This is Statement of Richard S. Fuld. Hearing on "Too Big To Fail: Expectations and Impact of Extraordinary Government Intervention and the Role of Systemic Risk in the Financial Crisis".

Chapter 5 - This is Statement of Harvey R. Miller. Hearing on "Too Big To Fail: Expectations and Impact of Extraordinary Government Intervention and the Role of Systemic Risk in the Financial Crisis".

Chapter 6 - This is Statement of Barry Zubrow. Hearing on "Too Big To Fail: Expectations and Impact of Extraordinary Government Intervention and the Role of Systemic Risk in the Financial Crisis".

Chapter 7 - This is Statement of Timothy F. Geithner. Hearing on "Public Policy Issues Raised by the Report of the Lehman Bankruptcy Examiner".

Chapter 8 - This is Statement of Federal Reserve Chairman Ben S. Bernanke. Hearing on "Public Policy Issues Raised by the Report of the Lehman Bankruptcy Examiner".

Chapter 9 - This is Testimony of SEC Chairman Mary L. Shapiro. Hearing on "Public Policy Issues Raised by the Report of the Lehman Bankruptcy Examiner".

Chapter 10 - This is Statement of Anton R. Valukas. Hearing on "Public Policy Issues Raised by the Report of the Lehman Bankruptcy Examiner".

Chapter 11 - This is Statement of Richard S. Fuld Jr. Hearing on "Public Policy Issues Raised by the Report of the Lehman Bankruptcy Examiner".

Chapter 12 - This is Statement of Thomas H. Cruikshank. Hearing on "Public Policy Issues Raised by the Report of the Lehman Bankruptcy Examiner".

Chapter 13 - This is Statement of William K. Black. Hearing on "Public Policy Issues Raised by the Report of the Lehman Bankruptcy Examiner".

Chapter 14 - This is Statement of Matthew Lee Hearing on "Public Policy Issues Raised by the Report of the Lehman Bankruptcy Examiner".

In: The Lehman Brothers Bankruptcy: Analyses
Editors: Gary E. Walker and Lindel D. Clarke
ISBN: 978-1-62081-730-8

Chapter 1

LEHMAN BROTHERS AND INDYMAC: COMPARING RESOLUTION REGIMES*

David H. Carpenter

SUMMARY

In the United States, the insolvencies of depository institutions are not handled according to the procedures of the U.S. Bankruptcy Code. Instead, they and their subsidiaries are subject to a separate regime prescribed in federal law, called a conservatorship or receivership. Under this regime, the conservator or receiver, which generally is the Federal Deposit Insurance Corporation (FDIC), is provided substantial authority to deal with virtually every aspect of the insolvency. The failure of most other financial institutions within bank, thrift, and financial holding company umbrellas (including the holding companies themselves) generally are dealt with under the Bankruptcy Code.

Two clear lessons of the 2008 recession are that no financial institution, regardless of its size, complexity, or diversification, is invincible, and the failure of large or highly interconnected financial firms can negatively impact other companies and the financial system as a whole. Congress, as a result, is left with the question of how best to handle the failure of these so-called "systemically significant financial companies" (SSFCs). Some have proposed legislation that would impose a conservatorship/receivership regime, much like that for depository institutions, on insolvent financial institutions that are deemed systemically significant. Others have proposed resolving these institutions through a new chapter of the Bankruptcy Code.

In order to make a policy assessment concerning the appropriateness and likely effectiveness of these proposals, it is important to understand both the similarities and differences between insured depositories and other financial institutions large enough or interconnected enough to pose systemic risk to the U.S. economy upon failure, as well as the

* This is an edited, reformatted and augmented version of the Congressional Research Service Publication, CRS Report for Congress R40928, dated October 12, 2009.

differences between the Bankruptcy Code and the FDIC's conservatorship/receivership authority.

To address these questions, other CRS reports analyze the FDIC's conservatorship and receivership powers over failed banks and thrifts and compare the FDIC's resolution regime with the Bankruptcy Code. This report seeks to build on those reports by examining the specific failures of two large financial institutions: IndyMac Bancorp, Inc. and Lehman Brothers Holdings Inc. (LBHI).

*It should be noted that the resolutions of these two companies and their subsidiaries hadn't been completed at the time this report was written. At times, there are gaps in the information provided in this report, either as a result of the dearth of information publicly available or the opaqueness of that which is available. For example, **Table 2** in this report generally does not include information regarding the primary business activities of LBHI's foreign subsidiaries, but certain foreign subsidiaries were included in the table to provide some perspective as to the breadth of LBHI's global reach, as well as in the financial services its subsidiaries provided. While this report is not an exhaustive analysis of the resolution of these two companies, in conjunction with our other reports, it does attempt to enhance the debate regarding how to structure the insolvency regimes for financial institutions.*

INTRODUCTION

In the United States, the insolvencies of depository institutions (i.e., banks and thrifts with deposits insured by the Federal Deposit Insurance Corporation (FDIC)) are not handled according to the procedures of the U.S. Bankruptcy Code.[1] Instead, they and their subsidiaries are subject to a separate regime prescribed in federal law, called a conservatorship or receivership.[2] Under this regime, the conservator or receiver, which generally is the FDIC, is provided substantial authority to deal with virtually every aspect of the insolvency. The failure of most other financial institutions within bank, thrift, and financial holding company umbrellas (including the holding companies themselves) generally are dealt with under the Bankruptcy Code.[3]

Two clear lessons of the 2008 recession are that no financial institution, regardless of its size, complexity, or diversification, is invincible, and the failure of large or highly interconnected financial firms can negatively impact other companies and the financial system as a whole. Congress, as a result, is left with the question of how best to handle the failure of these so-called "systemically significant financial companies" (SSFCs). In March of 2009, Treasury Secretary Timothy Geithner proposed legislation that would impose a conservatorship/receivership regime, much like that for depository institutions, on insolvent financial institutions that are deemed systemically significant.[4] Others have proposed resolving these institutions through a new chapter of the Bankruptcy Code. Representative Spencer Bachus, Ranking Member of the Financial Services Committee, offers such a proposal in H.R. 3310, the Consumer Protection and Regulatory Enhancement Act of 2009.

In order to analyze and assess these proposals, it is helpful to understand both the similarities and differences between insured depositories and other financial institutions large enough or interconnected enough to pose systemic risk to the U.S. economy upon failure, as well as the differences between the Bankruptcy Code and the FDIC's conservatorship/ receivership authority.

To address these issues, other CRS reports analyze the FDIC's conservatorship and receivership powers over failed banks and thrifts[5] and compare the FDIC's resolution regime with the Bankruptcy Code.[6] This report seeks to build on those reports by examining the specific failures of two large financial institutions: IndyMac Bancorp, Inc. and Lehman Brothers Holdings Inc. (LBHI).

BANKRUPTCY CODE VS. INSURED DEPOSITORY RESOLUTION

As previously mentioned, another CRS report (CRS Report R40530, *Insolvency of Systemically Significant Financial Companies: Bankruptcy vs. Conservatorship/Receivership*, by David H. Carpenter)[7] provides a more in-depth analysis of the differences between the Bankruptcy Code and the conservatorship/receivership regimes for banks and thrifts. However, a brief summary of that report's conclusions may provide some necessary background for the understanding of the resolution process of IndyMac and Lehman Brothers.

In sum, the U.S. insolvency regime for banks and thrifts is designed to provide the FDIC the ability to intervene early and resolve financially troubled banks and thrifts quickly. The FDIC is granted vast powers to make unilateral decisions, grounded in statutorily defined guidance, in an administrative setting with only limited judicial review, and where generally only ex post damages are available. The focus is primarily on protecting depositors and the FDIC's Deposit Insurance Fund, and little emphasis is placed on attempting to rehabilitate insolvent institutions.[8]

The Bankruptcy Code, on the other hand, is designed to give creditors and management in reorganizations a say in major decisions of bankruptcy proceedings. All bankruptcy proceedings are judicial in nature. Most decisions are reviewable by a higher court, and in some situations, decisions receive ex ante review. While the majority of corporate bankruptcies are liquidations, the Code puts much greater emphasis on rehabilitating default firms than the depository counterpart. As a result, complex bankruptcies can take years to complete.[9]

INDYMAC

IndyMac Bancorp, Inc. (IndyMac Bancorp) was a thrift holding company, which was regulated on a consolidated basis by the Office of Thrift Supervision (OTS).[10] It held four subsidiaries, including IndyMac Bank, F.S.B. (IndyMac Bank), a federally chartered thrift. (**Table I** provides a list of IndyMac Bancorp's subsidiaries, their places of incorporation, their primary business activities, and their primary regulators, if applicable, as of the company's 2007 10-K filing with the SEC. Table I also includes each subsidiary's current status.)

IndyMac Bank was largely engaged in residential mortgage activities. According to its 2007 10-K filing, it was the seventh largest thrift in the U.S.; the eighth largest mortgage servicer; and the ninth largest originator of residential mortgages.[11] By the end of March

2008, the thrift held a total of more than $30 billion in assets and more than $19 billion in deposits, the majority of which were FDIC-insured.[12]

On Friday, July 11, 2008, IndyMac Bank was closed by the OTS, and the FDIC was appointed its conservator (and, subsequently, receiver)[13] as a result of losses on mortgage-related assets and runs by depositors.[14] When an insured bank or thrift becomes insolvent, the institution's charterer,[15] its primary federal regulator, or the FDIC is authorized to act *ex parte* (i.e., without notice or a hearing) to seize the institution and its assets and install the FDIC as conservator or receiver.[16] The basic difference between a conservatorship and a receivership is that a conservatorship involves operating the institution as a going concern to protect its assets until it stabilizes or is closed and a receiver appointed.[17]A receiver is charged with liquidating the institution and winding up its affairs.

The FDIC transferred most of IndyMac Bank's assets, including its FDIC-insured deposits, to a newly chartered thrift, IndyMac Federal Bank, F.S.B. (IndyMac Federal).[18] On Monday, July 14, 2008, IndyMac Federal opened, under FDIC control as conservator, offering virtually all services that had been provided by IndyMac Bank prior to the thrift's closure three days before. Individuals were able to access, and if desired, withdraw all of their FDIC-insured deposits (at that time, up to $100,000). Additionally, individuals were able to immediately access 50% of all uninsured deposits based on the FDIC's preliminary assessment of returns from winding down the thrift.[19]

IndyMac Bank's failure also brought down the holding company (IndyMac Bancorp, Inc.), which filed a petition for a Chapter 7 bankruptcy liquidation on July 31, 2008.[20]

OneWest Bank, FSB (OneWest Bank) acquired most of IndyMac Federal's assets and all of its deposits in a deal that was finalized on March 19, 2009. As part of this deal, the FDIC agreed to guarantee against potential losses on certain loans acquired from IndyMac Federal.[21] Upon the acquisition, OneWest Bank had no immediate plans to close any of the former IndyMac Federal branches. OneWest Bank also offered positions to many of IndyMac Federal's former employees.[22] At the same time as the acquisition, the OTS appointed the FDIC as receiver of IndyMac Federal.[23]

Litigation after IndyMac's Failure

The conservatorship/receivership regime for insured-depositories is almost entirely administrative in nature with only limited judicial appeal. Judicialreview of the FDIC's actions as conservator or receiver is limited to a handful of situations. For instance, disputes about claims against a receiver are to be resolved first by the FDIC in accordance with its regulations, subject to judicial review under the Administrative Procedure Act.[35] Also, the FDIC has the power to repudiate certain contracts entered into by the institution, under certain conditions.[36] The statute limits damages to "actual direct compensatory damages."[37] Even when judicial review is allowed, the only remedy generally available is damages. In other words, aggrieved parties usually cannot stop or reverse FDIC decisions. Conflicts as to the amount of "actual direct compensatory damages" may be settled in court.[38]

A number of judicial actions have been raised against the FDIC as conservator or receiver of IndyMac Bank and IndyMac Federal. Many of these actions allege violations of the Truth in Lending Act, violations of the Real Estate Settlement Procedures Act, fraud, and other claims stemming from individual mortgages in foreclosure. However, these actions appear to have been largely dismissed or stayed until the conservatorship/receivership administrative proceedings have been exhausted.[39]

IndyMac Loan Modification Program

In August 2008, the FDIC, as conservator over IndyMac Federal, established a loan modification program for borrowers of mortgages—who were having difficulty meeting their payment obligations—either owned or serviced by IndyMac Federal. The FDIC set eligibility requirements based on both borrower-characteristics (e.g., debt-to-income thresholds) and mortgage-characteristics (e.g., only primary residence mortgages). According to FDIC Chairman Sheila Bair, approximately 13,000 mortgages were modified while IndyMac Federal was under conservatorship.[40] Additionally, OneWest agreed to continue the loan modification program as part of its acquisition agreement.[41]

Table 1. IndyMac Bancorp Subsidiaries: Pre- and Post-Bankruptcy

Company Name	Incorporation	U.S. Regulator	Primary Business Activities	Current Status
IndyMac Bank, F.S.B.	Federally chartered, but based in Pasedena, California	OTS	Banking and residential mortgages[24]	Closed by OTS, FDIC appointed conservator and then receiver; assets and liabilities largely transferred to IndyMac Federal;[25] subsequently, IndyMac Federal largely acquired by OneWest Bank[26]
IndyMac Intermediate Holdings, Inc.	Delaware	[27]	Wholly owned subsidiary of IndyMac Bancorp[28]	Unclear
Financial Freedom Senior Funding Corporation	Delaware	State regulated	Reverse mortgages[29]	Assets and liabilities largely transferred to IndyMac Federal;[30] subsequently, largely acquired by OneWest Bank
IndyMac Retained Assets, Inc.	Delaware	[31]	Mortgage-backed securities and mortgage servicing[32]	Assets and liabilities largely transferred to IndyMac Federal;[33] Largely acquired by OneWest Bank[34]

Source: Information in the Table comes from various sources, including SEC and bankruptcy filings.

The FDIC was able to establish and implement the loan modification program as a result of the authority granted to it as conservator. The FDIC, acting in its traditional role as regulator, likely would not have wielded so much control over IndyMac's (or any other insured depository institution's) mortgages outside of its conservatorship/receivership powers.

LEHMAN BROTHERS HOLDINGS INC.

LBHI Structure and Activities

Before filing a Chapter 11 bankruptcy petition on September 15, 2008, Lehman Brothers Holdings Inc. (LBHI) was a global financial institution providing "services in equity and fixed income sales, trading and research, investment banking, asset management, private investment management and private equity" in 40 different countries.[42] It was the fourth largest U.S. investment bank with $639 billion in assets.[43] The company was structured as a financial conglomerate with numerous subsidiaries and affiliates incorporated across the globe.[44] LBHI, incorporated in Delaware and headquartered in New York, was voluntarily regulated on a consolidated basis by the Securities and Exchange Commission (SEC) as part of the now defunct Consolidated Supervised Entity program.[45] LBHI employed close to 30,000 people as of the end of November 2007. LBHI management remains in control of the company as debtor-in-possession, subject to supervision of the bankruptcy court. After the holding company filed for bankruptcy, at least 19 of LBHI's subsidiaries petitioned for Chapter 11 protection (collectively, LBHI Chapter 11 debtors). These cases have been consolidated, for procedural purposes.[46] The docket for these cases consists of more than 5,500 documents as a result of more than 60,000 claims against the companies.[47]

However, not all of LBHI's subsidiaries and affiliates can be debtors under Chapter 11 of the U.S. Bankruptcy Code (the Code).[48] Consequently, various pieces of the Lehman family are subject to different resolution proceedings in this country and abroad. For instance, Lehman Brothers Inc. is subject to a Securities Investor Protection Act (SIPA) insolvency proceeding—a special resolution proceeding for SEC-registered broker-dealers.[49] Other companies under the LBHI umbrella are subject to insolvency regimes in other countries. To help coordinate these multi-nation proceedings, administrators from the U.S., Australia, Germany, Hong Kong, the Netherlands, and Singapore have signed on to a *nonbinding* insolvency proceeding protocol.[50] The holding of assets in multiple countries that are subject to claims by creditors incorporated in different countries and that are to be distributed in accordance with varying insolvency rules from multiple sovereign states has led to some confusion, conflict, and litigation.[51] Additionally, some subsidiaries, thus far, have avoided insolvency proceedings altogether.[52] Others have been acquired, in whole or (more often) in part, by other corporations.

Table 2 provides a list of many of the company's important subsidiaries, their places of incorporation, their primary business activities, and their primary U.S. regulators, if applicable, as of the company's 10-K filing (for fiscal year ending November 30, 2007) with the SEC. **Table 2** also includes each company's current status. **Table 3** at the end of this report is a more complete list of LBHI's subsidiaries and affiliates from the same 10-K filing.

This report also discusses some of the important developments since LBHI filed for bankruptcy, including acquisitions by Barclays Capital Inc. (Barclays) and Nomura Holdings Inc. (Nomura),[53] the termination and netting of hundreds of thousands of Lehman's derivative contracts, as well as relevant provisions of the U.S. Bankruptcy Code that guided these major developments.

Table 2. LBHI Subsidiaries and Affiliates: Pre- and Post- Bankruptcy

Company Name	Incorporation	U.S. Regulator	Primary Business Activities	Current Status
Lehman Brothers Inc.	Delaware	SEC; CFTC (Commodity Futures Trading ommission); SIPC (Securities Investor Protection Corporation); Ontario Securities Commission of Canada	SEC registered broker-dealer; SEC registered investment adviser; CFTC registered futures commission merchants	Subject to SIPC bankruptcy proceeding (U.S.); assets may have been largely either sold to Barclays or transferred to Neuberger Berman Group LC[54]
Neuberger Berman, LLC	Delaware	SEC; SIPC	SEC registered broker-dealer; SEC registered investment adviser; CFTC registered futures commission merchants; CFTC registered commodity pool operator and/or commodity trading advisers	Now Neuberger Berman Group LLC after an employee buyout of majority ownership; LBHI retains remaining ownership interest[55]
Neuberger Berman Management Inc.	New York	SEC	SEC registered broker-dealer; SEC registered investment adviser	Now Neuberger Berman Management LLC; remains a subsidiary of Neuberger Berman, LLC[56]
Lehman Brothers OTC Derivatives Inc.	Delaware	SEC	SEC registered over-the-counter (OTC) derivatives dealer	Voluntary Ch. 11 Bankruptcy (U.S.)[57]
Lehman Brothers Financial Products Inc.	Delaware	[58]	Financial services	Assets may have been largely acquired by either Barclays or Neuberger Berman Group LLC; remainder of company subject to voluntary Ch. 11 bankruptcy (U.S.)[59]
Lehman Brothers Derivative Products Inc.	Delaware	[60]	Derivatives	Assets may have been largely acquired by either Barclays or Neuberger Berman Group LLC; remainder of company subject to voluntary Ch. 11 bankruptcy (U.S.)[61]
Lehman Brothers Special Financing Inc.	Delaware	[62]	Financial services	Assets may have been largely acquired by either Barclays or Neuberger Berman Group LLC; remainder of company subject to voluntary Ch. 11 bankruptcy (U.S.)[63]

Table 2. (Continued)

Company Name	Incorporation	U.S. Regulator	Primary Business Activities	Current Status
Lehman Commercial Paper Inc.	New York	[64]	Financial services	Assets may have been largely acquired by either Barclays or Neuberger Berman Group LLC; remainder of company subject to voluntary Ch. 11 bankruptcy (U.S.)[65]
Lehman Brothers Asset Management Inc.	Delaware	SEC; CFTC	SEC registered investment adviser; CFTC registered commodity pool operator and/or commodity trading advisers	Assets may have been largely acquired by either Barclays or Neuberger Berman Group LLC
Lehman Brothers Bancorp, Inc.	Delaware	OTS	Bank holding company (holding only thrifts and industrial loan corporations)	Remained an active bank holding company as of October 13, 2009[66]
Lehman Brothers Bank, FSB	Delaware	OTS; FDIC	Federally chartered savings bank (lending, real estate financing, commercial and residential mortgage-backed securities)	Changed its name to Aurora Bank FSB on April 27, 2009; currently operative[67]
Lehman Brothers Commercial Bank	Utah	FDIC; Utah Commissioner of Financial Institutions	Industrial loan company	Changed its name to Wood-lands Commercial Bank on February 6, 2009;currently operative[68]
Lehman Brothers Trust Company N.A.	New York	OCC	National trust bank	Neuberger Berman Group LLC announced on July 23, 2009 it will acquire the trust company[69]
Lehman Brothers Trust Company of Delaware	Delaware	State Bank Commissioner of the State of Delaware	Non-depository limited purpose Delaware trust company	Neuberger Berman Group LLC announced on July 23, 2009 it will acquire the trust company[70]
Lehman Brothers Commodity Services Inc.	Delaware	Federal Energy Regulatory Commission (FERC)	FERC-authorized power marketer (sells wholesale physical power)	Sold to EDF Trading North America Management LLC and EDF Trading North America Inc.[71]
Eagle Energy Partners I, L.P.	Texas	FERC	Energy marketing and services company	Sold to EDF Trading North America Management LLC and EDF Trading North America Inc.[72]
Lehman Brothers Alternative Investment Management LLC	Delaware	N/A	Hedge fund manager	Changed name to NB Investment Management LLC[73]
Congress Life Insurance	Most U.S. States	Multiple State Insurance Departments	Insurance	Appears to remain operative, at least in some states[74]
Lehman Brothers International (Europe)	U.K. (United Kingdom)	N/A[75]	Investment bank	Resolution administration (U.K.)[76]

Company Name	Incorporation	U.S. Regulator	Primary Business Activities	Current Status
Lehman Brothers Finance S.A.	Switzerland	N/A[77]	Equity derivatives	Ch. 15 bankruptcy proceeding (U.S.); primary liquidation proceeding under the supervision of the Swiss Federal Banking Commission Switzerland)[78]
Lehman Brothers Treasury Co. B.V.	Netherlands	N/A	Derivatives[79]	Bankruptcy proceeding (Netherlands)[80]
Lehman Brothers Bankhaus AG	Germany	N/A[81]	German bank (lending, real estate financing, commercial and residential mortgage-backed securities; German Depositors Protection Fund participant)	Insolvency proceeding (Germany)[82]
MNG Securities	Turkey	N/A	Equity securities brokerage firm[83]	Unclear
Lehman Brothers Japan	Japan	N/A[84]	Investment banking and securities[85]	Bankruptcy proceeding (Japan)[86]; apparently largely acquired by Nomura[87]
Lehman Brothers Investments Pte. Ltd.	Singapore	N/A	Foreign financial activities	Voluntary creditor's liquidation(Singapore)[88]; apparently largely acquired by Nomura[89]
Sail Investor Pte. Ltd.	Singapore	N/A	Foreign financial activities	Voluntary creditor's liquidation (Singapore)[90]
Lehman Brothers Asia Pacific (Singapore) Pte. Ltd.	Singapore	N/A	Foreign financial activities	Voluntary creditor's liquidation (Singapore)[91]
Lehman Brothers Asia Holdings Limited	Hong Kong	N/A	Foreign financial activities	Liquidation (Hong Kong)[92]; apparently largely acquired by Nomura[93]
Lehman Brothers Asia Limited	Hong Kong	N/A	Foreign financial activities	Liquidation (Hong Kong)[94]
Lehman Brothers Futures Asia Limited	Hong Kong	N/A	Foreign financial activities	Liquidation (Hong Kong)[95]
Lehman Brothers Securities Asia Limited	Hong Kong	N/A	Foreign financial activities	Liquidation (Hong Kong)[96]
Lehman Brothers Asia Capital Company	Hong Kong	N/A	Foreign financial activities	Liquidation (Hong Kong)[97]
Lehman Brothers Commercial Corporation Asia Limited	Hong Kong	N/A	Foreign financial activities	Liquidation (Hong Kong)[98]; apparently largely acquired by Nomura[99]

Table 2. (Continued)

Company Name	Incorporation	U.S. Regulator	Primary Business Activities	Current Status
Lehman Brothers Australia Holdings Pty Limited	Australia	N/A	Foreign financial activities	Resolution administrators appointed (Australia)[100]; apparently largely acquired by Nomura[101]
Lehman Brothers Australia Limited	Australia	N/A	Foreign financial activities	Resolution administrators appointed (Australia)[102]; apparently largely acquired by Nomura[103]
Lehman Brothers Australia Granica Pty. Limited	Australia	N/A	Foreign financial activities	Resolution administrators appointed (Australia)[104]; apparently largely acquired by Nomura[105]

Source: Information in the Table comes from various sources, including SEC and bankruptcy filings.

Developments since LBHI's Bankruptcy Petition

Acquisition by Barclays

Barclays reportedly was interested in acquiring Lehman—or at least parts of Lehman—before LBHI filed for bankruptcy.[106] However, a deal could not be reached under the circumstances.[107]

Instead, Barclays acquired "Lehman Brothers' fixed income and equity sales, trading and research; prime services; investment banking; principal investing; and private investment management businesses in North America" and its Manhattan headquarters (valued at a minimum of $1 billion) [108] from the bankruptcy estate.[109] The two companies entered into a purchase agreement on September 16, 2008,[110] which ultimately was approved by Judge James Peck, a federal bankruptcy judge, in an order dated September 20, 2008. After a number of Lehman's creditors appealed the sale order, the order was affirmed by a U.S. district court on March 13, 2009.[111] Since the original document was signed, Barclays and LBHI have agreed to a number of amendments to the original terms.[112] A number of disputes over the specific terms of the agreement also have arisen.[113]

Two features of the Bankruptcy Code likely made the Lehman acquisition more appealing post-bankruptcy petition than it otherwise would have been outside of bankruptcy. The first is the debtor-in-possession (DIP) financing provisions of 11 U.S.C. § 364, and the second is the ability to purchase debtor assets "free and clear" of liabilities, as provided by 11 U.S.C. § 363.

DIP financing to allows a bankruptcy debtor to continue operations while it progresses through the bankruptcy process, which may help the company avoid the need for liquidation. Under the Bankruptcy Code, the debtor may seek to have DIP financing loans be accorded senior priority over debts acquired prior to the bankruptcy petition.[114] Issuing such debt outside of bankruptcy generally is not possible because loan agreements often include clauses limiting or prohibiting the borrowing company from subsequently incurring debt senior to that being provided.[115]

Barclays agreed to provide Lehman $500 million in DIP financing as part of its purchase agreement,[116] which was conditioned on being "free and clear" of all but a handful of voluntarily assumed liens and liabilities.[117] The liabilities voluntarily assumed by Barclays include certain real property leases, certain repurchase agreements, and various benefits of retained employees.[118] (Barclays announced that it offered employment to 10,000+ former Lehman employees.[119]) Disputes have arisen over the details of these assumed liabilities.[120]

Acquisition by Nomura

The Tokyo-based investment bank, Nomura, has regional headquarters in New York, London, and Hong Kong, and conducts business in approximately 30 different countries.[121] In October 2008, the company announced "the acquisition of Lehman Brothers' franchise in the Asia Pacific region, including Japan and Australia"; the purchase of Lehman Brothers' "European and Middle Eastern equities and investment banking operations"; and the acquisition of Lehman Brothers' "service platform in India[, including] Lehman Brothers Services India Private Limited, Lehman Brothers Financial Services (India) Private Limited, Lehman Brothers Structured Finance Services Private Limited."[122] Nomura also acquired around 8,000 former Lehman employees. The company expected the acquisition to cost approximately $2 billion.[123]

"Safe-Harbor Protections" of Qualified Financial Contracts

A "stay" is a power by which creditors are, at least temporarily, prevented from pursuing their claims against a default entity. As one commentator explains:

> Stays permit the resolution authority [the time to] collect and validate claims, to determine the best way to dispose of assets in an orderly, non-fire-sale manner, and to treat all like-priority creditors equally. Stays prevent creditor runs and keep contracts in force—the counter party is bound by the contract; claims on the insolvent firm remain pending; and collateral may usually not be liquidated. This facilitates the coordination of creditor claims.[124]

The stay is an important tool under the U.S. Bankruptcy Code, especially for reorganizations. The Code establishes a general stay automatically upon petitioning for bankruptcy.[125] However, the Code provides a number of exceptions to the automatic stay, including for many securities contracts, commodity contracts, forward contracts, repurchase agreements, swap agreements, and netting arrangements (collectively, "qualified financial contracts").[126] It is especially common for financial institutions to be parties to these contractual arrangements, making special protections provided for them all the more important in case of a financial institution's insolvency.

Additionally, the Bankruptcy Code provides trustees the authority to avoid, i.e. claw-back or reverse, certain transfers (subject to certain limitations[127]) made by debtors if five conditions are met: (1) the transfer was made "to or for the benefit of a creditor"; (2) the transfer was for a debt owed before the transfer; (3) the transfer "was made while the debtor was insolvent"; (4) the transfer occurred "on or within 90 days" of the petition or within one year if the transfer was made to an "insider"[128]; and (5) the creditor received more from the transfer than it would have through bankruptcy proceedings.[129] The purpose of this avoidance power is to facilitate the equitable distribution of the bankruptcy estate's assets among credit classes and to limit the "race to the courthouse" problem.[130] Most qualified financial contracts are exempted from the trustees' general avoidance power.[131]

These so-called "safe-harbor protections" were provided, in part, to reduce the disruption to international financial markets caused by a financial firm's bankruptcy.[132] They have the effect of allowing counterparties to these contracts to terminate or liquidate (the collateral[133] held against) the contracts and net or setoff each party's positions even after the default firm has filed a bankruptcy petition.[134] These legal constructs are explained by two prominent economists this way:

> Close-out and netting consist of two separate but related rights, often combined in a single contract: 1) the right of a counterparty to unilaterally terminate contracts under specified conditions (close-out), and 2) the right to offset amounts due at termination of individual contracts between the same counterparties when determining the final obligation [(netting)].[135]

Almost all qualified financial contracts have close-out and netting provisions that are triggered by an act of default, including filing for bankruptcy. These provisions have the potential to push ailing firms into insolvency and to deplete their assets.[136]

The LBHI Chapter 11 debtors estimated that they were a party to around 930,000 qualified financial contracts prior to the bankruptcy petition, of which approximately 733,000 had been terminated as of November 13, 2008.[137] Counterparties to the many of these 700,000+ contracts seem to have at least attempted to terminate the contracts within a few days of LBHI's bankruptcy.[138] However, problems appear to have arisen in the close-out and netting process, which led the International Swaps and Derivatives Association (ISDA), a major trade association representing derivatives participants, to develop a Lehman derivatives protocol to help rectify these problems.[139] Those counterparties that held collateral against their contracts were able to terminate the contracts and keep the collateral as settlement.[140] Qualified financial contracts that were not collateralized could be closed-out and positions could be netted, but the counterparties, otherwise, were not able to collect what they were owed.[141] These disruptions likely alleviated the strain that settling 700,000 contracts nearly simultaneously could have had on the derivatives market, as hundreds of counterparties sought replacement contracts/ counterparties, and the LBHI bankruptcy estate, as collateral was seized outside of the automatic stay's protection.[142]

The LBHI debtors alleged that, in many cases, the counterparties to the 200,000 or so qualified financial contracts that had not been terminated by mid-November were not doing so because they owed the debtors money (i.e. the LBHI Chapter 11 debtors were "in-the-money" on these contracts). The LBHI Chapter 11 debtors also claimed that, in other instances, counterparties were not making the payments required by the non-terminated contracts. As a result, the LBHI debtors sought approval from the bankruptcy court to assign the remaining qualified financial contracts to third parties in order to be able to collect value from the contracts.[143] The court received a number of objections to this motion from creditors. On December 16, 2008, the court issued its first ruling on the matter, granting the debtors' motion, in part, while making certain modifications to account for some of the creditors' objections.[144] Multiple other motions were raised and orders were issued in an attempt to settle disputes arising from the assumption of these qualified financial contracts.[145]

Table 3. List of LBHI Subsidiaries as of November 30, 2007

Pursuant to Item 601(b)(21)(ii) of Regulation S-K, subsidiaries of the Registrant have been omitted which, considered in the aggregate as a single subsidiary, would not have constituted a significant subsidiary (as defined in Rule 1-02(w) of Regulation S-X) as of November 30, 2007. Indentations indicate parent-subsidiary relationships.

Tier	Name	Jurisdiction of Organization
0	Lehman Brothers Holdings Inc.	Delaware
1	Appalachian Asset Management Corp.	Delaware
2	Lehman Risk Services (Bermuda) Ltd.	Bermuda
1	ARS Holdings I LLC	Delaware
1	Banque Lehman Brothers S.A.	France
1	LB 745 LLC	Delaware
1	LB 745 Leaseco I LLC	Delaware
1	LBAC Holdings I Inc.	Delaware
2	Lehman Brothers Asia Capital Company	Hong Kong
1	LBCCA Holdings I LLC	Delaware
2	Falcon Holdings I LLC	Delaware
3	Falcon Holdings II Inc.	Delaware
4	CIMT Limited	Cayman Islands
5	TMIC Limited	Cayman Islands
6	MICT Limited	Cayman Islands
7	Falcon Investor I-X Inc.	Cayman Islands
8	Global Thai Property Fund	Thailand
2	Lehman Brothers Asia Capital Company	Hong Kong
2	Lehman Brothers Commercial Corporation Asia Limited	Hong Kong
2	Revival Holdings Limited	Cayman Islands
3	Global Korea Investments Ltd.	Cayman Islands
4	SOGKI Development Inc.	Cayman Islands
5	GKI Korea Development Limited	Malaysia
6	Maewha K-STARS Ltd.	Republic of Korea
3	Sunrise Finance Co., Ltd.	Japan
1	LBCCA Holdings II LLC	Delaware
2	Falcon Holdings I LLC	Delaware
3	Falcon Holdings II Inc.	Delaware
4	CIMT Limited	Cayman Islands
5	TMIC Limited	Cayman Islands
6	MICT Limited	Cayman Islands
7	Falcon Investor I-X Inc.	Cayman Islands
8	Global Thai Property Fund	Thailand
2	Lehman Brothers Commercial Corporation Asia Limited	Hong Kong
2	Revival Holdings Limited	Cayman Islands
3	Global Korea Investments Ltd.	Cayman Islands
4	SOGKI Development Inc.	Cayman Islands
5	GKI Korea Development Limited	Malaysia
6	Maewha K-STARS Ltd.	Republic of Korea
3	Sunrise Finance Co., Ltd.	Japan

Table 3. (Continued)

Tier	Name	Jurisdiction of Organization
1	LB Delta Funding	Cayman Islands
2	LB Delta (Cayman) No 1 Ltd.	Cayman Islands
1	LBHK Funding (Cayman) No. 4 Ltd.	Cayman Islands
2	LBHK Funding (Cayman) No. 1 Ltd.	Cayman Islands
1	LB Russia Holdings LLC	Delaware
2	LB Russia Holdings Inc.	Delaware
3	OOO Lehman Brothers	Russia
1	Lehman ALI Inc.	Delaware
2	314 Commonwealth Ave. Inc.	Delaware
3	Alnwick Investments (UK) Ltd.	United Kingdom
3	Bamburgh Investments (UK) Ltd.	United Kingdom
4	Gainsborough Investments BV	The Netherlands
5	Kenilworth Investments 1 Ltd.	Cayman Islands
3	Kenilworth Investments 2 Ltd.	Cayman Islands
3	Brasstown LLC	Delaware
4	Brasstown Mansfield I SCA	Luxembourg
2	Lehman Capital Investments 2 Ltd.	Cayman Islands
2	Property Asset Management Inc.	Delaware
3	L.B.C. YK	Japan
3	LB Capital Investments 2 Ltd.	Cayman Islands
3	LBS Holdings SARL	Luxembourg
3	Lehman Brothers Global Investments LLC	Delaware
4	New Century Finance Co., LTD.	Japan
5	Lehman Brothers Commercial Mortgage K.K.	Japan
3	Lehman Brothers Hy Opportunities Korea Inc.	Republic of Korea
3	Lehman Brothers P.A. LLC	Delaware
1	Lehman Brothers AIM Holding LLC	Delaware
2	Lehman Brothers Alternative Investment Management LLC	Delaware
1	Lehman Brothers Asset Management Inc.	Delaware
1	Lehman Brothers Asset Management, LLC	Delaware
1	Lehman Brothers Asia Pacific (Singapore) PTE. Ltd.	Singapore
2	Lehman Brothers Asia Holdings Limited	Hong Kong
3	Lehman Brothers Equity Finance (Cayman) Limited	Cayman Islands
3	Lehman Brothers Securities N.V.	The Netherlands
2	Lehman Brothers Pacific Holdings Pte. Ltd.	Singapore
3	Lehman Brothers Asia Limited	Hong Kong
3	Lehman Brothers Futures Asia Limited	Hong Kong
3	Lehman Brothers Securities Asia Limited	Hong Kong
3	Lehman Brothers Investments PTE Ltd.	Singapore
4	Lehman Brothers Holdings Japan Inc.	Japan
5	Lehman Brothers Japan Inc.	Japan
4	Lehman Brothers Capital Private Limited	India
4	Lehman Brothers Securities Private Limited	India
3	Lehman Brothers Singapore PTE Ltd.	Singapore
3	SAIL Investor Pte Ltd.	Singapore

Tier	Name	Jurisdiction of Organization
1	Lehman Brothers Australia Holdings PTY Limited.	Australia
2	Lehman Brothers Australia Granica PTY Limited	Australia
3	Lehman Brothers Australia Limited	Australia
4	LB Asset Management Ltd.	Australia
1	Lehman Brothers Bancorp Inc.	Delaware
2	Lehman Brothers Commercial Bank	Utah
2	Lehman Brothers Bank, FSB	United States
3	Aurora Loan Services LLC	Delaware
2	Lehman Brothers Trust Company, National Association	United States
2	Lehman Brothers Trust Company of Delaware	Delaware
2	Lehman Brothers Bancorp UK Holdings Limited	United Kingdom
3	MABLE Commercial Funding Limited	United Kingdom
4	ELQ Holdings B.V.	The Netherlands
5	ELQ Hypothekan N.V.	The Netherlands
4	Resetfan Limited	United Kingdom
5	Capstone Mortgage Services Ltd.	United Kingdom
5	Southern Pacific Mortgage Limited	United Kingdom
5	Preferred Holdings Limited	United Kingdom
6	Preferred Group Limited	United Kingdom
7	Preferred Mortgages Limited	United Kingdom
4	Storm Funding Ltd.	United Kingdom
1	Lehman (Cayman Islands) Ltd.	Cayman Islands
1	Lehman Brothers Co-Investment Associates LLC	Delaware
1	Lehman Brothers Inc.	Delaware
2	Lehman Brothers Derivative Products Inc.	Delaware
2	Lehman Brothers Financial Products Inc.	Delaware
2	Lehman Brothers Investment Holding Company Inc.	Delaware
3	LB India Holdings Mauritius I Limited	Mauritius
3	LB India Holdings Mauritius II Limited	Mauritius
2	Lehman Brothers Securities Taiwan Limited	Taiwan
2	Lehman Brothers Special Financing Inc.	Delaware
3	LB3 GmbH	Germany
3	Lehman Brothers Commodity Services Inc.	Delaware
4	Eagle Energy Management, LLC	Delaware
5	Eagle Energy Partners I, L.P.	Texas
2	Lehman Commercial Paper Inc.	New York
3	Bromley LLC	Delaware
3	East Dover Limited.	Ireland
3	Ivanhoe Lane Pty Limited	Australia
4	Serafino Investments Pty Limited	Australia
3	LCPI Properties Inc.	New Jersey
4	LW LP Inc.	Delaware
3	M&L Debt Investments Holdings Pty Limited	Australia
4	M&L Debt Investments Pty Limited	Australia
3	Merit, LLC	Delaware
3	Pindar Pty Ltd.	Australia

Table 3. (Continued)

Tier	Name	Jurisdiction of Organization
4	Long Point Funding Pty Ltd.	Australia
2	LB I Group Inc.	Delaware
3	GRA Finance Corporation Ltd.	Mauritius
3	LB-NL Holdings I Inc.	Delaware
4	LB-NL Holdings L.P.	Delaware
5	LB-NL U.S. Investor Inc.	Delaware
6	NL Funding, L.P	Delaware
1	Lehman Brothers (Luxembourg) S.A.	Luxembourg
1	Lehman Brothers OTC Derivatives Inc.	Delaware
1	Lehman Brothers Private Equity Advisers L.L.C.	Delaware
1	Lehman Brothers Private Funds Investment Company GP, LLC	Delaware
2	Lehman Brothers Private Fund Advisers LP	Delaware
2	Lehman Brothers Private Fund Management LP	Delaware
1	Lehman Brothers U.K. Holdings (Delaware) Inc.	Delaware
2	Ballybunion Investments No. 2 Ltd.	Cayman Islands
3	Ballybunion Investments No. 3 Ltd.	Cayman Islands
4	Dynamo Investments Ltd.	Cayman Islands
5	Ballybunion Partnership	Hong Kong
2	LB India Holdings Cayman I Limited	Cayman Islands
3	Lehman Brothers Services India Private Limited	India
4	Lehman Brothers Fixed Income Securities Private Limited	India
2	LB India Holdings Cayman II Limited	Cayman Islands
2	LB Lease & Finance No 1. Ltd.	United Kingdom
2	Lehman Brothers Capital GmbH, Co.	Germany
2	LB UK RE Holdings Ltd.	United Kingdom
3	Falcon LB Sarl	Luxembourg
4	LB SPV SCA	Luxembourg
3	LB UK Financing Limited	United Kingdom
4	LB SF No. 1 Ltd.	United Kingdom
5	Lehman Commercial Mortgage Conduit Ltd.	United Kingdom
2	Lehman Brothers Holdings Scottish LP	United Kingdom
3	Lehman Brothers Spain Holdings Limited	United Kingdom
3	Lehman Brothers Luxembourg Investments Sarl	Luxembourg
4	Woori-LB Fifth Asset Securitization Specialty Co., Ltd.	Republic of Korea
4	Woori-LB Fourth Asset Securitization Specialty Co., Ltd.	Republic of Korea
4	Lehman Brothers Asset Management France	France
4	Lehman Brothers UK Investments Limited	United Kingdom
5	LB Investments (UK) Limited	United Kingdom
6	LB Alpha Finance Cayman Limited	Cayman Islands
6	LB Beta Finance Cayman Limited	Cayman Islands
4	Lehman Brothers U.K. Holdings Ltd.	United Kingdom
5	Lehman Brothers Holdings Plc	United Kingdom
6	Furno & Del Castano Capital Partners LLP	United Kingdom

Tier	Name	Jurisdiction of Organization
6	LB Holdings Intermediate 1 Ltd.	United Kingdom
7	LB Holdings Intermediate 2 Ltd.	United Kingdom
8	Lehman Brothers International (Europe)	United Kingdom
6	Lehman Brothers Asset Management (Europe) Ltd.	United Kingdom
6	MBAM Investor Limited	United Kingdom
6	Lehman Brothers Europe Limited	United Kingdom
6	Lehman Brothers Limited	United Kingdom
5	Lehman Brothers (PTG) Limited	United Kingdom
6	Eldon Street Holdings Limited	United Kingdom
7	Thayer Properties Limited	United Kingdom
8	Thayer Group Limited	United Kingdom
9	Thayer Properties (Jersey) Ltd.	United Kingdom
2	Lehman Brothers Holdings Scottish LP 2	United Kingdom
3	Lehman Brothers Holdings Scottish LP 3	United Kingdom
2	Lehman Brothers Treasury Co. B.V.	The Netherlands
1	Lehman Brothers Bankhaus Aktiengesellschaft	Germany
1	Lehman Re Ltd.	Bermuda
1	Lehman Risk Advisors Inc.	Delaware
1	LIBRO Holdings I Inc.	Delaware
2	Lehman Brothers do Brasil Ltda	Brazil
1	Neuberger Berman Inc.	Delaware
2	Neuberger Berman Asset Management, LLC	Delaware
2	Neuberger Berman Investment Services, LLC	Delaware
2	Neuberger Berman Management Inc.	New York
2	Sage Partners, LLC	New York
2	Executive Monetary Management, Inc.	New York
2	Neuberger Berman, LLC	Delaware
3	Neuberger Berman Pty Ltd.	Australia
3	Neuberger & Berman Agency, Inc.	New York
1	Principal Transactions Inc.	Delaware
2	Louise Y.K.	Japan
2	Y.K. Tower Funding	Japan
1	Real Estate Private Equity Inc.	Delaware
2	REPE LBREP III LLC	Delaware
1	Southern Pacific Funding 5	United Kingdom
1	Wharf Reinsurance Inc.	New York

Source: LBHI 2008 10-K, Exhibit 21.01.

LBHI Chapter 11 debtors and their counterparties also had a number of disputes regarding the value of certain qualified financial contracts. In late August 2008, the bankruptcy court ordered the parties to settle these disputes in mandatory arbitration to reduce the court's burden. However, the court also granted the parties more time to hammer out the details of the dispute resolution procedures after more than 50 counterparties raised objections to those procedures.[146]

Conclusion

While both failed financial companies were relatively large, Lehman's business activities were far more complex and spread out across the globe. IndyMac operated almost exclusively within the United States and primarily engaged in mortgage-related activities through its FDIC-insured thrift. On the other hand, Lehman operated in dozens of countries and engaged in a wide range of financial activities that were primarily conducted within its non-depository subsidiaries. Some of these subsidiaries were subject to extensive federal oversight and regulation, while many were not.

Lehman's complexity and the adversarial nature of the bankruptcy process likely have been the primary causes of the vast judicial wrangling over Lehman's assets and the delay of paying out claims. Because of the FDIC's deposit insurance and authority to act unilaterally subject to limited judicial appeal, many claims against IndyMac already have been paid out and there has been little post-failure litigation related to IndyMac. However, more legal disputes may be raised in the near future as the FDIC completes the winding down of the thrift.

End Notes

[1] 11 U.S.C. §§ 109(b)(2) and (d).

[2] The basic difference between a conservatorship and a receivership is that a conservatorship involves operating the institution as a going concern to protect its assets until it stabilizes or is closed and a receiver appointed. A receiver is charged with liquidating the institution and winding up its affairs. A conservatorship may indicate that the FDIC aims to restore the institution to solvency or that the FDIC had to act quickly without the usual lead time for investigation. In either case, a conservatorship may be followed by a receivership if a determination is made that the institution is not viable. For an in-depth analysis of the FDIC's conservatorship/receivership powers, *see* CRS Report RL34657, *Financial Institution Insolvency: Federal Authority over Fannie Mae, Freddie Mac, and Depository Institutions*, by David H. Carpenter and M. Maureen Murphy. Fannie Mae, Freddie Mac, and the Federal Home Loan Banks are subject to a conservatorship/receivership regime modeled after that for insured depositories.

[3] 11 U.S.C. § 109.

[4] The proposal is to be known as the "Resolution Authority for Systemically Significant Financial Companies Act of 2009." Text can be found at http://www.ustreas.gov/press/releases/ reports/032509%20legislation.pdf. It is unclear exactly which financial firms would be considered "systemically significant." For a detailed analysis of the proposal, *see* CRS Report R40526, *Insolvencies of "Systemically Significant Financial Companies" (SSFCs): Proposal for Federal Deposit Insurance Corporation (FDIC) Resolution*, by M. Maureen Murphy.

[5] CRS Report RL34657, *Financial Institution Insolvency: Federal Authority over Fannie Mae, Freddie Mac, and Depository Institutions*, by David H. Carpenter and M. Maureen Murphy.

[6] CRS Report R40530, *Insolvency of Systemically Significant Financial Companies: Bankruptcy vs. Conservatorship/Receivership*, by David H. Carpenter, Insolvency of Systemically Significant Financial Companies: Bankruptcy vs. Conservatorship/Receivership, by David H. Carpenter. The report discusses six important differences between the two resolution regimes:
(1) Overall objectives of each regime;
(2) Insolvency initiation authority and timing;
(3) Oversight structure and appeal;
(4) Management, shareholder, and creditor rights;
(5) FDIC "superpowers," including contract repudiation versus Bankruptcy's automatic stay; and
(6) Speed of resolution.

[7] *Id.*

[8] Eva H.G. Hüpkes, THE LEGAL ASPECTS OF BANK INSOLVENCY: A COMPARATIVE ANALYSIS OF WESTERN EUROPE, THE UNITED STATES AND CANADA (2000).

[9] Robert R. Bliss and George G. Kaufman, *U.S. Corporate and Bank Insolvency Regimes: A Comparison and Evaluation*, 2 Va. L. & Bus. Rev. 143 (2007).

[10] IndyMac Bancorp, Inc., S.E.C. Form 10-K, p. 8, filed Feb. 29, 2008, available at http://www.sec.gov/Archives/edgar/data/773468/000095014808000053/v38189e10vk.htm. As a consolidated regulator, OTS had the power to order reports and conduct examinations of the holding company and its subsidiaries with the requirement that OTS "to the extent deemed feasible, use ... reports filed with or examinations made by other Federal agencies or the appropriate State supervisory authority." 12 U.S.C. § 1467a(b)(4).

[11] *Id.*

[12] FDIC Press Release, *FDIC Establishes IndyMac Federal Bank, FSB as Successor to IndyMac Bank, F.S.B., Pasedena, California*, Jul. 11, 2008, available at http://www.fdic.gov/news/ news/press/2008/pr08056.html.

[13] FDIC Press Release, *FDIC Implements Loan Modification Program for Distressed IndyMac Mortgage Loans*, Aug. 20, 2008, available at http://www.fdic.gov/news/news/press/2008/ pr08067.html.

[14] FDIC Press Release, *FDIC Establishes IndyMac Federal Bank, FSB as Successor to IndyMac Bank, F.S.B., Pasedena, California*, Jul. 11, 2008, available at http://www.fdic.gov/news/ news/press/2008/pr08056.html.

[15] State-chartered banks are chartered by state banking authorities. The primary federal regulator of a federally chartered bank or thrift is its chartering authority. National banks are chartered by the Office of the Comptroller of the Currency (OCC); federal thrifts or savings associations are chartered by the Office of Thrift Supervision (OTS). The primary federal regulator of state-chartered banks is either the Board of Governors of the Federal Reserve System (Fed) or the FDIC, depending upon whether the institution is a member bank, i.e., a member of the Federal Reserve System (FRS).

[16] The Federal Deposit Insurance Act (FDI Act) specifies judicial review for only one type of conservatorship or receivership appointment—FDIC's appointment of itself as receiver or conservator if depositors have been unable to access their funds 15 days after the appointment by the state of a receiver or conservator. 12 U.S.C. § 1821(c)(4). There are also other statutes that provide for post- seizure judicial review in certain instances, e.g., 12 U.S.C. § 203(b) (appointment of a conservator for a national bank). It has also been held that judicial review is available under the Administrative Procedure Act. James Madison Ltd. By Hecht v. Ludwig, 82 F. 3d 1085 (D.C. Cir. 1996).

[17] A pass-through conservatorship, as used for IndyMac Bank, is chosen because there is no provision for a bridge bank for a thrift institution. In a straight conservatorship, which is rarer than the pass-through version, the institution is operated on a temporary basis under its existing charter. Robert R. Bliss and George G. Kaufman, *U.S. Corporate and Bank Insolvency Regimes: A Comparison and Evaluation*, 2 Va. L. & Bus. Rev. 143, 151, n. 20 (2007). *See also* Patricia A. McCoy, Banking Law Manual § 15.03 (Lexis Pub. (2d ed.)) (hereinafter, McCoy).

[18] FDIC Press Release, *FDIC Establishes IndyMac Federal Bank, FSB as Successor to IndyMac Bank, F.S.B., Pasedena, California*, Jul. 11, 2008, available at http://www.fdic.gov/news/ news/press/2008/pr08056.html.

[19] Kate Pickert and Fielding Cage, *The Making of a Panic*, Time Magazine, available at http:// www.time.com/ time/2008/indymac/.

[20] IndyMac Bancorp, Inc. Ch. 7 Bankruptcy Petition, U.S. Bankr. Ct. S.D.Cal. (2008), available at http://www.cacb.uscourts.gov/cacb/Notices.nsf/New%20Cases%20of%20Interest/4029A3 A3BDD0D72188257498005AB9E7/$FILE/08-21752_IndyMacBancorp.pdf.

[21] Share Loss Agreement Between FDIC and OneWest Bank, FSB, Mar. 19, 2009, available at http://www.fdic.gov/ about/freedom/IndyMacSharedLossAgrmt.pdf.

[22] OneWest Press Release, Transfer of IndyMac Federal Bank, FSB Assets to OneWest Bank, FSB Frequently Asked Questions For Customers, the Media and the Public, available at http://www.indymacbank.com/ bankauto/content/eng/OWB_Customer_FAQ.pdf.

[23] FDIC Press Release, *FDIC Closes Sale of IndyMac Federal Bank, Pasadena, California*, Mar. 19, 2009, available at http://www. fdic.gov/ news/news/press/2009/pr09042.html.

[24] IndyMac Bancorp, Inc., S.E.C. Form 10-K, p. 8, filed Feb. 29, 2008, available at http://www.sec.gov/Archives/edgar/data/773468/000095014808000053/v38189e10vk.htm.

[25] FDIC Press Release, *FDIC Establishes IndyMac Federal Bank, FSB as Successor to IndyMac Bank, F.S.B., Pasedena, California*, Jul. 11, 2008, available at http://www.fdic.gov/news/ news/press/2008/pr08056.html.

[26] Loan Sale Agreement Between FDIC and OneWest Bank, FSB, Mar. 19, 2009, available at http://www.fdic.gov/ about/freedom/IndyMacLoanSaleAgrmt.pdf.

[27] CRS could not identify this company's primary regulator. As a subsidiary to a thrift holding company, OTS had authority to regulate it on a consolidated basis, meaning OTS had the power to order reports and conduct examinations with the requirement that OTS "to the extent deemed feasible, use ... reports filed with or examinations made by other Federal agencies or the appropriate State supervisory authority." 12 U.S.C. § 1467a(b)(4).

[28] IndyMac Bancorp, Inc., S.E.C. Form 10-K, p. 8, filed Feb. 29, 2008, available at http://www. sec.gov/Archives/ edgar/data/773468/ 000095014808000053/v38189e10vk.htm.

[29] OneWest Press Release, Transfer of IndyMac Federal Bank, FSB Assets to OneWest Bank, FSB Frequently Asked Questions For Customers, the Media and the Public, available at http://www.indymacbank. com/bankauto/content/eng/OWB_Customer_FAQ.pdf.

[30] Amended and Restated Insured Deposit Purchase and Assumption Agreement Between FDIC as Receiver of IndyMac Bank and FDIC as Conservator of IndyMac Federal Bank, Jul. 11, 2008, available at http://www.fdic.gov/bank/individual/failed/IndyMac_P_and_A.pdf.

[31] CRS could not identify this company's primary regulator. As a subsidiary to a thrift holding company, OTS had authority to regulate it on a consolidated basis, meaning OTS had the power to order reports and conduct examinations with the requirement that OTS "to the extent deemed feasible, use ... reports filed with or examinations made by other Federal agencies or the appropriate State supervisory authority." 12 U.S.C. § 1467a(b)(4).

[32] IndyMac Bancorp, Inc., S.E.C. Form 10-K, p. 7-8, filed Feb. 29, 2008, available at http://www. sec.gov/Archives/ edgar/data/773468/000095014808000053/v38189e10vk.htm.

[33] Amended and Restated Insured Deposit Purchase and Assumption Agreement Between FDIC as Receiver of IndyMac Bank and FDIC as Conservator of IndyMac Federal Bank, Jul. 11, 2008, available at http://www. fdic.gov/bank/individual/failed/IndyMac_P_and_A.pdf.

[34] Loan Sale Agreement Between FDIC and OneWest Bank, FSB, Mar. 19, 2009, available at http://www. fdic.gov/about/freedom/IndyMacLoanSaleAgrmt.pdf.

[35] 12 U.S.C. §§ 1821(d)(3)-(8).

[36] 12 U.S.C. § 1821(e)(1). The statute contains specific provisions relating to various types of contracts and leases. These include contracts for the sale of real property, 12 U.S.C.§ 1821(e)(6); service contracts, 12 U.S.C. § 1821(e)(7); and any certain securities contract, commodity contract, forward contract, repurchase agreement, swap agreement, or similar agreement that the FDIC determines to be a "qualified financial contract." 12 U.S.C. §§ 1821(e)(8) - (10). Contracts with a Federal Home Loan Bank and the Federal Reserve Bank may not be repudiated. 12 U.S.C. § 1921)(e)(13).

[37] 12 U.S.C. § 1821(e)(3).

[38] Robert R. Bliss and George G. Kaufman, *U.S. Corporate and Bank Insolvency: An Economic Comparison and Evaluation*, Federal Reserve Bank of Chicago (2006), available at http://www.chicagofed.org/publications/ workingpapers/wp2006_01.pdf.

[39] See, e.g., Combs v. FDIC, 2009 U.S. Dist. LEXIS 77870 (E.D. Mich. 2009); Ibarra v. Plaza Home Mortgage, 2009 U.S. Dist. LEXIS 80581 (S.D. Cal. 2009); Madison v. First Magnus Financial Corporation, 2009 U.S. Dist. LEXIS 81452 (D. Ariz. 2009).

[40] Sheila Bair, Chairman of the FDIC, *Remarks by FDIC Chairman Sheila Bair to the National Association of Realtors Midyear Legislative Meeting and Trade Expo*, May 12, 2009, transcript available at http://www. fdic.gov/ news/news/ speeches/chairman/spmay1209.html.

[41] Share Loss Agreement Between FDIC and OneWest Bank, FSB, Mar. 19, 2009, available at http://www.fdic.gov/ about/freedom/IndyMacSharedLossAgrmt.pdf.

[42] Lehman Brothers Holdings Inc., S.E.C. Form 10-K, p. 5, filed Jan. 29, 2008, available at http:// www.sec.gov/Archives/edgar/data/806085/000110465908005476/a08-3530_110k.htm.

[43] Ben Hallman, *A Moment's Notice*, Amer. Lawyer, Dec. 1, 2008, available at http://www.law. com/jsp/ Pub Article.jsp? id=1202426213501.

[44] Some believe that LBHI's failure, along with the U.S. government's decision to not provide the company assistance, triggered the panic of 2008. See, e.g., William Sterling, *Looking Back at Lehman: An Empirical Analysis of the Size and Timing of the Shock and the Effectiveness of Countermeasures*, Oct. 30, 2009, available at http://www.trilogyadvisors.com/world report/200910.Lehman.pdf ("In this paper, we will argue that the facts are clear: The Lehman bankruptcy represented a massive financial shock that was clearly the trigger for the fall 2008 panic." Others believe the panic was triggered by other events. See, e.g., John Taylor, "How Government Created the Financial Crisis," Wall St. Journal, Feb. 9, 2009, available at http://online.wsj. com/article/SB123414310280561945.html ("Research shows the failure to rescue Lehman did not trigger the fall panic.").

[45] SEC Press Release, *Chairman Cox Announces End of Consolidated Supervised Entities Program*, Sept. 26, 2008, available at http://www.sec.gov/news/press/2008/2008-230.htm.

[46] Debtor's Motion for an Order Pursuant to Sections 105 and 365 of the Bankruptcy Code to Establish Procedures for the Settlement or Assumption and Assignment of Prepetition Derivatives Contracts, U.S. Bankr. Ct. S.D.N.Y., Case No. 08-13555, Docket No. 1498.

[47] Lehman Brothers Holdings Inc. (Chapter 11), Epiq Systems, available at http://lehman-docket. com.

[48] *See* 11 U.S.C. § 101.

[49] 15 U.S.C. §§ 78aaa, *et seq*. For a general overview of the SIPA resolution process, *see* U.S. Courts, Bankruptcy Basics: SIPA, available at http://www.uscourts.gov/bankruptcycourts/ bankruptcybasics/sipa.html. Lehman Brothers Inc. customer claims were still being settled as of July 1, 2009, with the expectation that settlement will continue for the foreseeable future. LBI Securities Investor Protection Corporation (SIPC) Proceeding, *Statement Regarding Customer Claims and Distributions*, Jul. 1, 2009, available at http://chapter11. epiqsystems.com/clientdefault.aspx?pk=978bd245-11be-4d4b-83db-d6a3283b2962&l=1 ("The Trustee [James W. Giddens] has received over 12,000 customer claim forms representing over 80,000 accounts. The Trustee has established teams of professionals who have been working to reconcile and resolve issues. These include

teams working on the multibillion dollar claims submitted on an omnibus or group basis by Barclays, LBIE [Lehman Brothers International (Europe)], and other Lehman entities' claims by prime brokerage account holders and over 7,000 timely filed individual customer claims after identification and elimination of duplicates. The Trustee has already determined 3,350 of these claims. The Trustee has also issued approximately 1,500 deficiency letters and reached out to customers to obtain required information with respect to claims that lack meaningful information or are defective on their face.

"The Trustee is reviewing remaining claims and issuing letters of determination as rapidly as possible. Under SIPA and the procedures approved by the Court, when the Trustee issues a determination denying a customer claim in whole or in part, the claimant has a right to object, and the dispute must be resolved or submitted for Court determination. Some of these disputes will involve whether certain categories of transactions qualify for customer treatment under SIPA as well as valuation questions. Some will involve substantial dollar amounts. It may be a considerable time before some of these disputes can be finally resolved through the Bankruptcy Court and appeals process. The Trustee will reserve for disputed claims until resolution becomes final.").

[50] Cross-Border Insolvency Protocol for the Lehman Brothers Group of Companies, LBHI Key Documents, available at http://chap11.epiqsystems.com/Documents.aspx?pk=de7ced2b-52e7-4172-92e1-9ec425933bd0. This protocol provides the following background:

Commencing on September 15, 2008 and periodically thereafter ..., the Debtors commenced (or in some cases, had initiated against them) plenary insolvency, administration, liquidation, rehabilitations, receivership, or like proceedings ("Plenary Proceedings") in different jurisdictions ("the Plenary Fora") and before different courts and governmental, regulatory, or administrative bodies ..., as well as proceedings that are secondary or ancillary to a Plenary Proceeding ... in different jurisdictions other than the Plenary Fora....

In certain of the Proceedings, the Debtors remain authorized to operate their businesses and manage their properties as "Debtors in Possession," while in others, liquidators, administrators, trustees, custodians, supervisors or curators have been appointed to manage the Debtors' affairs and represent their insolvency estates.... Furthermore, in certain of these Proceedings, one or more statutory committee of creditors or equity holders has or have been appointed....

*****

Given the integrated and global nature of Lehman's businesses, many of the Debtors' assets and activities are spread across different jurisdictions, and require administration in and are subject to the laws of more than one Forum. The efficient administration of each of the Debtors' individual Proceedings would benefit from cooperation....

Id. at 1-2.

[51] See, e.g., Randall Smith, Ianthe Jeanne Dugan, and Cassell Bryan-Low, *Lehman Creditors To Get Payout Plan*, Wall Street Journal, Oct. 5, 2009, available at http://online.wsj.com/ article/SB125470896979863433.html.

[52] For example, Lehman Brothers Bank, a federal savings bank, and Lehman Brothers Commercial Bank, an industrial loan company, are both active companies, albeit under different names (Aurora Bank FSB and Woodlands Commercial Bank, respectively). *See* Table I.

[53] Barclays and Nomura did not necessarily purchase entire subsidiaries. Instead, they may have purchased certain assets and liabilities of particular LBHI subsidiaries. Additionally, the purchase agreements do not clearly delineate from which subsidiaries the assets and liabilities were purchased. As a result, Table I uses language such as "assets may have been largely acquired" to describe the current status of particular subsidiaries.

[54] SIPC Press Release, *James W. Giddens, Lehman Brothers Inc. SIPC Trustee, Reports on Progress of Customer Claim Processing*, Feb. 25, 2009, available at http://www.sipc.org/ media/release25Feb09.cfm.

[55] Neuberger Berman Press Release, *Neuberger Berman Becomes Independent*, May 4, 2009, available at https://www.nb.com/MYP/NB/PUB/24771/NFA/H/K/E/S/ doc/050409_ NB_ Becomes_Independent_ Press_ Release.pdf.

[56] See SEC Filings for Neuberger Berman Management LLC.

[57] In re Lehman Brothers OTC Derivatives Inc., U.S. Bankr. Ct. S.D.N.Y. Case No. 08-13893, petition available athttp://chap11.epiqsystems.com/clientdefault.aspx?pk=de7ced2b-52e7-4172-92e1-9ec425933bd0&l=1.

[58] CRS could not identify this company's primary regulator; it could be an unregulated hedge fund.

[59] In re Lehman Brothers Financial Products Inc., Case No. 08-13902 Bankr. Ct. S.D.N.Y. (2009), petition available at http://chap11.epiqsystems.com/clientdefault.aspx?pk=de7 ced2b-52e7-4172-92e1-9ec425933bd0&l=1.

[60] CRS could not identify this company's primary regulator; it could be an unregulated hedge fund.

[61] In re Lehman Brothers Derivative Products Inc., Case No. 08-13899 Bankr. Ct. S.D.N.Y. (2009), petition available at http://chap11.epiqsystems.com/clientdefault.aspx?pk=de7ced2b-52e7-4172-92e1-9ec425933b d0&l=1.

[62] CRS could not identify this company's primary regulator; it could be an unregulated hedge fund.

[63] In re Lehman Brothers Special Financing Inc., Case No. 08-13888 Bankr. Ct. S.D.N.Y. (2009), petition available at http://chap11.epiqsystems.com/clientdefault.aspx?pk=de7ced2b-52e7-4172-92e1-9ec425933bd0&l=1.

[64] CRS could not identify this company's primary regulator; it could be an unregulated hedge fund.

[65] In re Lehman Commercial Paper Inc., Case No. 08-13900 Bankr. Ct. S.D.N.Y. (2009), petition available at http://chap11.epiqsystems.com/clientdefault.aspx?pk=de7ced2b-52e7-4172-92e1-9ec425933bd0&l=1.

[66] OTS Institution Search, Lehman Brothers Bancorp, Inc., available at http://www.ots.gov/?p=Institution Search&hid= H3497.

[67] Aurora Bank FSB, Frequently Asked Questions, available at https://www.aurorabankfsb.com/ faq.html.

[68] See FDIC, Institution Directory, Woodlands Commercial Bank history, available at http:// www2.fdic.gov/idasp/ confirmation_outside.asp?inCert1=58009.

[69] Neuberger Berman Group LLC Press Release, *Neuberger Berman to Acquire Trust Company*, July 23, 2009, available at https://www.nb.com/public/DMA/Japan/news/TrustCo% 20Agreement.pdf.

[70] Neuberger Berman Group LLC Press Release, *Neuberger Berman to Acquire Trust Company*, July 23, 2009,available at https://www.nb.com/public/DMA/Japan/news/TrustCo% 20A greement.pdf.

[71] FERC Press Release, *FERC Authorizes Lehman-EDF Transaction*, October 30, 2008, available at http://www.ferc.gov/news/media-alerts/2008/2008-4/10-30-08-factsheet.pdf.

[72] FERC Press Release, *FERC Authorizes Lehman-EDF Transaction*, October 30, 2008, available at http://www.ferc.gov/news/media-alerts/2008/2008-4/10-30-08-factsheet.pdf.

[73] London Stock Exchange Aggregated Regulatory News Service, *Lehman Brothers Diversified Arbitrage (Ireland) Fund Plc (the "Company") – Update to Operations*, RNS No. 7943R May 6, 2009.

[74] *See, e.g.*, Commonwealth of Massachusetts Division of Insurance, 2008 Annual Report, available at http://www.mass.gov/Eoca/docs/doi/Media/2008AnnualReport.pdf.

[75] Regulated by the U.K.'s Financial Services Authority, *see* Joint FSA/EUI Announcement, *Lehman Brothers International (Europe) in Administration*, Oct. 8, 2008, available at http:// www.fsa.gov.uk/pages/ About/ Media/notes/ bn030.shtml.

[76] FSA Press Release, Today, Lehman Brothers Holding Inc ("LBHI"), a U.S. investment bank, announced that it intends to file a petition under Chapter 11 of the U.S. Bankruptcy Code., Sept. 15, 2008, available at http://www.fsa.gov.uk/pages/Library/Communication/ State-ments/2008/lehman.shtml.

[77] Regulated by the Swiss Federal Banking Commission, *see* In re Lehman Brothers Finance SA, Case No. 09-10583 Bankr. S.D.N.Y. (2009), Ch. 11 dismissal available at http://chap11. epiqsystems.com/clientdefault. aspx?pk=de7ced2b52e7-4172-92e1-9ec425933bd0&l=1.

[78] In re Lehman Brothers Finance SA, Case No. 09-10583 Bankr. S.D.N.Y. (2009), Ch. 11 dismissal available at http://chap11.epiqsystems.com/clientdefault.aspx?pk=de7ced2b-52e7-4172-92e1-9ec425933bd0&l=1.

[79] Lehman Brothers Treasury Co. B.V. Bankruptcy Public Notice 1, available at http://www. lehmanbrotherstreasury.com/pdf/english/1st%20public%20bankruptcy%20report%20LBT%20(22%20December%202008)%20(w)%20(2).PDF.

[80] Cross-Border Insolvency Protocol for the Lehman Brothers Group of Companies, LBHI Key Documents, available at http://chap11.epiqsystems.com/Documents.aspx?pk=de7ced2b-52e7-4172-92e1-9ec425933bd0.

[81] Regulated by Germany's Federal Financial Supervisory Authority (BaFin), *see* BaFin Press Release, *BaFin orders moratorium on Lehman Brothers Bankhous AG*, Sept. 15, 2008, available at http://www.bafin.de/ cln_161/nn_720788/SharedDocs/Mitteilungen/EN/2008/ pm__080915__lehman.html.

[82] Cross-Border Insolvency Protocol for the Lehman Brothers Group of Companies, LBHI Key Documents, available at http://chap11.epiqsystems.com/Documents.aspx?pk=de7ced2b-52e7-4172-92e1-9ec425933bd0.

[83] Matthew Goldstein, *Lehman Brothers Holdings Inc. (Mexico Stock Exchange) Company Overview*, Reuters, available at http://www.reuters.com/finance/stocks/companyProfile? symbol=LEHMQ.MX.

[84] Regulated by the Japan's Financial Services Agency, *see* Associated Press, *Lehman Brothers Japan files for bankruptcy*, Japanese Times, Sept. 17, 2008, available at http://search.Japantimes.co.jp/cgi-bin/ nb20080917a2.html.

[85] BusinessWeek, *Lehman Brothers Holdings, Inc., Asia Pacific Operations Company Overview*, available at http://investing.businessweek.com/research/stocks/private/snapshot.asp? Priv capId=49093257.

[86] Associated Press, *Lehman Brothers Japan files for bankruptcy*, Japan Times, Sept. 17, 2008, available at http://search. japantimes.co.jp/cgi-bin/nb20080917a2.html.

[87] BusinessWeek, *Lehman Brothers Holdings, Inc., Asia Pacific Operations Company Overview*, available at http://investing.businessweek.com/research/stocks/private/snapshot.asp? privcapId=49093257.

[88] Cross-Border Insolvency Protocol for the Lehman Brothers Group of Companies, LBHI Key Documents, available at http://chap11.epiqsystems.com/Documents.aspx?pk=de7ced2b-52e7-4172-92e1-9ec425933bd0.

[89] BusinessWeek, *Lehman Brothers Holdings, Inc., Asia Pacific Operations Company Overview*, available at http://investing.businessweek.com/research/stocks/private/snapshot.asp? privcapId=49093257.

[90] Cross-Border Insolvency Protocol for the Lehman Brothers Group of Companies, LBHI Key Documents, available athttp://chap11.epiqsystems.com/Documents.aspx?pk=de7ced2b-52e7-4172-92e1-9ec425933bd0.

[91] *Id.*

[92] *Id.*

[93] BusinessWeek, *Lehman Brothers Holdings, Inc., Asia Pacific Operations Company Overview*, available at http://investing.businessweek.com/research/stocks/private/snapshot.asp? priv capId=49093257.

[94] Cross-Border Insolvency Protocol for the Lehman Brothers Group of Companies, LBHI Key Documents, available at http://chap11.epiqsystems.com/Documents.aspx?pk=de7ced2b-52e7-4172-92e1-9ec425933bd0.

[95] *Id.*

[96] *Id.*

[97] *Id.*

[98] *Id.*

[99] BusinessWeek, *Lehman Brothers Holdings, Inc., Asia Pacific Operations Company Overview*, available at http://investing.businessweek.com/research/stocks/private/snapshot.asp? privcapId=49093257.

[100] Cross-Border Insolvency Protocol for the Lehman Brothers Group of Companies, LBHI Key Documents, available at http://chap11.epiqsystems.com/Documents.aspx?pk=de7ced2b-52e7-4172-92e1-9ec425933bd0.

[101] BusinessWeek, *Lehman Brothers Holdings, Inc., Asia Pacific Operations Company Overview*, available at http://investing.businessweek.com/research/stocks/private/snapshot.asp? privcapId=49093257.

[102] Cross-Border Insolvency Protocol for the Lehman Brothers Group of Companies, LBHI Key Documents, available at http://chap11.epiqsystems.com/Documents.aspx?pk=de7ced2b-52e7-4172-92e1-9ec425933bd0.

[103] BusinessWeek, *Lehman Brothers Holdings, Inc., Asia Pacific Operations Company Overview*, available at http://investing.businessweek.com/research/stocks/private/snapshot.asp? privcapId=49093257.

[104] Cross-Border Insolvency Protocol for the Lehman Brothers Group of Companies, LBHI Key Documents, available at http://chap11.epiqsystems.com/Documents.aspx?pk=de7ced2b-52e7-4172-92e1-9ec425933bd0.

[105] BusinessWeek, *Lehman Brothers Holdings, Inc., Asia Pacific Operations Company Overview*, available at http://investing.businessweek.com/research/stocks/private/snapshot.asp? privcapId=49093257.

[106] For a glimpse into the circumstances that ultimately resulted in LBHI's bankruptcy and the subsequent Barclays acquisition from U.S. regulators' point-of-view, see David Wessel, *In Fed We Trust*, pp. 9-26 (Crown Publishing Group, a division of Random House, Inc., New York 2009). The following excerpts from an article written by Ben Hallman describe the situation from the point-of-view of the lawyers involved:

By the second week of September, investors had all but given up on Lehman Brothers Holdings Inc. Creditors wanted the 158-year-old investment bank to put up additional collateral to cover its bets in the derivatives market. Customers were scrambling to close accounts. Traders couldn't move the firm's commercial paper, or settle trades.

*****

On Friday, September 12, Lehman's stock price plunged 90 percent. At about 6 p.m., Fed officials and Treasury Secretary Paulson called for an emergency meeting of some of Wall Street's top bankers at the New York Federal Reserve office. They told the bankers that the government would not bail out Lehman, and that it was up to Wall Street to sort out the mess, according to press reports. But it was London that almost saved the day. Barclays, a British bank that had been eyeing various parts of the Lehman business for months, was interested. That evening, [law firm] Simpson Thacher partners John Finley and Andrew Keller, representing Lehman, delivered a draft of a merger agreement to Barclays.

*****

On Saturday, September 13, Weil[, Gotshal & Manges, another law firm,] ramped up its bankruptcy preparation efforts. A sale still seemed likely - even after word spread that Bank of America Corporation, which had also been in the running to buy Lehman, was instead purchasing Merrill Lynch & Co., Inc. for $50 billion-but the precipitous fall in Lehman's share price the day before, along with all the bank's other problems, convinced the players that something significant was in store.

*****

The Barclays deal fell apart on Sunday morning. ...

In the end, [Lehman's board of directors] felt that it had no choice. In a tearful session, they voted to dissolve. At 1 a.m. on Monday morning, [Harvey Miller, a Weil attorney,] filed papers with the U.S. Bankruptcy Court for the Southern District of New York, asking for Chapter 11 protection for Lehman Brothers Holding [Inc]. The long weekend was over, but for the weary Weil lawyers, the work had just begun. ...

Barclays ... wanted to buy Lehman's brokerage operation, Lehman Brothers Inc. How long would it take to put a deal together? [Miller] suggested 15 days. One of the Barclays representatives stood up, and said, "In that case, we're not interested." "Perhaps we can do better," Miller said.

*****

Over the next five days, the lawyers drove a sale of Lehman Brothers Inc., the brokerage unit, through U.S. Bankruptcy Court. They worked knowing that every minute wasted was a minute that the value of the underlying business diminished, "like a melting ice cube on the dock," as Miller said in court. More than 100 Weil, Gotshal lawyers would take part – many of them working around the clock to finalize deals that would normally take months to complete.

*****

Working around the clock, the lawyers crafted an agreement in about 40 hours. ... "We did in a few days what normally would take at least a month," says Lewkow, the Cleary lawyer. ... Time was so precious that the lawyers didn't even take the time to incorporate the final changes that had been handwritten in the margins of the sale agreement. They submitted it to Judge James Peck, a relatively new federal bankruptcy judge, after midnight, in the early hours of Wednesday morning, and immediately began work on an amendment to the agreement.

Judge Peck set an aggressive schedule, and on Friday, just 48 hours after the first hearing, the lawyers for all the parties, along with a motley collection of creditors, journalists, and hedge funders (including former first daughter Chelsea Clinton), packed into the claustrophobic courtroom. At 1 a.m. on Saturday, September 20, five days from the hour that the parent company had filed for protection in his court, Judge Peck approved a $1.35 billion sale of the brokerage arm to Barclays. 'I have to approve this transaction because it is the only available transaction,' he said.

The sale required the unusual intervention of the Securities Investor Protection Corporation (SIPC), a government-chartered entity created 37 years ago to protect investor accounts in the event of a brokerage firm failure. Miller asked the SIPC to initiate a liquidation proceeding for the brokerage that would correspond with the bankruptcy hearing. This was necessary to complete a sale because a brokerage can't technically file for Chapter 11 protection under federal bankruptcy law. The timing was important to allow for the seamless transfer of customer accounts from the Lehman to the Barclays platform.

Ben Hallman, A Moment's Notice, Amer. Lawyer, Dec. 1, 2008, available at http://www.law.com/jsp/PubArticle.jsp? id=1202426213501.

[107] David Wessel, *In Fed We Trust*, pp. 18-20 (Crown Publishing Group, a division of Random House, Inc., New York 2009).

[108] David Wessel, *In Fed We Trust*, p. 20 (Crown Publishing Group, a division of Random House, Inc., New York2009).

[109] Barclays Press Release, *Lehman Brothers Business Reopens Under Barclays Ownership*, Sept. 22, 2009, available at http://www.barcap.com/About+Barclays+Capital/Press+Office/News+releases/News,1031, Lehman+ Brothers+ Business+Reopens+Under+Barclays+Ownership.

[110] Asset Purchase Agreement, LBHI, Lehman Brothers Inc., LB 745 LLC, and Barclays Capital Inc., Sept. 16, 2009, available at http://chapter11.epiqsystems.com/ViewDocument. aspx?DocumentPk=2066f82a-f909-4491-b858ca5406b46827.

[111] Bay Harbour Management LC v. Lehman Brothers Holdings Inc., Nos. 08 Civ. 8869 (DLC), 08 Civ. 8914 (DLC), (S.D.N.Y. 2009).

[112] *See* Executed Sales Documents, LBHI Key Documents, available at http://chap11.epiqsystems.com/Documents.aspx?pk=de7ced2b-52e7-4172-92e1-9ec425933bd0.

[113] Objection of Barclays Capital Inc. to Proposed Joinders in Debtors' Motion For an Order Under Rule 2004Authorizing Discovery From Barclays Capital Inc., U.S. Bankr. Ct. S.D.N.Y. Case No. 08-13555, Docket No. 4093.*See, also*, Diane Davis, *Court Allows Lehman Brothers to Investigate Sale of Barclays Capital Through Discovery*,BNA Bankruptcy Law Reporter, Jul. 29, 2009.

[114] 11 U.S.C. § 364.

[115] Kenneth Ayotte and David A. Skeel, Jr., *Bankruptcy or Bailouts?*, Inst. for Law & Econ., Univ. of Penn., Research Paper No. 09-11 and Northwest Univ. School of Law, Research Paper No. 09-05, p. 8 (hereinafter Ayotte and Skeel).

[116] Diane Davis, *Bay Harbour, Hedge Funds Challenge Sale of Lehman Assets to Barclays Capital*, BNA Bankruptcy Law Reporter, Sept. 25, 2008.

[117] Asset Purchase Agreement, Art. II, LBHI, Lehman Brothers Inc., LB 745 LLC, and Barclays Capital Inc., Sept. 16, 2009, available at http://chapter11.epiqsystems.com/View Document.aspx?DocumentPk=2066f82a-f909-4491-b858ca5406b46827.

[118] *Id.*

[119] Barclays Press Release, *Lehman Brothers Business Reopens Under Barclays Ownership*, Sept. 22, 2009, available at http://www.barcap.com/About+Barclays+Capital/Press+Office/ News+releases/News,1031, Lehman+Brothers+Business+Reopens+Under+Barclays+Ownership.

[120] Order, Pursuant to Fed. R. Bankr. P. 2004, Authorizing Discovery From Barclays Capital, Inc., U.S. Bankr. Ct. S.D.N.Y. Case No. 08-13555, Docket No. 4164. *See, also*, Diane Davis, *Court Allows Lehman Brothers to Investigate Sale of Barclays Capital Through Discovery*, BNA Bankruptcy Law Reporter, Jul. 29, 2009.

[121] Nomura Press Release, *Nomura to further enhance global presence with acquisition of Lehman Brothers' service platform in India*, Oct. 6, 2008, available at http://www. nomuraholdings.com/news/nr/ holdings/ 20081006/20081006.html.

[122] Nomura Holdings Inc. Investor Summary, *Acquisition of Former Lehman Brothers Operations*, Oct. 2008, available at http://www.nomuraholdings.com/investor/summary/ financial/data/2009_2q_leh.pdf#page=5.

[123] *Id*

[124] Robert R. Bliss and George G. Kaufman, *U.S. Corporate and Bank Insolvency: An Economic Comparison and Evaluation*, Federal Reserve Bank of Chicago (2006), available at http:// www.chicagofed.org/publications/ workingpapers/wp2006_01.pdf.

[125] 11 U.S.C. § 362(a).

[126] 11 U.S.C. § 362(b).

[127] *See, e.g.*, 11 U.S.C. §§ 546, 547, 555, 556, 559, 560, 561.
[128] The term "insider" is defined at 11 U.S.C. § 101(31).
[129] 11 U.S.C. § 547(b).
[130] Collier on Bankruptcy § 5-547.01 (15th ed. rev.).
[131] 11 U.S.C. §§ 546(e)-(j).
[132] GuyLaine Charles, *OTC Derivative Contracts in Bankruptcy: The Lehman Experience*, NY Bus. L.J. Vol. 13, No. 1, p. 14 (Spring 2009) (hereinafter "*OTC Derivative Contracts in Bankruptcy*").
[133] The collateral held on these contracts generally is under the control of the counterparty and usually consists of liquid assets, such as securities or cash. Robert R. Bliss and George G. Kaufman, *Derivatives and Systemic Risk: Netting, Collateral, and Closeout*, Federal Reserve Bank of Chicago, p. 7 (2005), available at http://www.chicagofed.org/publications/workingpapers/wp2005_03.pdf (hereinafter "*Derivatives and Systemic Risk*").
[134] *OTC Derivative Contracts in Bankruptcy* at 15.
[135] *Derivatives and Systemic Risk* at 4.
[136] Ayotte and Skeel at 31.
[137] Notice of Debtors' Motion For an Order Pursuant to Sections 105 and 365 of the Bankruptcy Code to Establish Procedures for the Settlement or Assumption and Assignment of Prepetition Derivatives Contracts, U.S. Bankr. Ct. S.D.N.Y. Case No. 08-13555, Docket No. 1498.
[138] International Swaps and Derivatives Association, Inc. Press Release, *Lehman Risk Reduction Trading Session and Protocol Agreement*, Sept. 14, 2008, available at http://www.isda.org/ press/press091408lehman.html.
[139] ISDA 2008 Lehman CDS Protocol, available at http://www.isda.org/2008lehmancdsprot/2008 lehmancdsprot.html.
[140] Ayotte and Skeel at 31.
[141] *Id.*
[142] *Id.*
[143] Debtor's Motion for an Order Pursuant to Sections 105 and 365 of the Bankruptcy Code to Establish Procedures for the Settlement or Assumption and Assignment of Prepetition Derivatives Contracts, U.S. Bankr. Ct. S.D.N.Y. Case No. 08-13555, Docket No. 1498.
[144] Order Pursuant to Sections 105 and 365 of the Bankruptcy Code to Establish Procedures for the Settlement or Assumption and Assignment of Prepetition Derivatives Contracts, U.S. Bankr. Ct. S.D.N.Y. Case No. 08-13555, Docket No. 2257.
[145] *See, e.g.*, Order Approving Consensual Assumption of Prepetition Derivative Contracts, U.S. Bankr. Ct. S.D.N.Y. Case No. 08-13555, Docket No. 2667.
[146] Matthew Goldstein, *Lehman derivatives disputes must be mediated- NY court*, Reuters, Aug. 26, 2009, available at http://www.reuters.com/article/bankruptcyNews/idUSN2627330 320090826.

In: The Lehman Brothers Bankruptcy: Analyses
Editors: Gary E. Walker and Lindel D. Clarke
ISBN: 978-1-62081-730-8

Chapter 2

THE ORDERLY LIQUIDATION OF LEHMAN BROTHERS HOLDINGS INC. UNDER THE DODD-FRANK ACT*

Federal Deposit Insurance Corporation

INTRODUCTION

The bankruptcy filing of Lehman Brothers Holdings Inc. (Lehman or LBHI) on September 15, 2008, was one of the signal events of the financial crisis. The disorderly and costly nature of the LBHI bankruptcy—the largest, and still ongoing, financial bankruptcy in U.S. history—contributed to the massive financial disruption of late 2008. This paper examines how the government could have structured a resolution of Lehman under the orderly liquidation authority of Title II of the Dodd-Frank Wall Street Reform and Consumer Protection Act (Dodd-Frank Act) and how the outcome could have differed from the outcome under bankruptcy.

The Dodd-Frank Act grants the Federal Deposit Insurance Corporation (FDIC) the powers and authorities necessary to effect an orderly liquidation of systemically important financial institutions. These authorities are analogous to those the FDIC uses to resolve failed insured depository institutions under the Federal Deposit Insurance Act (FDI Act).[1] The keys to an orderly resolution of a systemically important financial company that preserves financial stability are the ability to plan for the resolution and liquidation, provide liquidity to maintain key assets and operations, and conduct an open bidding process to sell the company and its assets and operations to the private sector as quickly as practicable. The FDIC has developed procedures that have allowed it to efficiently use its powers and authorities to resolve failed insured institutions for over 75 years. The FDIC expects to adapt many of these procedures, modified as necessary, to the liquidation of failed systemically important financial institutions.

* This is an edited, reformatted and augmented version of the Federal Deposit Insurance Corporation Quarterly, Volume 5, No. 2, dated 2011.

THE EVENTS LEADING TO THE LEHMAN BANKRUPTCY

Background

The events leading up to Lehman's bankruptcy are documented in a number of books and articles; but perhaps most extensively in two documents: the Report of Anton R. Valukas, Examiner, Bankruptcy of Lehman Brothers Holdings Inc., and the Trustee's Preliminary Investigation Report of the Attorneys for James W. Giddens, Trustee for the Securities Investors Protection Act (SIPA) Liquidation of Lehman Brothers, Inc. The analysis in this paper assumes that the events leading up to Lehman's bankruptcy filing took place roughly as described in these two reports.

Prior to 2006, Lehman had been described as being in the "moving business," primarily originating or purchasing loans and then selling them through securitizations.[2] Beginning in 2006, the firm shifted to an aggressive-growth business strategy, making "principal" investments in long-term, high-risk areas such as commercial real estate, leveraged lending and private equity. Even as the sub-prime crisis grew, the firm continued its rapid growth strategy throughout 2007.

At the beginning of 2008, with no end of the sub-prime crisis in sight, Lehman again revised its business strategy and began the process of deleveraging. However, by the end of the first quarter of 2008, the firm had made no substantial progress in either selling assets or in raising large amounts of equity. Richard S. Fuld, Jr., Lehman's CEO, told the Examiner that he had decided that Lehman would not raise equity unless it was at a premium above book value.[3]

After Bear Stearns failed and was purchased by JPMorgan Chase on March 15, 2008, Lehman was seen by many as the next most vulnerable investment bank.[4] At this time, Lehman began raising equity and seeking investment partners. In late March, Lehman contacted Warren E. Buffett, unsuccessfully seeking an investment from either Mr. Buffett or one of Berkshire Hathaway's subsidiaries. At the beginning of April, Lehman completed a $4 billion convertible preferred stock issuance. In late May, Lehman began talks with a consortium of Korean banks, but no deal was reached. On June 7, Lehman announced a $2.8 billion loss for the second quarter and on June 12 it raised $6 billion in preferred and common stock, resulting in $10 billion in the aggregate of new capital for the second quarter of 2008.

By mid-June, Lehman recognized that its commercial real estate portfolio was a major problem and began to develop a "good bank-bad bank" plan to spin off the portfolio. It identified $31.6 billion in assets that would be placed in a so-called bad bank to be named SpinCo, which would reduce Lehman's balance sheet and shed risky assets. For a number of reasons, the plan never came to fruition.[5]

Although the consortium of Korean banks withdrew from negotiations, one of the consortium's banks, the government-owned Korean Development Bank (KDB), continued to express an interest in buying or making a substantial investment in Lehman. The talks between Lehman and KDB went through a number of iterations, with KDB becoming increasingly concerned about Lehman's risky assets. In August, KDB proposed an investment in a "Clean Lehman," where all risk of future losses (risky assets) would be spun off from Lehman. By late August, KDB decided that the deteriorating global financial situation and the declining value of Korea's currency made that transaction too problematic and withdrew from further negotiations.[6]

In July 2008, Lehman contacted Bank of America with a proposal whereby Bank of America would buy a 30 percent interest in LBHI, but the discussions never culminated in a transaction. In late August, Lehman again contacted Bank of America, this time about helping finance SpinCo. Lehman subsequently asked Bank of America to consider buying the entire firm, but Bank of America did not pursue a transaction.

MetLife had also been in contact with Lehman about a possible purchase. MetLife began due diligence in early August, but decided within a few days that Lehman's commercial real estate and residential real estate assets were too risky. Also in August, the Investment Corporation of Dubai explored a potential investment principally in Lehman's Neuberger Berman wealth and asset management business. Discussions ceased in early September.[7]

By the late summer of 2008, Lehman's liquidity problems were becoming acute. Lehman's urgent need to find a buyer was precipitated in part by panic in the financial markets following the two largest players in the U.S. mortgage market, Fannie Mae and Freddie Mac, being placed into conservatorship on September 7, 2008, and the ensuing devaluation of those institutions' common and preferred stock. On September 9, Treasury Secretary Henry M. Paulson, Jr. contacted Bank of America and asked it to look into purchasing Lehman.[8] During that conversation on September 9, Secretary Paulson informed Bank of America that the government would not provide any assistance.[9] Bank of America began due diligence, and on September 11 told Secretary Paulson that there were so many problems with the assets on Lehman's balance sheet that Bank of America was unwilling to pursue a privately negotiated acquisition. Secretary Paulson then told Bank of America that, although the government would not provide any assistance, he believed a consortium of banks could be encouraged by the government to assist Bank of America in an acquisition of Lehman by taking the bad assets in a transaction similar in certain respects to the 1998 rescue of Long-Term Capital Management.[10] Bank of America then agreed to continue to consider the purchase of Lehman. At various times in the following two days, Bank of America discussed its analysis of Lehman with the Treasury Department and concluded that Lehman had approximately $65-67 billion in commercial real estate and residential mortgage-related assets and private equity investments that it was unwilling to purchase in any acquisition without the government providing loss protection. Independently, on September 13, Merrill Lynch approached Bank of America and shortly thereafter Bank of America agreed to acquire Merrill Lynch.[11]

Lehman reported further losses on September 10, and announced plans to restructure the firm.[12] The panic also affected Lehman's trading counterparties, which began to lose confidence in the firm. Many of these counterparties withdrew short-term funding, demanded increasingly greater overcollateralization on borrowings or clearing exposures, demanded more collateral to cover their derivatives positions and subsequently began to move their business away from Lehman. Lehman's clearing banks also began to demand billions of dollars of additional collateral.

A final attempt at a sale of Lehman occurred on September 11, 2008, when Lehman was contacted by Barclays, a large U.K. commercial and investment bank.[13] Barclays commenced due diligence of Lehman on September 12 and soon identified $52 billion in assets that it believed Lehman had overvalued and that Barclays would not purchase as part of the transaction. As in the case of Bank of America, these assets were concentrated in commercial real estate, residential real estate, and private equity investments. For a variety of reasons, Barclays could not get immediate regulatory approval from the U.K. authorities and the transaction was abandoned on September 14.[14]

LBHI started work on a plan for an "orderly" wind-down. The plan estimated it would take six months to unwind Lehman's positions and made the assumption that the Federal Reserve Bank of New York would assist Lehman during the wind-down process.[15] On September 14, 2008, the Federal Reserve Bank of New York told LBHI that, without the Barclay's transaction, it would not fund Lehman.

Chapter 11 Filing

With no firm willing to acquire LBHI and without funding from the central bank, LBHI filed for Chapter 11 bankruptcy on September 15, 2008.[16] On that date, a number of LBHI affiliates also filed for bankruptcy protection and Lehman's U.K. broker-dealer, Lehman Brothers International (Europe) (LBIE), filed for administration in the United Kingdom. These events adversely affected the ability of Lehman's U.S. broker-dealer, Lehman Brothers Inc. (LBI), to obtain adequate funding and settle trades. LBI remained in operation until September 19, when it was placed into a SIPA liquidation.[17]

The Lehman bankruptcy had an immediate and negative effect on U.S. financial stability and has proven to be a disorderly, time-consuming, and expensive process.[18] Of Lehman's creditors, the one that experienced the most disruption was the Reserve Primary Fund, a $62 billion money market fund. On the day of the filing, the fund held $785 million of Lehman's commercial paper, representing 13.8 percent of the amount outstanding as of May 31, 2008.[19] The fund immediately suffered a run, facing redemptions of approximately $40 billion over the following two days. With depleted cash reserves, the fund was forced to sell securities in order to meet redemption requests, which further depressed valuations. The fund's parent company announced it would "break the buck" when it re-priced its shares at $0.97 on September 16, 2008. During the remainder of the week, U.S. domestic money market funds experienced approximately $310 billion in withdrawals, representing 15 percent of their total assets and eventually prompting the U.S. Treasury to announce a temporary guarantee of money market funds.[20]

LBHI's default also caused disruptions in the swaps and derivatives markets and a rapid, market-wide unwinding of trading positions for those financial markets contracts not subject to the automatic stay in bankruptcy. For example, LBHI's bankruptcy filing affected LBI's exposure in the commodities markets via its positions that settled on markets operated by CME Group. LBI's assets on CME Group markets were largely contracts to hedge risk for the energy business conducted in its other entities. LBHI typically was guarantor of the swap contracts of its subsidiaries and affiliates. For those derivative financial instruments for which LBHI acted as guarantor, the Chapter 11 filing of LBHI constituted a default under the International Swaps and Derivatives Association agreements governing the swaps, which had the effect of allowing termination of those trades. This left naked hedges and exposed LBI to considerable pricing risk since it was not able to offer both sides of the hedge when liquidating the portfolio.[21] Similarly, the Options Clearing Corporation (OCC) threatened to invoke its emergency clearing house rules which would allow it to liquidate all of LBI's positions unless a performing third party agreed to assume the positions. The Depository

Trust & Clearing Corporation (DTCC) shared the same concerns as the CME Group and the OCC, and was unwilling to perform settlement and transfer functions for LBI unless a performing third party assumed all potential liability. When Barclays refused to assume the potential liability, the DTCC began liquidating LBI's positions as a broker-dealer whose membership had been terminated on September 22, 2008. Consequently, account transfer requests from customers that were already in process were canceled. The DTCC also reversed all account transfers that had taken place on September 19, 2008, a Friday. As a result, $468 million of customer assets that otherwise would have been immune from seizure were seized.[22] It was not until February 11, 2009, that a court order restored the reversed transactions.

Other unsecured creditors of LBHI are projected to incur substantial losses. Immediately prior to its bankruptcy filing, LBHI reported equity of approximately $20 billion; short-term and long-term indebtedness of approximately $100 billion, of which approximately $15 billion represented junior and subordinated indebtedness; and other liabilities in the amount of approximately $90 billion, of which approximately $88 billion were amounts due to affiliates. The modified Chapter 11 plan of reorganization filed by the debtors on January 25, 2011, estimates a 21.4 percent recovery for senior unsecured creditors. Subordinated debt holders and shareholders will receive nothing under the plan of reorganization, and other unsecured creditors will recover between 11.2 percent and 16.6 percent, depending on their status.[23]

Just prior to Lehman's bankruptcy filing, the firm had identified $31.6 billion in commercial real estate assets of questionable value. Potential acquirers of Lehman had identified additional problematic assets—for a total value between $50 billion and $70 billion. Even if there had been a total loss on these assets, which would have eliminated any shareholder and subordinated debt holder potential for recovery, a quick resolution of LBHI that maintained the operational integrity of the company including its systems and personnel could have left general unsecured creditors with substantially more value than projected from the bankruptcy. By preserving the going-concern value of the firm, creditors could have been provided with an immediate payment on a portion of their claims through either an advance dividend or the prompt distribution of proceeds from the sale of assets. The panic selling that ensued—further precipitating a decline in asset values and a decline in the value of collateral underlying the firm's derivatives portfolio—could have been avoided and markets would likely have remained more stable.

The Resolution and Receivership Process for Failed Banks

Resolution Process

The FDIC has been successful in using its authority under the FDI Act to maintain stability and confidence in the nation's banking system, including in the resolution of large, complex insured depository institutions. The FDIC, as receiver for an insured depository institution, is given broad powers and flexibility under the FDI Act to resolve an insured depository institution in a manner that minimizes disruption to the banking system and maximizes value. The FDIC is given similar tools to those under the Dodd-Frank Act to accomplish these goals, including the ability to create one or more bridge banks, enforce cross-guarantees among sister banks, sell and liquidate assets, and settle claims.

When an insured bank fails, the FDIC is required by statute to resolve the failed bank in the least costly way, to minimize any loss to the deposit insurance fund, and, as receiver, to maximize the return on the assets of the failed bank.[24] Banks and thrifts are typically closed by their chartering authority when they become critically undercapitalized and have not been successful in their plan to restore capital to the required levels.[25] The FDIC is then appointed receiver.[26] When structuring a bank resolution, the FDIC can pay off insured depositors and liquidate the bank's assets, sell the bank in whole or in part (a purchase and assumption transaction, or P&A), or establish a bridge institution—a temporary national bank or federal thrift—to maintain the functions of the failed bank during the process of marketing the bank's franchise. Senior management and boards of directors are not retained, and no severance pay or "golden parachutes" are permitted.

Final planning and marketing for a bank resolution normally begins 90–100 days prior to the institution being placed into receivership, though the process may be accelerated in the event of a liquidity failure. It begins when a bank's problems appear to be severe enough to potentially cause it to fail. During this period, the FDIC coordinates its actions—including the scheduling of the failure—with other regulators. When a bank becomes critically undercapitalized, the primary federal regulator (PFR) has up to 90 days to close the institution and appoint the FDIC as receiver. The FDIC and the PFR require that the bank seek an acquirer or merger partner, and insist that top management responsible for the bank's failing condition leave in order to improve the prospects for such, before the FDIC has to exercise its powers as receiver. The FDIC's authority to take over a failed or failing institution, thus wiping out stockholders and imposing losses on unsecured and uninsured creditors, not only provides an incentive for management to actively seek an acquirer, but also encourages the institution's board of directors to approve (or recommend for approval to shareholders) such transactions to avoid the risk of an FDIC receivership.

During this planning phase, the FDIC collects as much information as possible about the bank and structures the resolution transaction. This information assists the FDIC in determining the best transaction structures to offer potential acquirers. The FDIC also values bank assets and determines which assets may be particularly problematic for an acquiring institution and may need to be retained in the receivership for disposition after resolution or covered by some level of risk protection. Qualified bidders are contacted to perform due diligence, subject to a confidentiality agreement. Due diligence is offered both on-site and off-site through the use of secure internet data rooms. Bidders are then asked to submit bids on the basis of the transaction structures offered by the FDIC. The FDIC analyzes the bids received and accepts the bid that resolves the failed bank in the least costly manner to the deposit insurance fund. The least-cost requirement ensures that the deposit insurance fund will not be used to protect creditors other than insured depositors and prevents differentiation between creditors except where necessary to achieve the least costly resolution of the failed bank. Then, at the point of failure, the institution is placed into receivership and immediately sold—with the sale resulting in a transfer of deposits and assets that renders the process seamless to insured depositors. The FDIC is also able to make an immediate payment, or advance dividend, to uninsured creditors not assumed by the assuming institution based upon estimated recoveries from the liquidation.

The Orderly Liquidation of Covered Financial Companies

Introduction

Title II of the Dodd-Frank Act defines the framework for orderly resolution proceedings and establishes the powers and duties of the FDIC when acting as receiver for a covered financial company.[27] The policy goal of the Dodd-Frank Act is succinctly summarized in section 204(a) as the liquidation of "failing financial companies that pose a significant risk to the financial stability of the United States in a manner that mitigates such risk and minimizes moral hazard." Creditors and shareholders are to "bear the losses of the financial company" and the FDIC is instructed to liquidate the covered financial company in a manner that maximizes the value of the company's assets, minimizes losses, mitigates risk, and minimizes moral hazard.[28]

This section discusses the key provisions of Title II and highlights the differences between the resolution of a systemically important financial institution under Title II of the Dodd-Frank Act and a proceeding under the Bankruptcy Code.[29] What follows is a brief summary of the appointment process and five of the most important elements of the authority available to the FDIC as receiver of a covered financial company. Those five elements are: (i) the ability to conduct advance resolution planning for systemically important financial institutions through a variety of mechanisms similar to those used for problem banks (these mechanisms will be enhanced by the supervisory authority and the resolution plans, or living wills, required under section 165(d) of Title I of the Dodd-Frank Act); (ii) an immediate source of liquidity for an orderly liquidation, which allows continuation of essential functions and maintains asset values; (iii) the ability to make advance dividends and prompt distributions to creditors based upon expected recoveries; (iv) the ability to continue key, systemically important operations, including through the formation of one or more bridge financial companies; and (v) the ability to transfer all qualified financial contracts[30] with a given counterparty to another entity (such as a bridge financial company) and avoid their immediate termination and liquidation to preserve value and promote stability.[31]

Appointment

Under section 203 of the Dodd-Frank Act, at the Secretary of the Treasury's (Secretary) request, or of their own initiative, the Board of Governors of the Federal Reserve System (Federal Reserve) and the FDIC are to make a written recommendation requesting that the Secretary appoint the FDIC as receiver for a systemically important financial institution that is in default or danger of default.[32] The recommendation to place a broker or dealer, or a financial company in which the largest domestic subsidiary is a broker or dealer, into receivership is made by the Federal Reserve and the Securities and Exchange Commission (SEC), in consultation with the FDIC. Similarly, the recommendation to place an insurance company or a financial company in which the largest domestic subsidiary is an insurance company, is made by the Federal Reserve and Director of the newly established Federal Insurance Office, in consultation with the FDIC.

The Secretary is responsible for making a determination as to whether the financial company should be placed into receivership, and that determination is based on, among other things, the Secretary's finding that the financial company is in default or in danger of default; that the failure of the company and its resolution under otherwise applicable State or Federal law would have serious adverse consequences on the financial stability of the United States; and that no viable private sector alternative is available to prevent the default of the financial company.[33]

The Dodd-Frank Act provides an expedited judicial review process of the Secretary's determination. Should the board of directors of the covered financial company object to the appointment of the FDIC as receiver, a hearing is held in federal district court, and the court must make a decision on the matter within 24 hours. Upon a successful petition (or should the court fail to act within the time provided), the Secretary is to appoint the FDIC receiver of the covered financial company.[34]

Special Powers under Title II

Ability to Preserve Systemic Operations of the Covered Financial Company. The Dodd-Frank Act provides an efficient mechanism—the bridge financial company—to quickly preserve the going-concern value of the firm's assets and business lines. There are no specific parallel provisions in the Bankruptcy Code,[35] and therefore it is more difficult for a debtor company operating under Chapter 11 of the Bankruptcy Code to achieve the same result as expeditiously, particularly where circumstances compel the debtor company to seek bankruptcy protection before a wind-down plan can be negotiated and implemented. Where maximizing or preserving value depends upon a quick separation of good assets from bad assets, implementation delays could adversely impact a reorganization or liquidation proceeding.

The Dodd-Frank Act authorizes the FDIC, as receiver of a covered financial company, to establish a bridge financial company to which assets and liabilities of the covered financial company may be transferred.[36] Fundamental to an orderly liquidation of a covered financial company is the ability to continue key operations, services, and transactions that will maximize the value of the firm's assets and operations and avoid a disorderly collapse in the marketplace. To facilitate this continuity of operations, the receivership can utilize one or more bridge financial companies. The bridge financial company is a newly established, federally chartered entity that is owned by the FDIC and includes those assets, liabilities, and operations of the covered financial company as necessary to achieve the maximum value of the firm. Shareholders, debt holders, and other creditors whose claims were not transferred to the bridge financial company will remain in the receivership and will receive payments on their claims based upon the priority of payments set forth in section 210(b) of the Dodd-Frank Act. Like the bridge banks used in the resolution of large insured depository institutions,[37] the bridge financial company authority permits the FDIC to stabilize the key operations of the covered financial company by continuing valuable, systemically important operations.

While the covered financial company's board of directors and the most senior management responsible for its failure will be replaced, as required by section 204(a)(2) of the Dodd-Frank Act,[38] operations may be continued by the covered financial company's employees under the strategic direction of the FDIC, as receiver, and contractors employed by the FDIC to help oversee those operations. These contractors would typically include firms with expertise in the sector of the covered financial company. In addition, former executives, managers and other individuals with experience and expertise in running companies similar to the covered financial company would be retained to oversee those operations.

A bridge financial company also provides the receiver with flexibility in preserving the value of the assets of the covered financial company and in effecting an orderly liquidation. The receiver can retain certain assets and liabilities of the covered financial company in the receivership and transfer other assets and liabilities, as well as the viable operations of the covered financial company, to the bridge financial company. The receiver may also transfer certain qualified financial contracts to the bridge financial company, as discussed below. The bridge financial company can operate until the receiver is able to stabilize the systemic functions of the covered financial company, conduct marketing for its assets and find one or more appropriate buyers.[39]

Transfer of Qualified Financial Contracts. Under the Bankruptcy Code, counterparties to qualified financial contracts with the debtor company are permitted to terminate the contract and liquidate and net out their position. The debtor company or trustee has no authority to continue these contracts or to transfer the contracts to a third party, absent the consent of the counterparty, after the debtor company's insolvency. A complex, systemic financial company can hold very large positions in qualified financial contracts, often involving numerous counterparties and back-to-back trades, some of which may be opaque and incompletely documented. A disorderly unwinding of such contracts triggered by an event of insolvency, as each counterparty races to unwind and cover unhedged positions, can cause a tremendous loss of value, especially if lightly traded collateral covering a trade is sold into an artificially depressed, unstable market. Such disorderly unwinding can have severe negative consequences for the financial company, its creditors, its counterparties, and the financial stability of the United States.

In contrast, the Dodd-Frank Act expressly permits the FDIC to transfer qualified financial contracts to a solvent financial institution (an acquiring investor) or to a bridge financial company.[40] In such a case, counterparties are prohibited from terminating their contracts and liquidating and netting out their positions on the grounds of an event of insolvency.[41] The receiver's ability to transfer qualified financial contracts to a third party in order for the contracts to continue according to their terms—notwithstanding the debtor company's insolvency—provides market certainty and stability and preserves the value represented by the contracts.[42]

By the time of the failure of the troubled financial company, most if not all of its qualified financial contracts would be fully collateralized as counterparties sought to protect themselves from its growing credit risk. As a result, it is likely that a transfer of qualified financial contracts to a third party would involve the transfer of fully collateralized transactions and not expose the receiver to risk of loss.[43] To the extent the derivatives portfolio included qualified financial contracts which were under-collateralized or unsecured, the FDIC, as receiver of the covered financial company, would determine whether to repudiate or to transfer those qualified financial contracts to a third party based upon the FDIC's obligation to maximize value and minimize losses in the disposition of assets of the entire receivership.

Funding. A vital element in preserving continuity of systemically important operations is the availability of funding for those operations. A Chapter 11 debtor operating under the Bankruptcy Code will typically require funds in order to operate its business—referred to as debtor-in-possession financing (DIP financing). Although the Bankruptcy Code provides for a debtor company to obtain DIP financing with court approval, there are no assurances that the court will approve the DIP financing or that a debtor company will be able to obtain sufficient—or any—funding or obtain funding on acceptable terms, or what the timing of such funding might be. For a systemically important financial institution, the market may be destabilized by any delay associated with negotiating DIP financing or uncertainty as to whether the bankruptcy court will approve DIP financing. Further, the terms of the DIP financing may limit the debtor's options for reorganizing or liquidating and may diminish the franchise value of the company, particularly when the DIP financing is secured with previously unencumbered assets or when the terms of the DIP financing grant the lender oversight approval over the use of the DIP financing.

The Dodd-Frank Act provides that the FDIC may borrow funds from the Department of the Treasury, among other things, to make loans to, or guarantee obligations of, a covered financial company or a bridge financial company to provide liquidity for the operations of the receivership and the bridge financial company. Section 204(d) of the Dodd-Frank Act provides that the FDIC may make available to the receivership funds for the orderly liquidation of the covered financial company.[44] Funds provided by the FDIC under section 204(d) of the Dodd-Frank Act are to be given a priority as administrative expenses of the receiver or as amounts owed to the United States when used for the orderly resolution of the covered financial company, including, *inter alia*, to: (i) make loans to or purchase debt of the covered financial company or a covered subsidiary; (ii) purchase (or guarantee) the assets of the covered financial company or a covered subsidiary; (iii) assume or guarantee the obligations of a covered financial company or a covered subsidiary; and (iv) make additional payments or pay additional amounts to certain creditors. In the unlikely event that recoveries from the disposition of assets are insufficient to repay amounts owed to the United States, there will be a subsequent assessment on the industry to repay those amounts. By law, no taxpayer losses from the liquidation process are allowed.

Once the new bridge financial company's operations have stabilized as the market recognizes that it has adequate funding and will continue key operations, the FDIC would move as expeditiously as possible to sell operations and assets back into the private sector. Under certain circumstances the establishment of a bridge financial company may not be necessary, particularly when the FDIC has the ability to pre-plan for the sale of a substantial portion of the firm's assets and liabilities to a third party purchaser at the time of failure.

The rapid response, preservation of systemically important operations and immediate funding availability under the Dodd-Frank Act may be expected to provide certainty to the market, employees, and potential buyers. This promotes both financial stability and maximization of value in the sale of the assets of the covered financial company.

Advance Dividends and Prompt Distributions. The FDIC, as receiver for a covered financial company, satisfies unsecured creditor claims in accordance with the relevant order of priorities set forth in section 210(b) of the Dodd-Frank Act. To provide creditors with partial satisfaction of their claims as expediently as practicable, the FDIC, as receiver, is able—though not required—to make advance dividends to unsecured general creditors based upon expected recoveries. The FDIC may use funds available to the receivership, including amounts borrowed as discussed above under "—Funding," to make these advance dividends in partial satisfaction of unsecured creditor claims.[45] These advance dividends would be made at an amount less than the estimated value of the receivership assets so as not to leave the receivership with a deficit in the event the realized value is less than the expected value of the liquidation.

The FDIC, as receiver, also makes periodic distributions to unsecured creditors from the sale of assets. Accordingly, an unsecured creditor will not be required to wait until all claims are valued, or until all assets are disposed of, before receiving one or more substantial payments on his claim. The ability promptly to provide creditors with partial satisfaction of claims following the failure of a covered financial company serves the Title II mandate of mitigating systemic impact, particularly in the case of key counterparties. The FDIC has successfully provided advance dividends to unsecured creditors (including uninsured depositors) and distributions from the sale of assets to unsecured creditors in the resolution of insured depository institutions under the FDI Act to quickly move funds to claimants and to help to stabilize local markets.

In large, complex bankruptcy cases such as Lehman, a creditor may not receive any payment on his claim for a considerable period of time following the commencement of the bankruptcy case. One reason for this is that it often takes a great deal of time to establish both the size of the pool of assets available for general unsecured creditors and the legitimate amounts of the claims held by such creditors. Litigation is typically needed to establish both of these numbers, which can require years of discovery followed by trial, then more years of appeals and remands.

If sufficient certainty can be attained regarding a portion of the claims, the Chapter 7 trustee will petition the court for permission to make an interim distribution, or the Chapter11 trustee or debtor-in-possession will provide in the plan of reorganization or plan of liquidation for interim distributions as various stages of the restructuring are reached.[46] However, except in the case of "prepackaged" plans of reorganization, even an interim distribution can take months or years to materialize. In the case of LBHI, there has been no distribution to general unsecured creditors more than two years after LBHI's initial bankruptcy filing.

Oversight and Advanced Planning. An essential prerequisite for any effective resolution is advance planning, a well-developed resolution plan, and access to the supporting information needed to undertake such planning.

Bankruptcy proceedings are typically challenging in the case of systemically important financial institutions in part because the participants have little notice or opportunity for advance preparation or coordination. The bankruptcy court, which must approve actions by the debtor outside of the ordinary course of business, may have little or no knowledge about the systemically important financial institution, and would have to rely upon the management of such institution for requisite information.

Title I of the Dodd-Frank Act significantly enhances regulators' ability to conduct advance resolution planning in respect of systemically important financial institutions through a variety of mechanisms, including heightened supervisory authority and the resolution plans, or living wills, required under section 165(d) of Title I of the Dodd-Frank Act.[47] The examination authority provided by Title I of the Dodd-Frank Act will provide the FDIC with on-site access to systemically important financial institutions, including the ability to access real-time data.[48] This will enable the FDIC, working in tandem with the Federal Reserve and other regulators, to collect and analyze information for resolution planning purposes in advance of the impending failure of the institution.

An essential part of such plans will be to describe how this process can be accomplished without posing systemic risk to the public and the financial system. If the company does not submit a credible resolution plan, the statute permits increasingly stringent requirements to be imposed that, ultimately, can lead to divestiture of assets or operations identified by the FDIC and the Federal Reserve to facilitate an orderly resolution. The Dodd-Frank Act requires each designated financial company to produce a resolution plan, or living will, that maps its business lines to legal entities and provides integrated analyses of its corporate structure; credit and other exposures; funding, capital, and cash flows; domestic and foreign jurisdictions in which it operates; its supporting information systems and other essential services; and other key components of its business operations, all as part of the plan for its rapid and orderly resolution. The credit exposure reports required by the statute will also provide important information critical to the FDIC's planning processes by identifying the company's significant credit exposures, its component exposures, and other key information across the entity and its affiliates. The elements contained in a resolution plan will not only help the FDIC and other domestic regulators to better understand a firm's business and how that entity may be resolved, but the plans will also enhance the FDIC's ability to coordinate with foreign regulators in an effort to develop a comprehensive and coordinated resolution strategy for a cross-border firm.[49]

Structure and Bidding

Once the structure is developed, the FDIC would seek bids from qualified, interested bidders for the business lines or units that have going-concern value. The FDIC would analyze the bids received and choose the bid or bids that would provide the highest recovery to the receivership. The winning bidder would be informed and would take control of the business lines or units concurrent with the closing of the institution. Losses would be borne by equity holders, unsecured debt holders, and other unsecured creditors that remain in the receivership. These creditors would receive payment on their claims in accordance with the priority of payment rules set forth in the Dodd-Frank Act.[50] The FDIC could make advance dividend payments to creditors based upon an upfront conservative valuation of total recoveries. As recoveries are realized, the FDIC could also pay out distributions to creditors as it has done successfully with failed insured banks. See "—Special Powers under Title II—Advance Dividends and Prompt Distributions," above.

ORDERLY RESOLUTION OF LEHMAN UNDER THE DODD-FRANK ACT

March–July, Due Diligence and Structuring the Resolution

Planning in the Crisis Environment: As the financial crisis enveloped Bear Stearns, the FDIC would have worked closely with the Federal Reserve and other appropriate regulators to gather information about the systemically important firms that may fall under the FDIC's resolution authority. At a minimum, the firms' resolution plans would have been reviewed jointly by the FDIC and the Federal Reserve to make sure that the plans were credible and up-to-date. The information supporting these plans and any additional information that the FDIC and Federal Reserve would have received through on-site discussions with the firms during their review of the resolution plans would have provided the FDIC with valuable information necessary for effective resolution planning, information not available to the FDIC prior to the passage of the Dodd-Frank Act. In this regard the FDIC's presence would not be indicative that a resolution is imminent, but rather that in a crisis the FDIC seeks to assure that all firms' resolution plans are sufficiently robust to allow an orderly liquidation of any particular firm that might fail.

For Lehman, if senior management had not found an early private sector solution, the FDIC would have needed to establish an on-site presence to begin due diligence and to plan for a potential Title II resolution. Lehman was not the only firm in possible trouble and the FDIC would likely have had a heightened presence in other subject firms at the time. Thus, the market would not necessarily have taken the FDIC's heightened presence as a signal that a failure was imminent as the market already was aware of Lehman's problems. While it is possible in this situation or in other situations that the FDIC's on site presence could create signaling concerns, this argues for the FDIC having a continuous on-site presence for resolution planning during good times.

Discussions with Lehman: In the various accounts of the failure of Lehman it is noteworthy that senior management discounted the possibility of failure until the very last moment.[51] There was apparently a belief, following the government's actions in respect of Bear Stearns, that the government, despite statements to the contrary, would step in and provide financial assistance and Lehman would be rescued. If Title II of the Dodd- Frank Act had been in effect, the outcome would have been considerably different. Lehman's senior management would have understood clearly that the government would not and could not extend financial assistance outside of a resolution because of the clear requirements in the Dodd-Frank Act that losses are to be borne by equity holders and unsecured creditors, and management and directors responsible for the condition of the failed financial company are not to be retained.

To convey this point to Lehman and its Board of Directors, the FDIC could have participated in a meeting in the spring of 2008, together with Lehman's Board of Directors, the Federal Reserve, and the SEC, to outline the circumstances that would lead to the appointment of the FDIC as receiver for one or more Lehman entities, and what that resolution would entail. The regulators would have emphasized that any open-company assistance or "too big to fail" transaction would be unavailable,[52] and that the alternative to a sale of the company or a substantial capital raising would be a bankruptcy under the Bankruptcy Code or a resolution under Title II with no expectation of any return to shareholders.

The regulators could have set a deadline of July to sell the company or raise capital. This would have clearly focused Lehman's Board of Directors on the urgency of the matter and encouraged the Board to accept the best non-government offer it received notwithstanding its dilutive nature; virtually any private sale would yield a better return for shareholders than the likely negligible proceeds shareholders would receive in an FDIC receivership, as equity holders have the lowest priority claims in a receivership.

Lehman's senior management and Board of Directors may have been more willing to recommend offers that were below the then-current market price if they knew with certainty that there would be no extraordinary government assistance made available to the company and that Lehman would be put into receivership. Such avenues may have been available. For instance, KDB is reported to have suggested paying $6.40 per share when Lehman's stock was trading at $17.50 on August 31—just 15 days prior to Lehman's bankruptcy filing.

Forcing Lehman to more earnestly market itself to a potential acquirer or strategic investor well in advance of Lehman's failure would serve several other goals, even if such private sector transaction were unsuccessful. The FDIC would be able to use this marketing information to identify appropriate bidders who would be invited to join in the FDIC-led due diligence and bidding process as described in "—Due Diligence" and "—Structuring the Transaction," below.

The preferred outcome under the Dodd-Frank Act is for a troubled financial company to find a strategic investor or to recapitalize without direct government involvement or the FDIC being appointed receiver. To that end, the recommendation and determination prescribed by section 203(a)(2)(E) and (b)(3) of the Dodd-Frank Act, respectively, concern the availability of a viable private sector alternative. Requiring a troubled financial company to aggressively market itself pre-failure helps to ensure that exercise of the orderly resolution authority in Title II is a last resort. In this matter, the FDIC's experience with troubled banks is instructive. The commencement of the FDIC's due diligence process has frequently provided the motivation senior management has needed to pursue sale or recapitalization more aggressively. Between 1995 and the end of 2007, the FDIC prepared to resolve 150 institutions. Of this number, only 56—that is, 37 percent—eventually failed. Of course, many fewer problem banks have been able to find merger partners or recapitalize since the crisis began. However, from 2008 to 2010, of the 432 banks where the FDIC began the resolution process, 110—25 percent—avoided failure, either by finding an acquirer or recapitalizing.

Due Diligence: Just as when an insured depository institution is a likely candidate for an FDI Act receivership, the FDIC will need to gather as much information as possible about a systemically important financial institution in advance of any Title II resolution. In the case of LBHI, the SEC and the Federal Reserve Bank of New York began on-site daily monitoring in March 2008, following the collapse and sale of Bear Stearns, at which point the FDIC would already have been on-site at Lehman to facilitate the FDIC's Title I resolution planning and monitoring activities.[53] The FDIC would have determined, jointly with other supervisors, the condition of the company for the purposes of ordering corrective actions to avoid failure, and it otherwise would have prepared for a Title II orderly resolution.

The FDIC would continue assembling information about the condition and value of Lehman's assets and various lines of business. In preparing for a Title II resolution of a company subject to heightened prudential standards under Title I, the FDIC will have access to the information included in such company's resolution plan, or living will.[54] Though that resolution plan is designed to provide for the resolution of the systemically important financial institution under the Bankruptcy Code, it would provide regulators with invaluable information about the institution's structure, organization, and key operations that could form the basis for an orderly liquidation under Title II. It is the FDIC's experience that management of a troubled institution often has an overly optimistic view of the value of its franchise and the firm's prospect for recovery. Thus, while the resolution plan would provide key financial and other data about the consolidated entity, an independent examination of the troubled firm may have been necessary. The FDIC will also have access to real-time data from on-site monitoring conducted by the FDIC and other prudential regulators.

The FDIC's participation in gathering information and in exercising its examination authority would be done in coordination with the on-site monitoring activities of the SEC and the Federal Reserve Bank of New York. The development of additional information to facilitate a potential resolution would be done in a manner that would not disrupt the business operations or indicate an imminent failure of the financial company. As regulated entities under the Dodd-Frank Act, heightened supervision by the FDIC, the Federal Reserve, and other prudential regulators will be normal. As a result, these information-gathering activities should neither signal increased distress nor precipitate market reaction.

While conducting due diligence, the FDIC would have begun developing the transaction and bid framework by analyzing the legal structure of the firm, its operations, and its financial data. In this case, LBHI was a large holding company with major overseas operations.[55] As with any large, complex financial company, there were many interrelations among the major affiliates of the group. LBHI was the guarantor of all obligations of LBI and the source of funding for a number of other Lehman entities. LBI was the employer of record for much of the company, including various foreign subsidiaries. LBI was also the owner and operator of key IT systems used throughout the company and provided custody and trade execution services for clients of foreign Lehman entities, primarily for trades conducted by LBIE in the United States. Likewise, LBIE provided custody and trade execution services for clients of LBI conducting trades outside of the United States. The interconnected nature of Lehman's operations would have argued for maintaining maximum franchise value by developing a deal structure that would have maintained the continuing uninterrupted operation of the major business lines of the firm by transferring those assets and operations to an acquirer immediately upon the failure of the parent holding company.[56]

During the FDIC's investigation of the Lehman group, it would have identified subsidiaries which would be likely to fail in the event of a failure of LBHI but would likely not be systemic and would provide little or no value to the consolidated franchise. The FDIC would not have recommended a resolution under Title II for those subsidiaries, and they would likely have been resolved under the Bankruptcy Code or other applicable insolvency regime.[57] The assets of these subsidiaries would not have been part of a Title II receivership, other than the receiver's equity claim; the FDIC would have had no expected return on the equity for any such non-systemic subsidiary placed into bankruptcy. The FDIC also would have identified any subsidiary that would be likely to fail in the event of a failure of LBHI, and whose failure likely would be systemic. The FDIC would have made an evaluation as to whether the resolution of any such subsidiary under Title II would have aided in the orderly resolution of the parent company.[58]

As is the case with insured depository institutions that have foreign operations, the FDIC would have begun contacting key foreign financial authorities on a discrete basis to discuss what legal or financial issues might arise out of an FDIC receivership, or out of foreign resolution regimes in the case of Lehman entities operating outside of the United States, and how those resolutions could be coordinated. In addition, foreign financial authorities would have been consulted when foreign financial companies and investors expressed interest in investing in or purchasing Lehman. These discussions would have addressed, at a minimum, the financial strength of the acquirer, types of approvals that would be required to consummate a transaction, and any identified impediments to the transaction. Regular, ongoing contact would be particularly important after the transaction structure was determined and qualified bidders had been contacted and had expressed interest.

Valuation and Identification of Problem Assets: On a consolidated basis, LBHI and its subsidiaries had total assets of $639 billion, with $26.3 billion in book equity and total unsecured long-term and short-term borrowings of $162.8 billion as of May 31, 2008. The parent company, LBHI, had $231 billion in assets, with $26.3 billion in book equity and $114.6 billion in unsecured long-term and short-term borrowings. On September 14 (just prior to bankruptcy), LBHI (unconsolidated) was slightly smaller with $209 billion in assets, $20.3 billion in book equity, and $99.5 billion in long-term and short-term unsecured debt, including $15 billion in subordinated debt. In addition, LBHI's short-term unsecured debt included $2.3 billion in commercial paper—almost 40 percent of the approximately $5.7 billion in commercial paper outstanding enterprise wide.

By March 2008, Lehman had recognized that its commercial real estate related holdings were a major impediment to finding a merger partner. Its SpinCo proposal identified $31.7 billion in significantly underperforming commercial real estate related assets. During the week leading up to Lehman's bankruptcy filing, Bank of America identified an additional $38.3 billion in suspect residential real estate related assets and private equity assets that it would not purchase in an acquisition. Barclay's identified $20.3 billion of similar potentially additional problem assets in its due diligence. In the FDIC's resolution process, the FDIC's structuring team as well as prospective bidders would have had sufficient time to perform due diligence and identify problem asset pools. While Lehman was seeking an investor pre-failure, the FDIC would have identified and valued these problem asset pools in order to set a defined bid structure for Lehman. The bid structure would have allowed prospective acquirers to bid upon options to purchase all of Lehman's assets in a whole financial company P&A with loss sharing on defined pools of problem assets, or a purchase which excludes those problem asset pools. In the latter bid option, the receivership estate would have purchased the problem assets out of Lehman's subsidiaries at their fair market value prior to consummating the purchase agreement with the acquirer. These problem assets, in addition to those directly owned by the holding company, could have been retained in the receivership or placed into a bridge financial company prior to future disposition. Either bid would have allowed a further option for the prospective acquirer to pay to assume the commercial paper and other critical short-term securities of Lehman. The bidding structure is discussed more fully in "—August, Begin Marketing Lehman," below.

Both bid structures are intended to provide comfort to not only the potential acquirer, but also to its regulators, concerning the potential down-side exposure to problem assets. In excluding pools of identified problem assets from a bid, an acquirer is protected directly by effectively capping its exposure to such assets—which are left with the receivership—at zero. This risk minimization comes at the cost of lost potential upside from returns on servicing the troubled assets, higher administrative costs of the receiver, and a less attractive bid. In the loss-sharing structure, a potential acquirer receives tail-risk protection: the acquirer is able to cap its exposure to an identified pool of problem assets at set levels. This comfort is particularly important where a potential acquirer is unable to undertake in-depth due diligence on such assets, or must do so on an abbreviated time table. This down-side protection will also be important to regulators, as it mitigates the risk of an acquirer experiencing financial distress due to the problem assets of an acquiree.[59]

Structuring the Resolution: During due diligence, the FDIC would have identified certain pools of assets of Lehman—including certain commercial real estate, residential real estate, and private equity assets—that would make a whole financial company P&A transaction difficult. See "—Valuation and Identification of Problem Assets," above. These troubled assets were estimated to be between $50 and $70 billion in book value.

The FDIC would have set up a data room to enable potential acquirers to conduct due diligence, and would have begun developing a marketing structure for Lehman and its assets. The FDIC would have identified potential acquirers of Lehman. Criteria would have included maximization of value on the sale, the stability of the potential acquirer, and the ability of the acquirer expediently to consummate an acquisition.[60] Having identified the potential acquirers, the FDIC would have explained the bid structure and invited the firms to conduct (or continue) due diligence of Lehman.

During this time, the FDIC would have continued to monitor Lehman's progress in marketing itself. This would have encouraged Lehman to consummate a non- government transaction, which remained the best outcome for all parties. It would also have provided the FDIC with key information concerning interested acquirers and potential issues and concerns of such acquirers in completing a transaction.

Also during this time, as is the case with insured depository institutions that have foreign operations, the FDIC would have continued a dialogue with key foreign financial authorities to discuss what legal or financial issues might arise out of an FDIC receivership, or out of foreign resolution regimes in the case of Lehman entities operating outside of the United States, and how those resolutions could be coordinated.[61] Specifically, the FDIC would address issues of ring-fencing of assets, particularly of Lehman's U.K.-based broker-dealer. See "—Due Diligence," above.

August, Begin Marketing Lehman

Assuming Lehman were unable to sell itself, the FDIC would have commenced with marketing Lehman.[62] The FDIC would have set a defined bidding structure. Prospective acquirers previously identified (as discussed in "—March–July, Due Diligence and Structuring the Resolution—Structuring the Transaction," above) would have been invited to bid based on the following options:

Option A: Whole financial company purchase and assumption with partial loss share (loss-sharing P&A). Under this option, the assets and operations of Lehman are transferred to the acquirer with no government control and no ongoing servicing of Lehman assets by the government. Due to the problem assets discussed above, however, it may be necessary for the receivership estate to offer a potential acquirer protection from loss in respect of that identified pool of problem assets. In this type of transaction, the acquirer purchases the assets at their gross book value, and assumes, at a minimum, the secured liabilities. Depending on the bid, other liability classes may be assumed as well. Since the book value of assets must always exceed the amount of liabilities assumed in this structure, the acquirer, after factoring its discount bid for the assets, must also provide a combination of cash and a note payable to the receivership estate to balance out the transaction.[63] The receivership estate's share of loss payments are made through reductions in the outstanding balance of the note payable as loss claims occur over time.

Transactions offering an option for a sharing of potential future losses between the acquirer and the FDIC have been frequently used to resolve failed banks. Loss-share transactions allow the FDIC to obtain better bids from potential assuming institutions by sharing a portion of the risk on a pool of assets. This has been particularly important during periods of uncertainty about the value of assets. The FDIC's experience has been that these transactions result in both better bid prices and improved recoveries for the receivership and receivership creditors.

Another benefit of loss sharing is that the FDIC is able to transfer administration of the failed financial company's problem assets to the assuming institution and receive a premium for the failed company's franchise value, thereby maximizing value. By having the assuming company absorb a portion of the loss, the FDIC induces rational and responsible credit management behavior from the assuming institution to minimize credit losses. Compared to the alternative of retaining problem assets in receivership, the loss-share structure tends to be more efficient, as it limits losses and administrative costs of the receivership.

The FDIC would therefore permit bidders to bid on a structure based on a sale of the whole financial company, with partial but substantial coverage of losses on those identified problem assets.[64] The loss-share structure encourages bidders to maximize their bids by offering downside credit risk protection from loss on an identified pool of problem assets. This can produce a more efficient outcome as it incentivizes the acquirer to maximize recoveries while reducing administrative costs of the receivership. See "The Resolution and Receivership Process for Failed Banks—Loss Share," above.

Option B: Modified purchase and assumption without loss share, which excludes certain identified problem assets (modified P&A, similar to a good bank–bad bank resolution strategy). Under this option, the majority of the assets and operations of Lehman are transferred to the acquirer. Identified pools of problem assets would not be included in the transaction, but retained for disposition at a later date.[65]

Liabilities: While the FDIC would transfer the assets of Lehman to the acquirer in accordance with Option A or Option B described above, most unsecured creditor claims would remain with the receivership, including shareholder claims and claims of holders of unsecured, long-term indebtedness. Fully secured claims would be transferred, along with the collateral, to the acquirer. The bid participants would have the opportunity to bid on acquiring certain short-term indebtedness of Lehman, particularly Lehman's outstanding commercial paper. In order for this bid structure to be successful, bidders would need to bid an amount sufficient to cover the loss that the commercial paper and other short-term creditors would have otherwise incurred had the creditors remained in the receivership.

In comparing bids under Option A and Option B, the receivership estate's cost of managing and disposing of the identified problem assets would be taken into consideration. Depending on the bid, the acquirer would purchase the acquired assets through a combination of one or more of cash, notes, and assumed liabilities.

It should be noted that the proposed bid structure represented by Option A and Option B represents one set of options for disposing of the assets and operations of a covered financial company in an efficient manner. The FDIC would have the flexibility to restructure these bids as the facts and circumstances of a particular covered financial company warrant in order to satisfy the FDIC's statutory mandates of promoting financial stability, maximizing recoveries, and minimizing losses.

Early September, Closing

Following due diligence, interested parties would have submitted closed, or sealed, bids. The FDIC would have evaluated the bids based upon the requirement under the Dodd-Frank Act to maximize value upon any disposition of assets.[66] Bids would have been evaluated on a present-value basis. The FDIC would have selected the winning bid, and the acquirer and the FDIC, as the receiver for LBHI, would enter into a conditional P&A agreement based upon the agreed upon bid structure.[67]

We have assumed, for the limited purpose of this discussion, that Barclays would have provided a winning bid to complete an acquisition of Lehman.[68]

We have further assumed that, as LBHI reached a point at which it was in default or in danger of default, a systemic determination would have been made by the Secretary of the Treasury and the FDIC would have been appointed receiver of LBHI.[69]

At the time a determination was made that Lehman should be put into receivership and the FDIC named receiver, the assets and select liabilities of Lehman would have been transferred to Barclays as the acquiring institution based upon the structure of the winning bid.[70] Barclays would have maintained the key operations of Lehman in a seamless manner, integrating those operations over time. Disruptions to the market likely would have been minimal. Barclays would have continued to make scheduled payments on liabilities transferred to it, including secured indebtedness and, to the extent assumed by Barclays, commercial paper.[71] To the extent Barclays' winning bid had been based upon a whole financial company with loss share, it would have been responsible for servicing problem assets in accordance with the terms of the loss-sharing P&A agreement.

Lehman's derivatives trading was conducted almost exclusively in its broker-dealer, LBI, and in LBI's subsidiaries.[72] As a result, Barclays' acquisition of the broker-dealer group would have transferred the derivatives operations, together with the related collateral, to Barclays in its entirety as an ongoing operation. At the moment of failure, Barclays would have assumed any parent guarantee by Lehman outstanding in respect of the subsidiaries' qualified financial contracts. This action should have substantially eliminated any commercial basis for the subsidiaries' counterparties to engage in termination and close-out netting of qualified financial contracts based upon the insolvency of the parent guarantor. This would have removed any financial incentive to do so as well, as a financially secure acquirer would have assumed the obligations and provided guarantees to the same extent as its predecessor, in part to preserve the significant franchise value of the derivatives portfolio (including the underlying collateral).[73] The more limited derivatives operations conducted by LBHI would have been subjected to haircuts to the extent that any net amount due to a counterparty was not collateralized or hedged. Particularly in the future, it is expected that the vast majority of the derivatives transactions of a covered financial company will be fully collateralized.

Barclays would have purchased the acquired assets through a combination of one or more of the following: cash, notes, and the assumption of liabilities. The FDIC, as receiver for Lehman, would have disposed of any problem assets left behind in the receivership or managed the loss-share agreement with Barclays in respect of those assets, and would have settled creditor claims in accordance with the priority for repayment set forth in the Dodd-Frank Act.[74]

The Likely Treatment of Creditors

As mentioned earlier, by September of 2008, LBHI's book equity was down to $20 billion and it had $15 billion of subordinated debt, $85 billion in other outstanding short- and long-term debt, and $90 billion of other liabilities, most of which represented intra-company funding. The equity and subordinated debt represented a buffer of $35 billion to absorb losses before other creditors took losses. Of the $210 billion in assets, potential acquirers had identified $50 to $70 billion as impaired or of questionable value. If losses on those assets had been $40 billion (which would represent a loss rate in the range of 60 to 80 percent), then the entire $35 billion buffer of equity and subordinated debt would have been eliminated and losses of $5 billion would have remained. The distribution of these losses would depend on the extent of collateralization and other features of the debt instruments. If losses had been distributed equally among all of Lehman's remaining general unsecured creditors, the $5 billion in losses would have resulted in a recovery rate of approximately $0.97 for every claim of $1.00, assuming that no affiliate guarantee claims would be triggered. This is significantly more than what these creditors are expected to receive under the Lehman bankruptcy. This benefit to creditors derives primarily from the ability to plan, arrange due diligence, and conduct a well structured competitive bidding process. The Dodd-Frank Act provides a further potential benefit to creditors: earlier access to liquidity. As described above, the acquirer would have provided a combination of cash and a note to the receiver. Under the Dodd-Frank Act, the FDIC could have promptly distributed the cash proceeds from the sale of assets to claimants in partial satisfaction of unsecured creditor claims.[75] The FDIC would also have been able to borrow up to 90 percent of the fair value of the note available for repayment—together with the fair value of any assets left in the receivership available for repayment—from the orderly liquidation fund and advance those funds to the receivership.[76] These borrowed funds could have been made available to creditors immediately in the form of advance dividends to satisfy a portion of creditor claims based upon the total expected recovery in the resolution. This is in contrast to the actual circumstances of the LBHI bankruptcy, in which there has been no confirmed plan of reorganization or cash distribution to unsecured creditors of LBHI more than two years after the failure of Lehman.

CONCLUSION

Title II of the Dodd-Frank Act provides "the necessary authority to liquidate failing financial companies that pose a systemic risk to the financial stability of the United States in a manner that mitigates such risk and minimizes moral hazard."[77] These powers and authorities are analogous to those the FDIC uses to resolve failed insured depository institutions under the FDI Act. In the case of Lehman, following appointment by the Secretary of the Treasury, the FDIC could have used its power as receiver and the ability to facilitate a sale under Title II of the Dodd-Frank Act to preserve the institution's franchise value and transfer Lehman's assets and operations to an acquirer. The FDIC would have imposed losses on equity holders and unsecured creditors, terminated senior management responsible for the failure of the covered financial company, maintained Lehman's liquidity, and, most importantly, attempted to mitigate and prevent disruption to the U.S. financial system, including the commercial paper and derivatives markets. The very availability of a comprehensive resolution system that sets forth in advance the rules under which the government will act following the appointment of a receiver could have helped to prevent a "run on the bank" and the resulting financial instability. By maintaining franchise value and mitigating severe disruption in the financial markets, it is more likely that debt holders and other general creditors will receive greater recoveries on their claims under the Dodd-Frank Act than they would have otherwise received in a Chapter 7 liquidation or a Chapter 11 reorganization.

The key to an orderly resolution and liquidation of a systemically important financial institution is the ability to plan for its resolution and liquidation, provide liquidity to maintain key assets and operations, and preserve financial stability. During the planning phase, the FDIC, working in tandem with the Federal Reserve and the SEC, would have been able to identify problem assets; require management to raise capital or find an acquirer; gather information about the institution's structure, organization, and key operations; prepare the resolution transaction structure and bids; and seek potential acquirers. During this phase, the FDIC would have contacted the relevant foreign and domestic regulatory authorities and governments to coordinate the resolution. Through this process, the FDIC would have minimized losses and maximized recoveries in the event the systemically important financial institution failed and was put into receivership.

Perhaps most importantly, the Dodd-Frank Act provides the means to preserve systemically important operations and reduce systemic consequences while limiting moral hazard by imposing losses on the stockholders and unsecured creditors of the failed systemically important financial institution rather than on the U.S. taxpayer. In so doing, the FDIC is able to fulfill its statutory mandate to preserve financial stability and serve the public interest.

AFTERWORD

This paper has focused on how the government could have structured a resolution of Lehman under Title II of the Dodd-Frank Act following the failure of such firm. In so doing, we have made a number of assumptions and caveats to provide a framework for the analysis and to maintain consistency with the historical record. That is, while we have assumed that the Dodd-Frank Act had been enacted pre-failure, and that the FDIC would have been able to avail itself of the pre-planning powers available under Title I, including having access to key data of subject institutions through resolution plans and on-site monitoring, we have not assumed-away the failure of Lehman.

The orderly liquidation authority of Title II would be a remedy of last resort, to be used only after the remedies available under Title I—including the increased informational and supervisory powers—are unable to stave off a failure. In particular, it is expected that the mere knowledge of the consequences of a Title II resolution, including the understanding that financial assistance is no longer an option, would encourage a troubled institution to find an acquirer or strategic partner on its own well in advance of failure. Likewise, on-site monitoring and access to real-time data provided under Title I is expected to provide an early-warning system to the FDIC and other regulators well in advance of a subject institution's imminent failure.

We have also stuck closely to the facts in identifying the most likely acquirer of Lehman as Barclays, while also discussing the potential role played by Bank of America and KDB. Lehman, while a complex firm, had value primarily as an investment bank. Thus, its resolution was focused on keeping the investment bank's operations intact in order to preserve its going-concern value. In other cases, a large financial firm with many pieces such as a large commercial bank, an insurance company, and a broker-dealer, might represent a financial firm that is no longer too big to fail, but may be too big to continue to exist as one entity.[78] Over the longer term, the development of resolution plans will enable the FDIC to prepare to split up such a firm in order to facilitate a Title II liquidation. The FDIC could pursue a number of alternatives instead of a whole financial company purchase-and-assumption transaction, including a spin-off of assets, an initial public offering, a debt-to-equity conversion, or some other transaction that would satisfy regulatory concerns about concentration while minimizing losses to the failed company's creditors.

End Notes

[1] 12 U.S.C. § 1811 *et seq.*

[2] Anton R. Valukas, *Examiner's Report: Bankruptcy of Lehman Brothers Holdings Inc.*, Vol. 2, 43, (Mar. 11, 2010) (hereinafter, Examiner's Report).

[3] *Id.* at 150–52. Lehman did raise capital at a later date. Presumably more could have been raised at this time if Lehman had been willing to consider less favorable terms to the then-current shareholders.

[4] *Id.* at 612–13.

[5] *Id.* at 640–62.

[6] *Id.* at 668–81.

[7] *Id.* at 687–94.

[8] Henry M. Paulson, Jr., *On the Brink: Inside the Race to Stop the Collapse of the Global Financial System*, 177 (2010) (hereinafter, *On the Brink*).

[9] *Id.* at 177, 184–85.

[10] *Id.* at 199–206.

[11] Examiner's Report at 696–703.

[12] Lehman Brothers Holdings Inc., Periodic Report on Form 8-K, Sept. 10, 2008.

[13] Similar to the case of Bank of America, Barclays contacted Lehman at Treasury's encouragement. Barclays and Bank of America were proceeding under similar expectations that there would not be any government assistance.

[14] Examiner's Report at 703–11 and *On the Brink* at 203–11.

[15] Examiner's Report at 720–21.

[16] LBHI filed for bankruptcy protection on Monday, September 15, 2008, at 1:30 am EDT. *Id.* at 726.

[17] LBHI's demise left LBI unable to obtain adequate financing on an unsecured or secured basis. LBI lost customers and experienced both an increase in failed transactions and additional demands for collateral by clearing banks and others. See *Trustee's Preliminary Investigation Report of the Attorneys for James W. Giddens, Trustee for the SIPA Liquidation of Lehman Brothers, Inc.*, 10, 25-26, 56.

[18] After more than two years in bankruptcy proceedings, total fees paid to advisers involved in the Lehman bankruptcy have exceeded $1 billion. *See* Liz Moyer, *Lehman Fees Hit $1 Billion and Counting*, Wall Street Journal, Nov. 23, 2010, *available at* http://online.wsj.com/article/ SB20001424052748 70424390 4575630653803513816.html.

[19] Lehman used November 30 as its year end for financial reporting purposes. Accordingly, May 31, 2008, was the date of the close of its second quarter financial period.

[20] *President's Working Group on Financial Markets: Money Market Fund Reform Options* (Oct. 2010), *available at* http://www.treasury.gov/press-center/press-releases/Documents/10.21% 20PWG%20Report%20Final.pdf.

[21] SIPA Trustee Report Section V.B., p. 66.

[22] *Id.* at 73.

[23] Joseph Checkler, *Lehman's New Creditor Plan Doesn't Factor in Key Group*, Wall Street Journal, Jan. 27, 2011. The plan of reorganization is subject to approval by creditors.

[24] The FDIC is required, pursuant to 12 U.S.C. § 1823(c)(4), to resolve failed insured depository institutions in the manner that is least costly to the deposit insurance fund. The Dodd-Frank Act does not require that a least cost determination be made in respect of a covered financial company, though the FDIC is required, to the greatest extent practicable, to maximize returns and minimize losses in the disposition of assets. *See* section 210(a)(9)(E) of the Dodd-Frank Act, 12 U.S.C. § 5390(a)(9)(E).

[25] Some banks, particularly large banks, may also be closed due to a liquidity failure (an inability to pay debts as they become due).

[26] As a receiver, the FDIC succeeds to the rights, powers, and privileges of the failed bank and its stockholders, officers, and directors. It may collect all obligations and money due to the institution, preserve and liquidate the institution's assets and property, and perform any other function of the institution consistent with its appointment as receiver. It has the power to sell a failed bank to another insured bank, and to transfer the failed bank's assets and liabilities without the consent or approval of any other agency, court, or party with contractual rights. The FDIC may also, as permitted by statute, repudiate contracts such as leases that are burdensome to the receivership and may rid the receivership of burdensome obligations. The FDIC operates its receiverships independently of the court or bankruptcy system, although certain of the FDIC's actions are subject to judicial review.

[27] A failed systemically important financial institution is deemed a covered financial company for purposes of Title II of the Dodd-Frank Act once a systemic determination has been made by the Secretary of the Treasury pursuant to section 203(b) thereof, 12 U.S.C. § 5383(b). *See* "—Appointment," *infra.*

[28] *See* sections 204(a)(1) and 210(a)(9)(E) of the Dodd-Frank Act, 12 U.S.C. §§ 5384(a)(1) and 5390(a)(9)(E).

[29] 11 U.S.C. § 101 *et seq.*

[30] Generally, qualified financial contracts are financial instruments such as securities contracts, commodities contracts, forwards contracts, swaps, repurchase agreements, and any similar agreements. *See* section 210(c)(8)(D)(i) of the Dodd-Frank Act, 12 U.S.C. § 5390(c)(8) (D)(i).

[31] *See generally* section 165 of Title I of the Dodd-Frank Act, 12 U.S.C. § 5365 and "The Orderly Resolution of Covered Financial Companies—Special Powers under Title II—Oversight and Advanced Planning," *infra.*

[32] Upon a 2/3 vote by the boards of both the FDIC and the Federal Reserve, a written recommendation is delivered to the Secretary. The recommendation includes: an evaluation of whether the financial company is in default or is in danger of default; a description of the effect the failure of the financial company would have on U.S. financial stability; an evaluation of why a case under the Bankruptcy Code is not appropriate; an evaluation of the effect on creditors, counterparties, and shareholders of the financial company and other market participants, and certain other evaluations required by statute. *See* section 203(a)(2) of the Dodd-Frank Act, 12 U.S.C. § 5383(a)(2).

[33] *See* section 203(b) of the Dodd-Frank Act, 12 U.S.C. § 5383(b).

[34] *See* section 202(a)(1)(A) of the Dodd-Frank Act, 12 U.S.C. § 5382(a)(1)(A).

[35] Similar to the FDIC's repudiation powers provided by section 210(c)(1) of the Dodd-Frank Act, 12 U.S.C. § 5390(c)(1), a bankruptcy trustee is authorized to reject certain contracts (which may be related to certain problem assets) of the debtor.

[36] *See* section 210(h) of the Dodd-Frank Act, 12 U.S.C. § 5390(h). There are statutorily imposed limitations upon the transfer of assets and liabilities from the receiver to the bridge financial company, including a prohibition against a bridge financial company assuming any liability that is regulatory capital of the covered financial company. *See* section 210(h)(1)(B)(i) of the Dodd-Frank Act, 12 U.S.C. § 5390(h)(1)(B)(i). Additionally, the liabilities transferred from a covered financial company to a bridge financial company are not permitted to exceed the assets so transferred. *See* section 210(h)(5)(F) of the Dodd-Frank Act, 12 U.S.C. § 5390(h)(5)(F).

[37] *See* 12 U.S.C. § 1821(n).

[38] This may be contrasted with a typical Chapter 11 resolution, in which the management of the pre-insolvency institution will continue to manage the operations of the debtor institution.

[39] In 2008, the FDIC implemented a successful resolution of IndyMac Bank through a transaction involving a "pass-through conservatorship," which is similar to the utilization of a bridge financial company. The transfer of assets to a *de novo* institution, named IndyMac Federal Bank, and its subsequent sale to a private investor in 2009 enabled the FDIC to sell the core business intact. This was more efficient and less costly than a liquidation and retained the value of the institution's assets. As of January 31, 2009, IndyMac Federal Bank had total assets of $23.5 billion and total deposits of $6.4 billion. The assuming institution agreed to purchase all deposits and approximately $20.7 billion in assets at a discount of $4.7 billion. The FDIC retained the

remaining assets for future disposition. *See* Press Release, FDIC, *FDIC Closes Sale of IndyMac Federal Bank*, Pasadena, California (March 20, 2009), *available at* http://www.fdic.gov/news/news/press/2009/pr09042.html.

[40] *See* section 210(c)(9) of the Dodd-Frank Act, 12 U.S.C. § 5390(c)(9).

[41] The exemption from the automatic stay under the Bankruptcy Code in the case of qualified financial contracts generally works well in most cases. However, for systemically important financial institutions, in which the sudden termination and netting of a derivatives portfolio could have an adverse impact on U.S. financial stability, the nullification of the *ipso facto* clause is needed. By removing a right of termination based solely upon the failure of the counterparty, the bridge financial company structure provides the flexibility to incentivize qualified financial contract counterparties to either maintain their positions in such contracts, or exit their positions in a manner which does not jeopardize U.S. financial stability.

[42] There are implications under the Dodd-Frank Act to transferring all of a covered financial company's qualified financial contracts to a bridge financial company in order to avoid such contracts' termination by their counterparties. As such contracts continue, following such transfer, to be valid and binding obligations of the bridge financial company (before being eventually wound down), the bridge financial company is required to perform the obligations there under, including in respect of meeting collateral requirements, hedging, and being liable for gains and losses on the contracts.

[43] Title VII of the Dodd-Frank Act, 15 U.S.C. § 8301 *et seq.*, contemplates requirements for increased initial and variation margin.

[44] The FDIC may issue or incur obligations pursuant to an approved orderly liquidation plan (up to 10 percent of the total consolidated assets of the covered financial company) and pursuant to an approved mandatory repayment plan (up to 90 percent of the fair value of the total consolidated assets of the covered financial company that are available for repayment). *See* section 210(n)(6) and (9) of the Dodd-Frank Act, 12 U.S.C. § 5390(n)(6) and (9). To the extent that the assets in the receivership are insufficient to repay Treasury for any borrowed funds, any creditor who received an additional payment in excess of what other similarly situated creditors received, which additional payment was not essential to the implementation of the receivership or the bridge financial company, may have the additional payment clawed back. See section 210(o)(1)(D)(i) of the Dodd-Frank Act, 12 U.S.C. § 5390(o)(1)(D)(i). This provision is consistent with Title II's directive to minimize moral hazard. To the extent that the clawbacks of additional payments are insufficient to repay Treasury for any borrowed funds, the FDIC is required to assess the industry. *See* section 210(o)(1)(B) of the Dodd-Frank Act, 12 U.S.C. § 5390(o)(1)(B).

[45] Amounts which may be borrowed from the Department of the Treasury are based upon the assets, or assets available for repayment, of the covered financial company. *See* footnote 44, *supra*.

[46] In recent years a common practice has developed in bankruptcy cases of allowing payments shortly after the filing of a Chapter 11 petition to certain priority creditors (wage claimants (up to $11,725), employee benefits claimants (up to $11,725), taxing authorities and several less frequently used groups) if sufficient assets are at hand, on the theory that such creditors will be paid first anyway at the time final distributions are made (thus, no creditor's rights will be impaired so long as the equity in available assets clearly exceeds the total priority claims). Permission to make such payments is generally sought as part of the debtor-in-possession's "first day motions," and such creditors generally receive payment within three to five days of the date of filing of the petition. A secondary consideration for paying prepetition wages is the desire on the part of management to retain an experienced work force at a time of turmoil. A second practice has developed in large Chapter 11 bankruptcy cases of paying "critical vendors" after obtaining a "first day order" shortly after the petition is filed. While such vendors have the status of general unsecured creditors, an argument is typically made to the Bankruptcy Court that certain trade creditors are considered key suppliers to the debtor-in-possession, and may refuse to do business with the Chapter 11 debtor unless they receive immediate payment on their prepetition claim, thus causing the entire reorganization effort to fail through loss of the going concern. This practice is more controversial than that of paying priority claimants, since (except in "prepackaged" bankruptcy cases) it is often very difficult to predict at the outset of the case what the percentage payout to general unsecured creditors will be at the end of the case. The practice has also come under criticism in recent years and has been cut back. One reason for the cutback is that there is little formal support in the Bankruptcy Code for the practice. *See In re Kmart Corp.*, 359 F. 3d 866 (7th Cir. 2004) and discussion in Turner, Travis N., "Kmart and Beyond: A 'Critical' Look at Critical Vendor Orders and the Doctrine of Necessity," 63 Wash. & Lee L.Rev. 431 (2006).

[47] *See generally* section 165 of Title I of the Dodd-Frank Act, 12 U.S.C. § 5365.

[48] *See* "Orderly Resolution of Lehman under the Dodd-Frank Act—March–July, Due Diligence and Structuring the Resolution—Planning in the Crisis Environment," infra.

[49] Domestic and foreign regulators are currently actively involved through the Financial Stability Board's Cross-Border Crisis Management Group to develop essential elements of recovery and resolution plans that will aid authorities in understanding subject firms' global operations and planning for the orderly resolution of a firm across borders. A number of jurisdictions are currently working to develop legislative and regulatory requirements for recovery and resolution plans, and domestic U.S. authorities are working to align regulatory initiatives in order to have a comprehensive and coordinated approach to resolution planning. For example, in

January 2010, the FDIC and the Bank of England entered into a Memorandum of Understanding concerning the consultation, cooperation, and exchange of information related to the resolution of insured depository institutions with cross-border operations in the United States and the United Kingdom.

[50] *See* section 210(b)(1) of the Dodd-Frank Act, 12 U.S.C. § 5390(b)(1).

[51] According to the Examiner's Report, following the near collapse of Bear Stearns in March 2008, "Lehman knew that its survival was in question." Lehman's management believed, however, that government assistance would be forthcoming to prevent a failure. *See* Examiner's Report at 609, 618.

[52] The Preamble to the Dodd-Frank Act notes that it was enacted, *inter alia*, "to end 'too big to fail' [and] to protect the American taxpayer by ending bailouts."

[53] *See* "Orderly Resolution of Lehman under the Dodd-Frank Act—March–July, Due Diligence and Structuring the Resolution—Planning in the Crisis Environment," *supra.*

[54] Had the Dodd-Frank Act been enacted sufficiently far in advance of Lehman's failure, undoubtedly much more supervisory information would have been available in March 2008. The Federal Reserve and the FDIC would have had the detailed information presented in Leh-man's statutorily required resolution plan under Title I of the Dodd-Frank Act. *See* section 165(d) of Title I of the Dodd-Frank Act, 12 U.S.C. § 5365(d).

[55] The principal operating entities in the holding company were LBI, the U.S. broker-dealer, and LBIE, the U.K.-based broker-dealer. Lehman also had a smaller Asian trading operation headquartered in Japan, and various smaller subsidiaries in other countries

[56] By completing a sale at the time of failure of the parent holding company, the acquirer would have been able to "step into the shoes" of LBHI and provide liquidity, guarantees, or other credit support to the newly acquired subsidiaries. Were the FDIC unable to promptly complete such a transaction, it could provide any necessary liquidity to certain key subsidiaries, such as LBIE, pending a sale of those assets. *See* footnote 58, *infra.*

[57] *See* section 202(c)(1) of the Dodd-Frank Act, 12 U.S.C. § 5382(c)(1).

[58] Upon a parent entering a Title II receivership, the FDIC may appoint itself receiver over one or more domestic covered subsidiaries of a covered financial company in receivership in accordance with the self-appointment process set forth in section 210(a)(1)(E) of the Dodd-Frank Act, 12 U.S.C. § 5390(a)(1)(E). This appointment process requires a joint determination by the FDIC and the Secretary of the Treasury that the covered subsidiary is in default or danger of default, that putting it into receivership would avoid or mitigate serious adverse effects on U.S. financial stability, and that such action would facilitate the orderly liquidation of the covered financial company parent. Once in receivership, the covered subsidiary would be treated in a similar manner to any other covered financial company: its shareholders and unsecured creditors would bear the losses of the company, and management and directors responsible for the company's failure would not be retained. The receiver, to aid in the orderly liquidation of the company, could extend liquidity to it in accordance with section 204(d) of the Dodd-Frank Act, 12 U.S.C. § 5384(d).

[59] Both Barclays and its U.K. regulators were concerned with exposure to problem assets of Lehman following a potential acquisition by Barclays. *See* footnote 68, *infra.*

[60] We also note the impact of section 622 of the Dodd-Frank Act, 12 U.S.C. § 1852, which could prohibit a large financial company from entering into a transaction to acquire another financial company if the *pro forma* liabilities would exceed certain statutory levels.

[61] For example, in the case of East West Bank's acquisition of United Commercial Bank, San Francisco, California, the FDIC engaged with the China Banking Regulatory Commission and the Hong Kong Monetary Authority in advance of the resolution to discuss potential acquirers, regulatory approvals and options for resolving or selling the assets and liabilities of United Commercial Bank's wholly owned subsidiary in China and its foreign branch in Hong Kong.

[62] Any agreement reached in respect of Lehman would be contingent upon its failure, a systemic determination under sections 203(b) or 210(a)(1)(E) of the Dodd-Frank Act, 12 U.S.C. §§ 5383(b) or 5390(a)(1)(E), as applicable, and the appointment of the FDIC as receiver under section 202 of the Dodd-Frank Act, 12 U.S.C. § 5382. In the case of Lehman, and for purposes of our analysis, had there been a viable acquirer or strategic investor pre-failure, no Title II resolution would be required. As discussed in "The Events Leading to the Lehman Bankruptcy," *supra,* and in footnote 68, *infra*, no such private sector alternative was available.

[63] A simple formula to reflect the amount of the acquirer's note payable is: Book value of assets purchased less the sum of (book value of liabilities assumed plus discount bid plus cash payment) is equal to note payable.

[64] To the extent problem assets were held directly by LBHI, or LBHI experienced significant intercompany exposures to losses in subsidiaries and affiliates, loss sharing would be more likely to be a preferred bid structure.

[65] As discussed under "—March–July, Due Diligence and Structuring the Resolution—Due Diligence," *supra*, subsidiaries holding such assets would generally be resolved under the Bankruptcy Code. To the extent any subsidiary was deemed systemic, it could be put into a separate receivership under Title II, its assets liquidated and its claims resolved in accordance with the Dodd-Frank Act.

[66] *See* section 210(a)(9)(E) of the Dodd-Frank Act, 12 U.S.C. § 5390(a)(9)(E).

[67] *See* footnote 62, *supra.*

[68] We note that this analysis is purely hypothetical in nature, and a bid conducted by the FDIC could have produced strong bids by a number of potential acquirers. Barclays, however, was close to completing a transaction with Lehman in September 2008. It was unable to proceed based upon the risk of financial loss due to problem assets it identified in its due diligence and the inability to gain an exemption from U.K. regulators from the requirement to hold a shareholder vote prior to approving a transaction with Lehman based upon the proposed structure. The FDIC believes it would have been able to alleviate Barclays' concerns—and facilitate requisite regulatory approvals—by structuring the transaction as a loss-sharing P&A or as a modified P&A. For the purpose of this discussion, therefore, a winning bid from Barclays would be one reasonable outcome from the bidding process outlined in "—August, Begin Marketing Lehman," *supra.*

[69] For a detailed discussion of the recommendation, determination, and appointment process under sections 203 and 202 of the Dodd-Frank Act, 12 U.S.C. §§ 5383 and 5382, *see* "The Orderly Liquidation of Covered Financial Companies—Appointment," *supra.*

[70] There is a danger of value dissipation—in proportion to the size and complexity of the covered financial company—the longer such covered financial company stays in receivership prior to a sale being consummated. Accordingly, the FDIC would generally prefer, where possible, to time a sale of the assets and operations of the covered financial company at or near the date of failure. The FDIC may also transfer key operations to a bridge financial company, as described under "The Orderly Resolution of Covered Financial Companies—Special Powers under Title II—Ability to Preserve Systemic Operations of the Covered Financial Company," *supra.* These same challenges are faced in the resolution of larger insured depository institutions under the FDI Act.

[71] Despite paying a premium to assume the commercial paper obligations, an acquirer may have been incentivized to bid on such business due to the incremental franchise value of the business line and to preserve customer goodwill.

[72] LBHI conducted its derivatives activities primarily in subsidiaries of LBI (the broker-dealer), including Lehman Brothers Special Financing Inc., Lehman Brothers Derivatives Products, Inc., and Lehman Brothers Financial Products, Inc.

[73] Under the International Swaps and Derivatives Association master agreements (and trades placed thereunder), parties may choose whether to be governed by New York or English law. To the extent that parties to a particular qualified financial contract are validly governed by English law (and a court recognizes and applies such choice of law), such contract may not be subject to the Dodd-Frank Act in terms of nullification of its *ipso facto* clause.

[74] *See* section 210(b)(1) of the Dodd-Frank Act, 12 U.S.C. § 5390(b)(1).

[75] *See* "The Orderly Resolution of Covered Financial Companies—Special Powers under Title II—Advance Dividends and Prompt Distributions," *supra*, for a discussion of the ability to make both prompt distributions and advance dividends in a Title II receivership.

[76] *See* footnote 44 and accompanying discussion, *supra.*

[77] Section 204(a) of the Dodd-Frank Act, 12 U.S.C. § 5384(a).

[78] *See* e.g., Simon Johnson & James Kwak, 13 Bankers: *The Wall Street Takeover and the Next Financial Meltdown* (2010); Michael McKee and Scott Lanman, "Greenspan Says U.S. Should Consider Breaking Up Large Banks," Bloomberg, Oct. 15, 2009, *available at* http:// www.bloomberg.com/apps/news? pid=newsarchive& sid=aJ8HPmNUfchg; Lita Epstein, "Breaking up 'too big to fail' banks: Britain leads, will U.S. follow," DailyFinance, Nov. 2, 2009, available at http://www.dailyfinance.com/story/ investing/breaking-up-banks-too-big-to-fail-britian-leads-but-will-u-s/19220380/. The Dodd-Frank Act includes provisions intended to prevent the creation of ever-larger financial companies, including section 622 thereof, 12 U.S.C. § 1852. *See* footnote 60, *supra.*

In: The Lehman Brothers Bankruptcy: Analyses
Editors: Gary E. Walker and Lindel D. Clarke
ISBN: 978-1-62081-730-8

Chapter 3

Statement of Thomas C. Baxter Jr. Hearing on "Too Big To Fail: Expectations and Impact of Extraordinary Government Intervention and the Role of Systemic Risk in the Financial Crisis"*

Chairman Angelides, Vice Chairman Thomas, and members of the Commission, thank you for the opportunity to appear before you today. For the past 15 years, I have been privileged to serve as the General Counsel of the Federal Reserve Bank of New York. I welcome the opportunity to speak to you about the events that brought Lehman Brothers to bankruptcy, events that occurred during 2008 when our Nation was in the midst of the worst financial crisis it has experienced since the Great Depression.

During the crisis, Federal Reserve policy makers needed to respond to a series of extraordinary and hugely consequential problems, usually with little time and imperfect information. Today I will be speaking to you about the facts surrounding one of these problems, Lehman Brothers. In 2008, my job was to provide legal advice to Federal Reserve policy makers, and so while I am happy to share with the Commission my recollections of the events that I will describe, I do not want to exaggerate my own importance. It was Chairman Bernanke, the Board of Governors, and President Geithner who made the policy determinations on behalf of the Federal Reserve System—determinations that in my view were careful, creative, and right.

With this introduction, I would like to start with a question that I am often asked about Lehman: "Why did you allow Lehman to fail?" It is an understandable question, but one that nevertheless contains a false premise. The Federal Reserve did not "allow" Lehman Brothers to die, bankruptcy being the equivalent of death to a financial company. Instead, the Federal Reserve, the United States Treasury Department, the Securities and Exchange Commission, and others tried hard to save it—not for its own sake, of course, but for the sake of all the families and businesses who would be harmed by the devastating effects of a Lehman

* This is an edited, reformatted and augmented version of the remarks given on September 1, 2010 before the Financial Crisis Inquiry Commission.

bankruptcy. We did not succeed, but the effort made was serious and determined. We came very close.

In my remarks today, I will summarize the Federal Reserve's actions to address the Lehman problem in two parts. In the first part, I will describe how the Federal Reserve monitored Lehman's efforts to stabilize itself and pressed its most senior management to find a long-term solution for its liquidity and capital problems. In the second part, I will review how we attempted to facilitate a rescue from bankruptcy and, when this failed, to mitigate the impact of Lehman's demise on the economic system as a whole.

LEHMAN'S DECLINE

The New York Fed had no role in supervising Lehman Brothers. The SEC supervised Lehman's broker-dealer pursuant to express statutory authority, and, as Chairman Mary Shapiro pointed out in her testimony before the House Financial Services Committee, the SEC also supervised Lehman's parent holding company under a voluntary program called the Consolidated Supervised Entity ("CSE") program.[1] The Federal Reserve had a business relationship with Lehman's broker-dealer, but our transactions with the broker-dealer were for the most part repurchase agreements done for monetary policy purposes, and purchases and sales of Treasury and agency securities.

In March, events in our financial system caused several responses that expanded the Federal Reserve's business relationship with Lehman Brothers and certain other investment banks. First, the Federal Reserve announced, on March 11, 2008, what became known as the Term Securities Lending Facility ("TSLF"). The TSLF was designed to address a liquidity problem that we had observed with respect to certain types of mortgage-backed securities. The TSLF addressed this problem by enabling primary dealers to borrow from the Federal Reserve certain securities that they could more easily exchange for cash and secure these borrowings by pledging securities to the Federal Reserve that were less easy to exchange. This enabled the primary dealers to obtain much-needed liquidity from the market.

Second, at around the time this program was announced, one of the primary dealers, Bear Stearns, was experiencing an extraordinary liquidity run. On Friday, March 14, 2008, the New York Fed received authority from the Board of Governors of the Federal Reserve to make a loan that enabled Bear Stearns to avoid a bankruptcy filing and to continue in operation through the weekend of March 15 and 16. During that weekend, the Federal Reserve and the United States Treasury Department facilitated an acquisition of Bear Stearns by J.P. Morgan Chase. The Federal Reserve also developed a new liquidity facility to lend cash directly to primary dealers, the Primary Dealer Credit Facility ("PDCF"). The PDCF became operational on Monday, March 17, 2008, and it was intended to provide a liquidity backstop for primary dealers who might face circumstances similar to Bear Stearns. Lehman Brothers was one of these dealers.

It is impossible to know what would have happened to Lehman without the TSLF and the PDCF, but it is safe to say that these facilities calmed markets and allowed Lehman and others more time to examine available options and to seek potential solutions. As history shows, Lehman had six months from the date of the Bear Stearns transaction to find a long-term solution to its myriad problems. Of course Lehman's challenges were very serious—it suffered from capital deficiency, liquidity drain, and a low level of market confidence. Any of these three could potentially prove fatal to a publicly traded financial company, even in the healthiest of economies. Lehman had the misfortune of trying to solve all three at once.

With the introduction of the TSLF and the PDCF, the New York Fed sent small teams of two monitors into each of the four remaining investment banks, Goldman Sachs, Merrill Lynch, Morgan Stanley, and Lehman Brothers—something it had never done before. Let me again emphasize that we were not intending to conduct supervisory activities with our personnel, nor were we attempting to displace the SEC, the primary regulator of the investment banks. To the contrary, we were acting as a potential lender to these potential borrowers, and we wanted to know our new borrowers better. Because of concern that our monitoring role could be misunderstood or misconstrued, Vice Chairman Donald Kohn described our objectives in public testimony. He said that the on-site monitors had two narrowly tailored goals: (1) to ensure that any credit that the Fed extended to the investment banks would be repaid, and (2) to ensure that the investment banks did not become too dependent upon Federal Reserve credit and would continue to work on improving their liquidity positions and financial strength.[2] The Federal Reserve monitors did not take on the broader responsibility of supervising Lehman. The SEC continued to be the supervisor of the broker-dealers and their parents, including Lehman's broker-dealer and its parent, Lehman Holdings.

Lehman showed some signs of recovery during this period. It raised capital in June of 2008. But liquidity continued to be a significant disability. As part of its monitoring, the New York Fed, in conjunction with the SEC, conducted liquidity stress analyses of the investment banks, in part to evaluate their creditworthiness. Those analyses suggested that Lehman needed to improve its liquidity should the credit crisis intensify. Again, to Lehman's credit, and in response to our analyses, Lehman took steps to, and did, improve its liquidity. At no time, however, did anyone at the New York Fed believe that Lehman had sufficient liquidity to withstand what was to come in September, events that Richard Fuld, Lehman's former chief executive officer, has described as the "perfect storm."[3]

Accordingly, as has been well-documented in the press and in the comprehensive report by Anton Valukas, the Lehman Brothers' Bankruptcy Examiner (the "Valukas Report"), senior Federal officials, including President Geithner, continually pressed Lehman to find workable solutions for its capital and liquidity problems from March to September 2008. Lehman executives pursued potential merger partners. They engaged in discussions with potential Korean buyers and approached Warren Buffett. At no time did the New York Fed tell Lehman that it would be bailed out with taxpayer money, nor did the New York Fed instruct Lehman to act as if such an option was available. Lehman's CEO, Mr. Fuld, and the Chairman of the Lehman board of directors, Thomas Cruikshank, have made clear that Lehman was not expecting any Federal bailout.[4] Both men fully understood that Lehman was a public company and needed to be fully responsible for its own financial situation.

"Lehman Weekend"

September of 2008 will likely be remembered as an epochal period in the history of American finance. The bankruptcy filing by Lehman occurred during that month, and it must be analyzed in the context of that most distressing time. On September 7, the Federal Housing Finance Agency placed Fannie Mae and Freddie Mac into conservatorship, and the Treasury Department used its authority, granted by Congress in July 2008, to make financial support available to these two government-sponsored entities. While Lehman is often considered the trigger for the systemic consequences that were to come later in the month, it is also clear that Fannie and Freddie's decline, among other factors, caused a number of market participants to begin "hunkering down" to protect their balance sheets. Exposure to Lehman was one of the items to be addressed. Counterparties' reluctance to deal with Lehman intensified starting on Monday, September 8, 2008, such that by Thursday, September 11, 2008, it was apparent to us that Lehman faced a liquidity crisis—i.e., it would not be able to pay its debts as they came due. The issue was no longer whether this public company could fashion its own rescue. We had come to the point of no return, where Lehman faced two alternatives: bankruptcy, or some kind of third-party rescue.

The United States Treasury Department, working in conjunction with the Federal Reserve and the SEC, convened a meeting of the Chief Executive Officers of major financial institutions at the New York Fed after the close of markets on Friday, September 12, 2008. Secretary Paulson opened the meeting with a short and plain declaration that there would be no public money to support Lehman. The Government then gave the CEOs two tasks. First, it was suggested they form a consortium to finance certain of Lehman's illiquid assets in order to facilitate an acquisition. Second, as a contingency, should the banking organizations fail to come up with a workable rescue plan, they should present an alternative plan to address the effects of a Lehman bankruptcy, because they should anticipate that would happen Monday morning.

As was the case with Bear Stearns, the Government knew that a third party would have to finance a portfolio of Lehman's illiquid assets in order to make Lehman acceptable as a merger partner. In this case, drawing upon the precedent of the rescue of Long Term Capital Management in 1998, the Government arranged for a consortium of private banks to provide the financing. And in fact, after much discussion and some disagreeable moments, the private banks agreed to do so. By Sunday, September 14, the counterparties had agreed to finance approximately $30 billion of Lehman's illiquid assets in order to facilitate Lehman's rescue. While the structure was never finalized, it would presumably have resembled a private sector version of Maiden Lane LLC, the vehicle used to acquire the assets from Bear Stearns. The banks would have lent $30 billion to their SPV, and the SPV would have purchased largely real estate-related assets from Lehman. This would have made Lehman more attractive to a potential acquirer.

Lining up financing for the illiquid assets was a necessary condition for a rescue, but it was not sufficient. The *sine qua non* of the plan, as Secretary Geithner and others have pointed out, was a willing and capable merger partner.[5] In the end, the rescue failed because we had no willing and capable merger partner able to provide the necessary commitments to stabilize Lehman. And, lest there is confusion on the point, this would be true no matter who was financing the acquisition of Lehman's illiquid assets, the counterparties or the New York Fed.

As of that Friday, there were two prospective Lehman acquirers: Bank of America and Barclays. On Saturday, September 13, Bank of America abandoned the potential acquisition of Lehman and reached an agreement to acquire Merrill Lynch. Barclays was the only remaining suitor. On Sunday, September 14, with the consortium financing committed, we learned for the first time that Barclays would not be able to deliver a key document to carry the merger to conclusion: a guarantee of Lehman's trading obligations between the signing of the merger agreement and its closing.

The Bear Stearns transaction taught us the importance of the guarantee to a successful rescue. A guarantee maintains the ability of the troubled company to operate as a going concern and, thus, preserves value. It does this by providing protection to counterparties during an especially vulnerable period—the period between merger contract and merger closing. Without such a guarantee, the creditors and counterparties of the firm would be at risk in the event that the merger fell apart because of a failed shareholder vote or some other contingency. Consequently, as a market matter, the guarantee is an indispensable part of any such rescue operation.

On Sunday, September 14, we learned that Barclays could not proffer the needed guarantee without a shareholder vote. This vote would take days, if not weeks or months, and there was no way to predict if the shareholders would even vote for the transaction to proceed. I explored with counsel whether the U.K. government, or one of its instrumentalities like the FSA, might waive this U.K. requirement, such that the guarantee could be delivered and the rescue effected. I learned that the U.K. authorities were not amenable to a waiver. Thus, Barclays ceased to be available as the willing buyer that we needed to rescue Lehman, and there was no other interest from any firm of sufficient size and capability that could acquire Lehman, a company with consolidated assets of about $600 billion.

Many have asked why, when the Barclays guarantee problem presented itself, the Federal Reserve did not step forward and guarantee the trading obligations of Lehman pending its merger with Barclays. They observe that we lent approximately $29 billion to Maiden Lane LLC to facilitate the merger of J.P. Morgan Chase and Bear Stearns, and they look at our commitment to lend up to $85 billion to AIG.

Under the law, the New York Fed does not have the authority to provide what I would characterize as a "naked" guarantee—one that would be unsecured and not limited in amount, and would put the U.S. taxpayers at risk for the *entirety* of Lehman's trading obligations. As Chairman Bernanke has observed, "the Federal Reserve has done, and will continue to do, *everything possible within the limits of its authority* to assist in restoring our nation to financial stability and economic prosperity…."[6] In this case, Lehman had no ability to pledge the amount of collateral required to satisfactorily secure a Fed guarantee, one large enough to credibly withstand a run by Lehman's creditors and counterparties. As events subsequently played out, several weeks after Lehman weekend, on October 2, 2008, Congress passed the Emergency Economic Stabilization Act ("EESA"), which provides the U.S. Treasury Department with legal authority to issue a guarantee.[7] Again, the Federal Reserve did not then, and does not now, have such authority.

Even if it had been legally possible, a Government guarantee would have also placed the taxpayer at enormous risk because it would have undermined deal certainty. It is important for the acquirer—and not a third party—to issue the guarantee because it gives the acquirer a strong incentive to close the deal and assume control of the target. For example, J.P. Morgan Chase, which proffered the guarantee needed to merge with Bear Stearns, negotiated a host of provisions from Bear Stearns that assured deal certainty. And, during the period between March 2008 (when J.P. Morgan Chase and Bear Stearns agreed to merge) and June 2008 (when the merger closed), counterparties of Bear Stearns continued to do business with it because of the J.P. Morgan Chase guarantee.

On the other hand, where a third party provides the guarantee, the acquirer enjoys all the benefits if the target's condition improves and none of the burdens if the target's condition declines. It is the third party who is on the hook, and in this case that third party would have been the taxpayer. Similarly, from the perspective of the merger target, an unlimited guarantee by the Government could provide the merger target with the means to try to stay independent— its shareholders might vote the merger down with an unlimited Government guarantee.

Some observers ask why if we were not able to backstop Lehman, we were able to provide substantial credit to AIG immediately afterwards. The answer is that in the case of AIG, there was sufficient collateral to support the commitment to lend. Unlike the naked guarantee needed to facilitate the merger of Barclays and Lehman, our committed credit to AIG on September 16, 2008 was fully secured by good collateral, namely, AIG's sound retail insurance businesses. In fact, before any money was disbursed to AIG on September 16, AIG delivered share certificates to the New York Fed that we continue to hold as collateral in our vaults. These shares fully secured every penny we lent to AIG on September 16, 2008. And today, the credit extended to AIG by the New York Fed remains fully secured.

Likewise, the Federal Reserve's loan to Maiden Lane LLC, which facilitated the Bear Stearns rescue, was and is fully secured. The security is important because it is the taxpayer's protection in the event of a default. There is no similar protection to the issuer of a naked guarantee; if the obligor of the guaranteed obligation fails to perform, the guarantor is liable.

On Sunday, September 14, with an acquisition of Lehman no longer possible, a working group of market participants focused on the best way to mitigate the effects of a Lehman bankruptcy. They concluded that a contingency plan developed by the SEC, the Treasury, and the New York Fed was the best option. Under this plan, Lehman's parent would file a Chapter 11 petition, but the broker-dealer subsidiary would continue to operate. It would operate with intra-day credit from its clearing bank, J.P. Morgan Chase, and overnight credit from the Federal Reserve.

The Federal Reserve would provide credit that was fully secured by the collateral of the broker-dealer and this would continue for a period of time to enable the broker-dealer to wind down its trading book in an orderly manner—thereby mitigating to some degree the impact of the failure on financial markets and the economy. At the point in time when an orderly liquidation of the broker-dealer became practical, a petition would be filed for a receivership under the Securities Investor Protection Act. This became the contingency plan, although it was always subject to the Lehman board of directors deciding to file a Chapter 11 petition, a matter that was their responsibility and not ours. On September 15, Lehman's board of directors elected to place the parent company in Chapter 11 while leaving Lehman's broker-dealer open for business so it could wind down its operations.

A look at the hypothetical alternative of lending to the Lehman holding company itself reveals that it was in fact not viable. By Monday, September 15, Lehman faced a total erosion of market confidence, and so the Federal Reserve would have been lending into a classic run. Had Lehman not filed for bankruptcy on September 15, but opened as if it were business as usual, creditors and counterparties would have rushed to protect their positions, using all legal remedies, causing the liquidity crisis to spread throughout Lehman's organization.

By contrast, the New York Fed affirmatively decided to continue extending credit to Lehman Brothers' broker-dealer. This decision was made to facilitate the broker-dealer's orderly winddown. Then, when Barclays returned to the negotiating table on Tuesday,

September 16, with an offer to purchase substantially all of the assets of Lehman's broker-dealer, the New York Fed used this financing to facilitate a transition of certain broker-dealer operations from Lehman to Barclays. Once Judge Peck of the United States District Court for the Southern District of New York approved the arrangement at the end of the week, those operations were in Barclays' hands.

While there was nothing truly "orderly" about the Lehman bankruptcy, the New York Fed's overnight financing of the Lehman broker-dealer avoided further market disruption. This piece of the overall Lehman story is rarely told, and yet it deserves attention. In contrast, Lehman Brothers International Europe ("LBIE"), the U.K. broker-dealer, was immediately placed into administration, its employees were sent home without paychecks, and the U.K. broker-dealer had no opportunity to wind down its positions. As such, its counterparties' positions were likewise frozen, which created liquidity problems and significant market exposures as asset prices moved in the wake of Lehman's failure.

Conclusion

In conclusion, let me say a few words about regulatory reform and the tools we had to work with. I mentioned earlier the guarantee tool that the Congress added when the EESA was enacted. Another important development is the Dodd-Frank legislation, which promises more effective comprehensive consolidated supervision of systemically significant organizations like Lehman. This supervision will demand higher levels of capital and liquidity, precisely the type of medicine that Lehman needed. Systemically significant non-banking financial companies, like Lehman, will also be obliged to submit resolution plans which will help to avoid some of the problems experienced after Lehman filed its Chapter 11 petition. Further, if a systemically significant organization like Lehman needs to be resolved, Dodd-Frank creates a new resolution procedure that should facilitate a more orderly winddown.

Thank you again for the opportunity to appear before you today, and I look forward to answering your questions.

End Notes

[1] Mary L. Schapiro, Chairman, U.S. Securities and Exchange Commission, Testimony Concerning the Lehman Brothers Examiner's Report, before the United States House of Representatives Committee on Financial Services, April 20, 2010.

[2] Donald L. Kohn, Vice Chairman, Board of Governors of the Federal Reserve System, Risk management and its implications for systemic risk, before the Subcommittee on Securities, Insurance, and Investment, Committee on Banking, Housing, and Urban Affairs, United States Senate, June 19, 2008.

[3] Richard S. Fuld, Jr., Statement before the United States House of Representatives Committee on Financial Services, April 20, 2010.

[4] Transcript, Hearing on Lehman Brothers Bankruptcy Examiner Report, United States House of Representatives Committee on Financial Services, April 20, 2008, pp. 136, 153.

[5] Timothy F. Geithner, Secretary of the Treasury, Statement before the United States House of Representatives Committee on Financial Services, April 20, 2010.

[6] Ben S. Bernanke, Chairman, Board of Governors of the Federal Reserve System, Speech at the National Press Club Luncheon, National Press Club, Washington, D.C., February 18, 2009 (emphasis added).

[7] *See* EESA, §102(c)(4), "Adjustment to purchase authority" ("The purchase authority limit in section 115 shall be reduced by an amount equal to the difference between the total of the outstanding guaranteed obligations and the balance in the Troubled Assets Insurance Financing Fund.")

In: The Lehman Brothers Bankruptcy: Analyses
Editors: Gary E. Walker and Lindel D. Clarke
ISBN: 978-1-62081-730-8

Chapter 4

STATEMENT OF RICHARD S. FULD. HEARING ON "TOO BIG TO FAIL: EXPECTATIONS AND IMPACT OF EXTRAORDINARY GOVERNMENT INTERVENTION AND THE ROLE OF SYSTEMIC RISK IN THE FINANCIAL CRISIS"*

Chairman Angelides, Vice Chairman Thomas and Members of the Commission, I appreciate the invitation to appear before you today. I am proud to have spent my entire business career of over forty years at Lehman Brothers and to have been its Chairman and CEO for its last fourteen years.

Lehman's demise was caused by uncontrollable market forces and the incorrect perception and accompanying rumors that Lehman did not have sufficient capital to support its investments. All of this resulted in a loss of confidence, which then undermined the firm's strength and soundness. Those same forces threatened the stability of other banks -- not just Lehman. Other firms were hurt by their plummeting stock prices and widening CDS spreads. But Lehman was the only firm that was mandated by government regulators to file for bankruptcy. The government then was forced to intervene to protect those other firms and the entire financial system.

Looking back, Lehman Brothers grew its business during a period of huge capital accumulation and easy access to liquidity and asset financing. During that time, Lehman Brothers' profitability and balance sheet grew accordingly.

In 2007, when the U.S. housing market began to show signs of weakening, Lehman Brothers and many of its competitors had already accumulated large positions in what were considered less liquid assets. Many market observers, including government officials charged with oversight of the financial markets, believed that the problems in the subprime residential mortgage market were and would be contained.

In retrospect, one can now see that as 2007 progressed, the weakening in the U.S. housing market was worse than predicted and spread to other sectors of the financial system.

* This is an edited, reformatted and augmented version of the remarks given on September 1, 2010 before the Financial Crisis Inquiry Commission.

Those adverse market conditions accelerated in March 2008 after Bear Stearns nearly failed. I believed then, and still do now, that had the Fed opened the financing window to investment banks just before the Bear Stearns problem, that decision might have provided the necessary liquidity to keep Bear Stearns operational and, more importantly, might have lessened the need for additional government intervention. Still, having acted, the intervention of the federal government set a precedent in the marketplace that impacted liquidity, capital formation and the expectations of creditors and stockholders for at least the next six months. At the same time, the federal government and the individual regulators involved were criticized for using taxpayers' money to rescue a financial company, which then set another precedent of how "not" to handle the next problem.

With Bear Stearns gone, Lehman, as the next smallest investment bank, became the focus of the marketplace and was subject to increasingly negative and inaccurate market rumors.

Critically, in 2008, Lehman reduced its total exposure to less liquid assets by almost 50%, from approximately $126 billion to $69 billion. We further strengthened our capital and liquidity positions by raising $10 billion of new equity.

During that same period, Lehman fully welcomed and cooperated with SEC and Fed officials, who were physically present in our offices monitoring our liquidity, funding, capital, risk management and mark-to-market process. Lehman also proposed to government regulators certain measures that could have helped Lehman and bolstered confidence in the financial markets. Those measures included (i) permitting Lehman to convert to a bank holding company, (ii) granting Lehman's Utah bank an exemption under Section 23A of the Federal Reserve Act to raise deposits, which would have given the firm additional liquidity and (iii) imposing a ban on naked short selling. Each of those requests was denied at the time. Tellingly, though, each measure was later implemented in some form for other investment banks during the days and weeks following Lehman's bankruptcy filing.

Despite all those efforts, unfounded rumors about Lehman continued to besiege the firm and erode confidence. An investment bank's very existence depends on confidence to consummate transactions, pledge collateral and repay loans. Without that confidence, no bank can function or continue to exist. This loss of confidence, although unjustified and irrational, became a self-fulfilling prophecy and culminated in a classic run on the bank starting on September 10, 2008, that then led Lehman to file for bankruptcy four days later, in the early morning hours of September 15.

In broad summary, on Sunday, September 7, 2008, the federal government placed Freddie Mac and Fannie Mae in conservatorship, destroying the value of their recently issued preferred shares. Two days later, on September 9, there were news reports that Lehman's talks with the Korean Development Bank had faltered. That day Lehman's stock dropped 45%. The next day, September 10, Lehman pre-released its third quarter 2008 results. The firm reported a net $3.9 billion loss, including $7.8 billion in gross writedowns on its residential mortgage and commercial real estate holdings. Even with this loss, Lehman still reported an equity capital position of $28.4 billion ($2.2 billion higher than the previous quarter). Lehman also announced plans to divest $25 billion of its commercial real estate assets into a separately capitalized entity. More rumors swirled that led the market to believe that Lehman's assets were not adequately marked to market and that Lehman did not have enough capital to withstand further writedowns. Those rumors proved to be completely false. Lehman's stock dropped further.

The run on the bank then started. Lehman's principal clearing banks demanded that Lehman post additional collateral. Counterparties to the numerous repurchase transactions that Lehman conducted on a daily basis began to withdraw business and to demand increased collateral to consummate trades. Liquidity was frozen by those clearing banks, and hedge fund customers began migrating to other firms.

On Friday, September 12, and through that Sunday, the Federal Reserve Bank of New York held emergency meetings with the major financial institutions to explore financing facilities and strategic alternatives with both Bank of America and Barclays. By Sunday night, Treasury and Fed officials decided not to provide temporary financing or support to any of those possibilities. Lehman then was mandated by government regulators to file for bankruptcy before the Asian markets opened the next day.

Notably, on that same Sunday, the Fed expanded for investment banks the types of collateral that would qualify for borrowings from its Primary Dealer Credit Facility. Only Lehman was denied that expanded access. I submit, that had Lehman been granted that same access as its competitors, even as late as that Sunday evening, Lehman would have had time for at least an orderly wind down or for an acquisition which would have alleviated the crisis that ensued.

There are a number of completely incorrect claims which have been held up as explanations for the demise of Lehman Brothers. To this day, those incorrect claims still persist in the public domain. Just because those incorrect assertions are repeatedly made does not make them true. I highlight these claims only because I believe this Committee needs to hear what is true:

First, there was no capital hole at Lehman Brothers. In contrast to the false market rumors about Lehman's mark-to-market determinations, even the Lehman bankruptcy examiner found immaterial differences in the firm's asset valuations, ranging from a low of $500 million to a high of $1.7 billion. As of August 31, 2008, two weeks prior to the bankruptcy filing, Lehman had $28.4 billion in equity capital. Assuming a full $1.7 billion in additional writedowns, as estimated by the examiner, Lehman still would have had $26.7 billion in equity capital. Positive equity of $26.7 billion is very different from the negative $30 or $60 billion "holes" claimed by some.

Second, Lehman had adequate financeable collateral. Many people, to this day, do not know that on September 12, the Friday night preceding Lehman's bankruptcy filing, Lehman financed itself and did not need access to the Fed's discount window. In addition, on that Monday, September 15, the day of the filing, Lehman Brothers Inc., the U.S. broker-dealer subsidiary, borrowed about $50 billion from the New York Fed by pledging acceptable collateral. The Fed was paid back 100 cents on the dollar. What Lehman needed on that Sunday night was a liquidity bridge. We had the capital. Along with its excess available collateral, Lehman also could have used whole businesses as collateral -- such as its Neuberger Berman subsidiary -- as did AIG some two days later.

Third is the notion that Lehman did not do enough to try to seek solutions to the crisis. As I have stated, Lehman made proposals about changes to its corporate structure to government officials, new ways to create liquidity and changes to regulations to prevent continued manipulation of stocks of financial companies. Lehman strengthened its position in 2008 by decreasing its exposure to less liquid assets by almost 50%, by writing down asset values by almost $25 billion, by raising $3.8 billion of equity capital more than its total net losses, by cutting its dividend and by increasing its long-term debt. Lehman pursued new capital opportunities with numerous potential investors, potential strategic partners and potential buyers of the firm. Lehman created an SEC-approved plan to spin off certain illiquid commercial real estate assets. Lehman created alternative capital options, which included changing convertible and preferred securities to common stock, further decreasing its less liquid assets, and selling all or part of its Investment Management Division. Those options, taken together, could have created \$7 to \$11 billion of additional equity capital. In the end, however, Lehman was forced into bankruptcy not because it neglected to act responsibly or seek solutions to the crisis, but because of a decision, based on flawed information, not to provide Lehman with the support given to each of its competitors and other non-financial firms in the ensuing days.

In retrospect, there is no question we made some poorly timed business decisions and investments, but we addressed those mistakes and got ourselves back to a strong equity position with a Tier I capital ratio of 11%. We also had financeable collateral and solidly performing businesses. There is nothing about this profile that would indicate a bankrupt company.

I thank the Commission for its time and look forward to addressing any questions.

In: The Lehman Brothers Bankruptcy: Analyses
Editors: Gary E. Walker and Lindel D. Clarke
ISBN: 978-1-62081-730-8

Chapter 5

STATEMENT OF HARVEY R. MILLER[1]. HEARING ON "TOO BIG TO FAIL: EXPECTATIONS AND IMPACT OF EXTRAORDINARY GOVERNMENT INTERVENTION AND THE ROLE OF SYSTEMIC RISK IN THE FINANCIAL CRISIS"*

I greatly appreciate the opportunity to participate in this hearing and in assisting the Financial Crisis Inquiry Commission ("Commission") in its investigation of the financial crisis which erupted in September of 2008 and was highlighted by the financial collapse of Lehman Brothers Holdings Inc. ("LBHI") and its affiliates (collectively, "Lehman"). The demise of Lehman precipitated consequences for the financial system and the worldwide economy that were largely unanticipated.

I am a practicing attorney and a senior member of the international law firm of Weil, Gotshal & Manges LLP ("Weil") that maintains its principal office in New York, New York. During my professional career, I have represented debtors, secured and unsecured creditors, trustees in bankruptcy, creditors' committees, equity interest holders, asset purchasers, and I have served as a trustee and as an attorney in cases under the Securities Investor Protection Act of 1970 (15 U.S.C. 78aaa et seq.).[2] Currently, I am the lead bankruptcy attorney for Lehman and also for Motors Liquidation Company, formerly known as General Motors Corporation, in the prosecution of their respective bankruptcy cases under chapter 11 of title 11 of the United States Code ("Bankruptcy Code") that are pending in the United States Bankruptcy Court for the Southern District of New York (Case Nos. 08-13555 (JMP) & 09-50026 (REG)).

I am currently an Adjunct Professor of Law at the New York University School of Law, where I have taught a seminar on chapter 11 bankruptcy and reorganization law since 1975. I also am an Adjunct Lecturer in Law at Columbia University School of Law, where I have taught a course on Corporate Reorganization and Bankruptcy Law for the past ten years. I have also lectured and written extensively on the subject of bankruptcy and reorganization.

---

* This is an edited, reformatted and augmented version of the remarks given on September 1, 2010 before the Financial Crisis Inquiry Commission.

It is my understanding that the Commission is seeking information as to (i) the circumstances surrounding the commencement of the Lehman chapter 11 bankruptcy case on September 15, 2008, and (ii) whether the failure by the government or other parties to support or assist Lehman was ill-advised and may have been a major factor in the economically devastating events that followed the commencement of the chapter 11 bankruptcy case. Those consequences included a severe loss of public confidence in the financial markets and almost caused an implosion of the financial system. In that context, the Commission has asked the penultimate question, "was Lehman Too Big To Fail?"

Lehman's Retention of Weil

Weil's representation of Lehman extended back to 1984. During the course of this relationship, Weil was never engaged to or acted as general counsel for Lehman, or was involved in the issuance of securities by LBHI. Rather, Weil represented Lehman in connection, generally, with independent specific transactions and matters as requested. Weil provided legal services on behalf of Lehman that involved almost all legal disciplines, including but not limited to services relating to banking, finance, corporate governance, securities, mergers and acquisitions, taxes, real estate and litigation. As a result, Weil became familiar with many aspects of Lehman's various business activities and to a limited degree, Lehman's financial affairs and capital structure. Likewise, Lehman became familiar with the broad range of legal services provided by Weil, including its widely recognized business finance & restructuring expertise. As a result, during the week of September 8, 2008, as the economy continued on a downward spiral and Lehman was confronting a potentially fatal liquidity crisis, it turned to Weil for assistance.

The first communication to Weil as to possible contingency planning was during the middle of the week of September 8, 2008. Steven Berkenfeld, the then head of Lehman's Legal, Compliance and Audit Division, called Steven J. Dannhauser, Weil's Chairman, to engage Weil on a confidential basis to assist Lehman in contingency planning if Lehman was unable to resolve its evolving liquidity crisis. Soon after that call, Mr. Dannhauser alerted me to the engagement and on Thursday, September 11, 2008, I began to assemble a small working group to perform preliminary organizational work gathering information as to Lehman's financial affairs. The Weil working group had no contact with Lehman and during that period no information was furnished by Lehman. The focus of the Weil team was on publicly available information regarding Lehman. Weil also was admonished that the engagement should be treated as highly confidential.

Discussions with Government Regulators Regarding a Potential Lehman Bankruptcy

During the late afternoon of Friday, September 12, 2008, I received a telephone call from Thomas A. Russo, then Lehman's Chief Legal Officer, requesting attendance at a meeting at the Lehman headquarters that was about to start with representatives of the Federal Reserve Bank of New York ("NY Fed"). It was my understanding that the meeting had been requested by the NY Fed to discuss Lehman's liquidity. By the time that I arrived at Lehman with my partner, Richard P. Krasnow, the meeting had begun. Approximately four or five representatives of the NY Fed were in attendance. Mr. Russo initially presided over the meeting. A number of representatives of Lehman's financial staff were also in attendance, including Ian Lowitt, then Lehman's Chief Financial Officer and Co-Chief Administrative Officer. Mr. Lowitt and his associates attempted to provide the meeting with a report as to Lehman's liquidity. The essence of Mr. Lowitt's presentation was that Lehman would be unable to produce a definitive conclusion as to its liquidity until late that evening or early Saturday morning because of the complex calculations that would have to be made after the close of financial markets and the receipt of financial information from Lehman's global offices. In addition, Mr. Lowitt noted that the calculations would have to take into account the effect of the increasing demands for collateral security made by Lehman's clearing banks and, particularly, JPMorgan Chase. Before the end of the meeting, Mr. Russo had to leave to attend another meeting concerning a potential transaction that might alleviate Lehman's financial needs.

At the September 12, 2008 meeting, there was no discussion as to the probability of Lehman seeking or being subject to the commencement of a bankruptcy case. No urgency was expressed as to the need to prepare any pleadings or other documents necessary to a bankruptcy filing. There were very brief comments made that intensive negotiations were in progress as to a potential sale or merger of Lehman with another financial institution.

Later, during the evening of September 12, 2008, I received a telephone call from James L. Bromley, a Partner in the New York law firm of Cleary Gottlieb Steen & Hamilton LLP, which was acting as attorneys for the NY Fed. Mr. Bromley inquired as to what preparations were being made to deal with the potential bankruptcy contingency. I explained to Mr. Bromley that during the meeting earlier that day at Lehman's headquarters, neither NY Fed representatives nor the Lehman representatives indicated any urgency to accelerate preparation for a potential bankruptcy contingency. I asked Mr. Bromley if anything had changed and he suggested that we should meet Saturday morning, September 13, 2008. During that conversation, I told Mr. Bromley that gathering the necessary information from Lehman was very difficult because almost all of the senior Lehman personnel were consumed in the pending sale or merger negotiations and were not accessible by the Weil team.

During the morning of Saturday, September 13, 2008, Mr. Bromley and four or five representatives of NY Fed met with me and other members of the Weil team at Weil's office. At that meeting, I again reiterated that progress in preparing for the bankruptcy contingency was very slow because of the lack of access to responsible Lehman personnel and resulting inability to obtain necessary financial information. The representatives from the NY Fed and Mr. Bromley appeared more concerned as to the need for accelerating the preparation of pleadings necessary for the bankruptcy contingency. However, they were not specific as to why or whether the situation had changed in any material manner. The meeting lasted from one to two hours. After the meeting, the Weil team, using publicly available information, attempted to prepare the necessary pleadings to be used if the bankruptcy contingency arose. During the course of that day, it appeared that the bankruptcy contingency remained a remote possibility and that a transaction involving a merger or sale with Barclays or Bank of America appeared promising.

During the morning of Sunday, September 14, 2008, there were many telephone exchanges and conferences with Lehman representatives. It appeared from those communications that Bank of America had withdrawn from any sale or merger negotiations and that there were reservations as to the probability of any transaction with Barclays.

During that Sunday afternoon, the situation began to appear more tenuous. I was advised that a request was made by the NY Fed for Lehman representatives to attend a meeting at the NY Fed in lower Manhattan. The meeting took place in a large conference room at the NY Fed. Lehman was represented by Bart McDade, Lehman's then President and Chief Operating Officer, Alex Kirk, Lehman's then Global Head of High Yield and Leveraged Loans, and an additional Lehman officer, as well as representatives from Weil, including me, Stephen J. Dannhauser, Thomas A. Roberts, Co-Chair of Weil's Corporate Department, and Lori R. Fife, a senior partner from Weil's Business, Finance & Restructuring Department. Representatives of the NY Fed, the United States Securities and Exchange Commission ("SEC"), and, I believe, the Securities Investor Protection Corporation ("SIPC") were in attendance. There were approximately 25 or more persons facing Lehman's representatives across the conference room table[3]. The meeting had started before the Weil team arrived. The discussion at the meeting was led by Thomas C. Baxter, Jr., the General Counsel of the NY Fed, an unidentified senior staff member of the NY Fed, and Mark A. Walker, the Managing Partner of Cleary Gottlieb Steen & Hamilton LLP. While the primary spokesman for the NY Fed was Mr. Baxter, comments were made by others present.

In substance, the Lehman representatives were advised that a transaction with Barclays was not going to occur and, further, that there would be no federal assistance provided to save or support Lehman. Despite requests for elucidation as to the basis of the decision, Lehman's representatives were instructed that there would be no further information provided as to the basis of the decision to refrain from providing Lehman with financial support or other assistance.

Lehman's representatives emphasized that assistance from the NY Fed was necessary for Lehman to open for business the following Monday, September 15, 2008. Notwithstanding, it was clear that governmental assistance was not to be provided, except as to Lehman's primary broker/dealer subsidiaries, as discussed below. Inquiries were made by Lehman's representatives as to whether there had been a realistic and comprehensive evaluation as to the potential consequences of Lehman's failure. The responses from the NY Fed and others was not illuminating. It appeared that the definitive decision not to assist or support Lehman had been made before the meeting with Lehman had commenced and the government representatives were not prepared to discuss the rationale underlying the decision or their evaluation of the potential consequences.

The only discussion of any assistance related to Lehman Brothers Inc. ("LBI"), Lehman's New York based primary broker-dealer subsidiary. It was acknowledged that LBI, as a "stock broker," did not qualify as a "debtor" under the Bankruptcy Code for the purposes of chapter 11. The discussion as to LBI focused on its ability to continue to operate for a limited period to facilitate transfers of customer accounts. The NY Fed indicated that it would continue to provide overnight repurchase loan transactions for LBI through the Primary Dealer Credit Facility that had been earlier established, provided that LBI pledged collateral security consistent with the requirements established by the NY Fed, albeit that in the existing circumstances, those requirements would be relaxed to some extent.

Throughout the meeting, Lehman's representatives continued to describe the gravity of Lehman's situation, arguing that a global financial crisis would result from the failure of Lehman that could best be described as a financial "Armageddon." After listening to comments from Lehman and Weil, Mr. Baxter stated that the government representatives would caucus to consider Lehman's comments. The government representatives then left the conference room for approximately one hour. When they returned, Mr. Baxter reported that after consideration of all of the contentions made on behalf of Lehman, the decision not to support Lehman had been reaffirmed. Accordingly, he stated that the only alternative was that Lehman had to fail. Mr. Baxter then directed that the Lehman and Weil teams should promptly return to Lehman's headquarters and arrange for a meeting of Lehman's Board of Directors to be convened for the purpose of adopting a resolution authorizing and directing LBHI to commence a bankruptcy case before 12:00 midnight of that day.

At that juncture the Lehman representatives reiterated that allowing Lehman to fail and commence a bankruptcy case would have dire consequences. The Lehman representatives urged the need for more information as to the rationale so they might adequately explain the position of the government to Lehman's Board of Directors. The response was that the NY Fed and others was that there existed no obligation or duty to provide such information or to substantiate the basis for the decision not to aid or support Lehman. In response to questions of whether or how the NY Fed evaluated the risks and consequences of Lehman's failure, the response was that the government had evaluated the attendant risks and intended to take appropriate action to offset any potential consequences and thereby calm any negative response of the financial markets.

The Lehman representatives were informed that press releases had been prepared that would be issued after the announcement of Lehman's bankruptcy which the government believed would have the desired effect of calming the financial markets and public investors. The direction to return to the Lehman headquarters was repeated. The Lehman and Weil teams were encouraged to promptly leave the premises and did so.

Lehman's Board of Directors previously had been convened for a meeting at 1:30 P.M. that day at Lehman's headquarters to approve the potential transaction with Barclays. As a result, Lehman's Board of Directors was present at Lehman's headquarters when Messrs. McDade and Kirk, and the Weil team, returned form the meeting at the New York Fed. Messrs. McDade and Kirk, and the Weil team, reported to the Board of Directors the events that had occurred during the earlier meeting with the government representatives.

The report was followed by an active discussion among Lehman's Directors. The discussion was interrupted when Richard Fuld, then Lehman's Chairman and Chief Executive Officer, was advised that a telephone call had been received from Christopher Cox, the Chairman of the SEC, requesting the opportunity to address the Board of Directors. The Board of Directors concluded that in the circumstances it would be appropriate to hear from Mr. Cox. The telephone conference was opened and Mr. Cox introduced himself and Mr. Baxter. They then addressed the Directors.

In substance, Messrs. Cox and Baxter stated that it was in the best interests of the financial system and the United States economy for Lehman's Board of Directors to pass a resolution approving the commencement of a bankruptcy case prior to 12:00 midnight of that day. Several Directors asked Messrs. Cox and Baxter whether they, on behalf of the NY Fed and the SEC, were directing the Board of Directors to adopt a bankruptcy resolution. In response, Mr. Cox hesitated, and Mr. Baxter suggested they hold an offline caucus. After five or ten minutes, Messrs. Cox and Baxter rejoined the conference call with the Directors.

Mr. Cox stated that he and Mr. Baxter were not issuing a direction to the Lehman Board of Directors to pass a resolution authorizing the commencement of a bankruptcy case. Rather, he indicated that the decision was for Lehman's Directors to make in the exercise of their business judgment and discretion. Such response notwithstanding, Lehman's Directors persisted in asking for a clear and definitive answer to the question of whether the NY Fed and SEC were directing the passage of a bankruptcy resolution. These questions precipitated another caucus that extended for another five to ten minutes. When Messrs. Cox and Baxter rejoined the conference call, they reiterated that the decision of whether to adopt a bankruptcy resolution was a decision for Lehman's Board of Directors to make and, further, that neither the SEC nor the NY Fed was directing the adoption of such a resolution. However, Mr. Cox stated that he believed that the preferences of the NY Fed and the SEC had been made unequivocally clear to Messrs. McDade, Kirk and others at the meeting that had been held earlier that day at the NY Fed.

After the conference call with Messrs. Cox and Baxter ended, Lehman's Board of Directors reviewed the facts and circumstances in light of the liquidity crisis confronting Lehman. The Board concluded that the commencement of a bankruptcy case by or against Lehman was inevitable. The Board then determined and exercised its judgment to adopt a resolution authorizing the commencement of a chapter 11 bankruptcy case by LBHI.

Pursuant to the Board's resolution, and in an atmosphere of ex re e to oil, anxiety and a level of chaos, a chapter 11 bankruptcy petition was cobbled together. At approximately 2:00 a.m. during the morning of September 15, 2008, LBHI electronically filed a petition for relief under chapter 11 of the Bankruptcy Code in the United States Bankruptcy Court for the Southern District of New York ("Bankruptcy Court").

The Lehman Bankruptcy Case

The commencement of the chapter 11 bankruptcy case by Lehman was the spark that ignited the simmering economic crisis that began in 2007. The Lehman chapter 11 bankruptcy case represents the largest, most complex, multi-faceted and far-reaching bankruptcy case ever filed in the United States. At the time that the bankruptcy case began, Lehman was the fourth largest investment banking firm in the United States. It had previously reported recorded assets in excess of $600 billion and liabilities of almost that amount. Lehman operated its business pursuant to a classic holding company structure. As the parent corporation, LBHI managed and directed the affairs of the Lehman enterprise. The enterprise maintained a global network of subsidiaries and affiliates with offices in every major financial center in the world that processed many thousands of transactions each business day. At the time of the commencement of the bankruptcy case, LBHI, directly and indirectly, had approximately 8,000 subsidiary entities and affiliates, of which over 100 were actively engaged in the various business activities of Lehman. These activities ranged from derivatives, commercial loans, underwriting, real estate, bank ownership and broker/dealer operations. Through its subsidiaries and affiliates, Lehman employed approximately 26,000 persons immediately preceding the commencement of the chapter 11 bankruptcy case.

LBHI managed the cash generated by the enterprise. Generally, all such cash was swept each night into cash concentration accounts at LBHI and each day LBHI disbursed cash to its various subsidiaries and affiliates, as needed. Lehman's cash needs also were supported by substantial borrowings that created a high debt-to-equity leverage ratio. A large portion of

Lehman's borrowings were short term loans which negatively affected Lehman's ability to refinance as the economy slowed and was adversely affected by the 2007 subprime mortgage crisis that continued to expand in 2008

The Lehman bankruptcy was unplanned. As a financial institution, Lehman's viability depended to a large extent on the confidence of the financial markets and the public. Accordingly, the disclosure of bankruptcy consideration and planning would have been disastrous to the continued operations of such a financial institution. Indeed, the public comments by various persons as to Lehman's vulnerability to bankruptcy subsequent to the financial distress of Bear Stearns & Co., in March, 2008, had negatively affected Lehman.

The commencement of the chapter 11 bankruptcy case had immediate and severe consequences. Lehman operated as a global organization with an integrated electronic accounting and reporting system for the many thousands of daily transactions that in the aggregate involved billions of dollars. The bankruptcy filing by LBHI, and the separate, almost contemporaneous initiation of administration proceedings of Lehman Brothers Inc. (Europe) ("LBIE"), the major London based LBHI subsidiary, under the insolvency laws of the United Kingdom, had the immediate effect of a worldwide collapse of the Lehman accounting and reporting system. As a result, the ability to determine the status of transactions and to ascertain assets and liabilities was substantially diminished. Within days of the commencement of the bankruptcy case, approximately 80 insolvency proceedings affecting Lehman subsidiaries and affiliates were initiated in 18 foreign countries. In those proceedings, receivers or administrators were appointed to oversee and administer the disposition of those entities and their respective assets and liabilities.

As of September 15, 2008, Lehman was a party to over 10,000 derivatives contracts relating to approximately 1.7 million transactions. Lehman was also a major participant in hundreds of substantial real estate and loan transactions. Those investments and transactions in the aggregate involved billions of dollars. The commencement of the Lehman bankruptcy case caused disruptions and systemic consequences in all of those situations. These disruptions abetted the crisis of confidence that occurred after the bankruptcy filing. To a limited degree, however, the ramifications of the Lehman bankruptcy case were alleviated by the ability to use the provisions of the Bankruptcy Code to effectuate the sale of the Lehman North American Capital Markets business to Barclays Capital Inc. ("BarCap").

During the morning of September 15, 2008, negotiations began with BarCap as to a possible sale of Lehman's North American Capital Markets business to BarCap. Those negotiations culminated in the Bankruptcy Court approved sale of that business to BarCap within five days of the commencement of the Lehman bankruptcy case[4].

The sale resulted in the transfer of essentially all of the New York-based Lehman employees to BarCap and enabled the expeditious transfer and satisfaction of customer accounts. It was accomplished because of the ability to effectively use the provisions of the Bankruptcy Code and to obtain the cooperation of SIPC to innovatively coordinate and integrate the bankruptcy case with the LBI case under the Securities Investor Protection Act ("SIPA") that was commenced on Friday, September 19, 2008 in coordination with the BarCap sale. The sale avoided potentially harsh consequences to Lehman customers and employees. The transfer of the North American Capital Markets business essentially was seamless. The sale enabled the North American Capital Markets business to continue operations on Monday, September 22, 2008. However, it did leave the Lehman chapter 11 bankruptcy administration with few Lehman employees. To overcome this problem and facilitate the administration of the Lehman bankruptcy case, BarCap and LBHI entered into a Transition Support Agreement ("Agreement"). To provide the necessary personnel, for administrative purposes, LBHI engaged Alvarez and Marsal Holdings LLC ("Alvarez & Marsal"). Approximately 180 to 200 employees of A&M became the basic core staff for Lehman. The Agreement, together with the support of A&M and the over $1 billion in cash received as a result of the BarCap sale, enabled the administration of the Lehman chapter 11 bankruptcy case to proceed.

The bankruptcy of Lehman was a catalyst for systemic consequences throughout the world. It fostered a negative reaction that endangered the viability of the financial system. As a result of failed expectations of the financial markets and others, a major loss of confidence in the financial system occurred. The consequences of that crisis of confidence are still a matter of debate and final accounting. Nevertheless, it is abundantly clear that the financial world almost went into a tailspin and is still suffering from the panic that occurred during the fall of 2008.

The actual costs of the Lehman chapter 11 bankruptcy case and other significant facts are:

1. Through July 31, 2010, the cost of administering the Lehman bankruptcy case, based upon the filed operating reports and applications by professionals for compensation and reimbursement of expenses, but including the costs of the A&M employees necessarily engaged to replace the Lehman employees transferred to BarCap is approaching $1 billion. Those costs include approximately $100 million incurred in connection with the independent examination of Lehman's affairs made by Anton R. Valukas, the Senior Partner of Jenner & Block, a Chicago-based law firm, as the Bankruptcy Court appointed Examiner[5]. There is no current estimate of the future costs of administration. However, it is likely over the next two years the expenses of administration may approximate a like amount.
2. The second anniversary of the bankruptcy filing is approaching and the expected duration of the Lehman bankruptcy case is estimated to be an additional two years or more.
3. Since September 15, 2008, approximately 66,000 claims against Lehman have been filed against Lehman in the bankruptcy case. The gross amount of these claims exceeds $873 billion. Many of the filed claims assert unliquidated damages. Currently, it is estimated that the total allowed amount of claims will be under $300 billion. The process of claims reconciliation is underway, but extremely difficult, as the nature of many of the transactions involved are extremely complex and present numerous difficulties in unwinding.
4. There has been a substantial amount of litigation commenced in the Bankruptcy Court and elsewhere relating to claims and other possible causes of action. Recently, Lehman commenced an adversary proceeding in the Bankruptcy Court against JPMorgan Chase Bank N.A. ("JPMorgan") seeking the recovery of billions of dollars based upon asserted avoidable transfers and other claims. JPMorgan has denied the claims asserted and litigation is contemplated to extend into 2010. As the expiration of applicable statutes of limitations approach, it is anticipated that additional substantial litigation will be initiated[6]. As to derivatives and the complexity associated with such transactions, the Bankruptcy Court has approved the adoption of

Alternative Dispute Resolution ("ADR") procedures for derivatives transactions. Because of the nature of those transactions, the progress is slow involving extensive discovery. Three independent mediators have been appointed in connection with the ADR process. Thus far, as a result of this process, over $181 million has been recovered for the benefit of the Lehman.

5. There has been no tabulation of the actual and expected costs of administration of foreign insolvency proceedings. However, the costs of the insolvency proceedings of LBIE, as publicly reported, reflect the substantial costs of administration of that case. Those costs are running at a pace that basically parallels the administrative costs of the Lehman chapter 11 bankruptcy case, notwithstanding its smaller size.
6. The extent of the foreign insolvency proceedings directly related to Lehman illustrate the systemic consequences of the Lehman bankruptcy and does not take into account the bankruptcy and insolvency proceedings of other entities that was caused by the Lehman chapter 11 bankruptcy case. In the United States there have been a significant number of bankruptcy cases commenced because of Lehman's financial collapse. Currently there are no statistics as to the number of proceedings commenced by or against non-Lehman entities because of Lehman's failure.
7. The public stockholders of LBHI have lost all of the value of their investments. The general unsecured creditors of Lehman have suffered substantial losses and their recoveries from the administration of the Lehman bankruptcy case will result in very substantial losses of principal. Estimated recoveries will be below 20% of allowed claims.
8. Of particular significance is that the administration of the Lehman bankruptcy case has not directly cost the U.S. taxpayers a single dollar. It is the stockholders of LBHI and the Lehman creditors who are bearing the brunt of the direct costs of the Lehman chapter 11 bankruptcy case.

WAS LEHMAN TOO BIG TO FAIL

The phrase "Too Big To Fail" is seductive and somewhat inflammatory. In reality there is no entity that is too big to fail. The real issue is to determine how to deal with potential failure. It is the consequences of failure that must be realistically evaluated. Such evaluation may lead to the loose application of the phrase "Too Big To Fail." Inevitably, there always will be situations in which the consequences of naked failure and collapse of a major entity will so materially affect the economy and the public interests that intervention and remedial action may be mandatory. That does not mean that the potentially failing entity has to be "bailed out" without loss to its owners and creditors. Rather, the potential systemic risks attendant to failure need to be ascertained and, if appropriate, action taken to ameliorate those risks that endanger the public interests.

In the case of Lehman, it appears that the decision to apply moral hazard was ill- advised. Lehman's bankruptcy precipitated a crisis that almost resulted in the destruction of the financial system. It shocked the financial markets and the investing public. It disrupted thousands of financial transactions on a global basis, with the consequential loss of value.

The Lehman bankruptcy caused a failure of expectations held by the financial markets and investors. Essentially in all prior like situations, the potential affects of contemplated failures were diminished by third party actions such as those taken by the financial community, with the encouragement of the Federal Reserve Bank in connection with the crisis relating to the hedge fund, Long-Term Capital Management, in 1998, or the more recent government action taken in the case of Bear Stearns & Co. The practice of third party intervention to mitigate the potential systemic consequences of failure has a long history. It goes back in recent times to the intervention of the New York Stock Exchange ("NYSE") in the context of the so-called Salad Oil Scandal of 1963 to protect the public customers of NYSE member firms, as well as the creation of the Resolution Trust Corporation to deal with bank failures in the Southwestern United States in the late 1980s. It was reaffirmed with respect to Bear Stearns & Co. and the conservatorships adopted for Fannie Mae and Freddie Mac in September, 2008.

The bankruptcy of Lehman may have directly resulted in the freezing of the financial markets that occurred during the week of September 15, 2008. By Wednesday, September 17. 2008, the commercial paper market had materially contracted to the point that major U.S. corporations were confronting potential illiquidity. A situation that caused such corporations to be concerned as to their ability to have sufficient cash to meet their obligations. In addition, the viability of firms such as Morgan Stanley & Co., the Wachovia Bank, and even Goldman Sachs & Co. was being questioned during the calamitous days and weeks of September and October, 2008.

It has been estimated by various commentators that during the week of September 15, 2008, over $700 billion of value disappeared. In that perspective, it is reasonable to question the decision of the government to abandon the notion of any conceivable assistance or support for Lehman that would have served to alleviate the potential financial distress and possibly have saved the financial markets from the turmoil that occurred. It did not have to be a "bail out" of Lehman creditors or its stockholders but, rather, a means to mitigate the costs and severe disruptions that resulted from the decision to allow Lehman to fail and commence a bankruptcy case without any government support.

A government sponsored plan to support an orderly wind-down of Lehman's business over a reasonable period of time might have negated or substantially eliminated the risks to the financial system and the public that were actually encountered. It has been estimated by some commentators that a government sponsored wind-down, with limited guaranties, might have cost $40 to $50 billion. That cost would have been far less than the initial $700 billion of value that disappeared during the first week of Lehman's chapter 11 bankruptcy case and the additional costs to the economy that followed in subsequent weeks. In addition, it is conceivable that the costs incurred by the government and others in connection with supporting or saving other entities and the automobile industry might have been substantially less.

Fowler Secretary or the Treasury, Henry C. Paulson, Jr and others have made various comments concerning the demise of Lehman. Secretary Paulson has commented that (1) the government did not have the tools to deal with Lehman, and (2) Lehman lacked adequate collateral to secure any government financing. Those comments are not persuasive. On Tuesday, September 16, 2008, the government did find the tools to free up approximately $80 billion as an initial investment in American International Group ("AIG"), and to subsequently increase that amount to over $100 billion. Of course, there may be many facts that are not within my knowledge that may have influenced the government's decision. If so, they have not been substantiated. It is also difficult to evaluate the impact on the Lehman situation on September 14, 2008 of the then developing AIG crisis.

The damages and harm precipitated by the Lehman bankruptcy could have been substantially reduced by innovative actions of the government. Instead, the government miscalculated and the financial system was pushed to the brink of total collapse, as Secretary Paulson subsequently explained to the leaders of Congress in requesting approval of the Toxic Assets Repurchase Program ("TARP"). As a consequence, intervention by the government was once again was recognized as necessary to preserve the national economy and the public interests.

THE GOVERNMENT FAILURE TO PROVIDE ASSISTANCE TO LEHMAN

The government did not provide any assistance to Lehman. The results are a matter of history. The reasons why the government did not provide assistance to Lehman has been the subject of speculation by many authors and others. The failure of the government to provide assistance to Lehman may have resulted from a serious miscalculation of the potential systemic risks that were presented by the proscribed Lehman's failure and collapse.

Possibly the government believed that in September, 2008, the financial markets already had taken into account and were prepared for the eventuality of Lehman's bankruptcy. The government may have assumed that because of all the notoriety created by certain hedge fund spokesmen as to Lehman's financial condition and media reports, that the financial markets and, perhaps the public, had factored into their operations and activities Lehman's potential failure. It is in that context that the government representatives, during the September 14, 2008 meeting, may have assumed that the referenced press releases would adequately serve to calm the financial markets and the public.

The government failed to take into account the expectations that had been created by prior governmental action and the history of third-party interventions in circumstances of financial crises. The government appears to have concluded that during the day of Lehman's bankruptcy it would be tumultuous, widely publicized and disconcerting, but that by Tuesday, September 16, 2008, the concern would have contracted, and by Wednesday, September 17, 2008, Lehman's bankruptcy mostly would be a historical fact. If that was the government's belief, it was a serious miscalculation. Lehman's bankruptcy, as noted, was the spark that inflamed the existing financial distress and may have caused it to quickly blossom into a major debacle. Appropriate intervention may have prevented, or at least materially lessened, the full impact of the financial panic that did occur.

Thank you for the privilege of being able to testify before this Commission.

End Notes

[1] Senior Partner, Weil, Gotshal & Manges LLP, New York, New York. The views expressed in this testimony are expressed solely on behalf of myself and not on behalf of any other person or entity.

[2] Since approximately 1973, I have been a conferee and member of the National Bankruptcy Conference and I also am a fellow of the American College of Bankruptcy.

[3] To the best of my knowledge, the government attendees were not identified.

[4] The sale was consummated on September 22, 2008 and involved the transfer of over approximately $47 billion of assets and the assumption of substantial liabilities. Subsequently, LBHI, the SIPA Trustee of LBI and the Lehman Statutory Creditors' Committee joined in proceedings against BarCap challenging the sale or, alternatively, varying aspects of the sale. To date, approximately 17 hearing days have been consumed in those proceedings and it is likely that the hearings will not be completed until October, 2010. Those proceedings are currently pending in the Bankruptcy Court (Case No. 08-13555 and Adversary Proceeding Nos. 09-1731 and 09-1733).

[5] In March, 2010, Mr. Valukas filed his Examiner's Report with the Bankruptcy Court. The Examiner's Report, exclusive of exhibits, totals 2209 pages plus approximately 1800 pages of appendices. The Report is a public document. Mr. Valukas was assisted by the accounting firm of Duff & Phelps in discharging his obligations as Examiner. The Examiner's Report includes an extensive section covering Lehman's relationship with government regulators. It is entitled, "The Interaction Between Lehman and the government" and consists of 54 pages. A copy of Mr. Valukas's related written testimony before the Committee on Financial Services of the United States House of Representatives on April 20, 2010 is attached as Exhibit 1.

[6] The Complaint and JPMorgan's Motion to Dismiss the complaint filed in the Adversary Proceeding (No. 10-03266 (JMP)) are attached as Exhibits 2.

In: The Lehman Brothers Bankruptcy: Analyses
Editors: Gary E. Walker and Lindel D. Clarke
ISBN: 978-1-62081-730-8

Chapter 6

STATEMENT OF BARRY ZUBROW. HEARING ON "TOO BIG TO FAIL: EXPECTATIONS AND IMPACT OF EXTRAORDINARY GOVERNMENT INTERVENTION AND THE ROLE OF SYSTEMIC RISK IN THE FINANCIAL CRISIS"*

Chairman Angelides, Vice-Chairman Thomas, and Members of the Commission, my name is Barry Zubrow. I am the Chief Risk Officer of JPMorgan Chase & Co., and have served in that role since I began working for the bank in December 2007. I thank the Commission for the invitation to appear, and I hope that my testimony will assist the Commission in its efforts to examine the causes of the financial crisis.

The Commission has asked me to address several topics related to JPMorgan, including its triparty repo program generally and its relationship with Lehman Brothers specifically. This is an important topic of inquiry for the Commission, as the triparty repo market is of vital importance to broker-dealers and others in the financial industry. It contributes significantly to the liquidity and efficiency of the securities markets in the United States. Indeed, the average daily volume of the triparty repo market grew to *$2.8 trillion* in 2008. The importance of the U.S. triparty repo market is underscored by the fact that it facilitates the financing by dealers of their U.S. Government and Agency securities inventories, an important source of liquidity through which the Federal Reserve operationally implements U.S. monetary policy.

JPMorgan is one of two major banks providing triparty repo clearing services in the United States. In its role as clearing bank, JPMorgan serves as the agent between a broker-dealer, on the one hand, and repo investors, such as money-market funds, on the other. In a typical transaction, the broker-dealer sells securities to repo investors in the evening with a promise to buy them back at a slight premium in the morning. JPMorgan provides services such as obtaining prices for the collateral pledged by the broker-dealers, applying and enforcing specific rules dictated by the investors regarding collateralization, and moving cash and collateral among accounts belonging to the broker-dealers and the investors.

* This is an edited, reformatted and augmented version of the remarks given on September 1, 2010 before the Financial Crisis Inquiry Commission.

JPMorgan served as triparty agent for Lehman's broker-dealer subsidiary, Lehman Brothers Inc. ("LBI"). At the beginning of each trading day, in a process known as the "unwind," JPMorgan would repay LBI's triparty repo investors the cash they had provided overnight, and move LBI's securities into accounts on which JPMorgan held a lien. JPMorgan thus would advance for LBI the large amounts of cash needed to buy back the securities LBI had sold the night before. These advances always were entirely discretionary, as JPMorgan was not contractually obligated to make them. In addition, as LBI's principal clearing bank, JPMorgan typically made substantial discretionary advances on LBI's behalf in connection with other repurchase agreement and financing activity, as well as advances in connection with the clearance and settlement of other LBI securities trading activity. Before LBI's final week, JPMorgan's intraday advances typically exceeded $100 billion daily.

JPMorgan's intraday exposure from the triparty repo program would last until the triparty investors and other financing sources returned in the evening for a new round of repos. During the day, JPMorgan thus faced the risk that the securities it held as collateral would drop in value, that the broker-dealer would default, and that the triparty investors and other financing sources would not re-invest with the broker-dealer in the evening to allow the broker-dealer to repay JPMorgan.

As of late 2007, JPMorgan took no margin on the large discretionary loans it made each morning in connection with the triparty repo unwind. Whereas the triparty investors would take a "haircut" overnight — paying less that 100 cents for each dollar of securities — JPMorgan took no such haircut when it took over the investors' position each morning. This enhanced the risk that JPMorgan would be unable to recoup the full amount of its advances through the liquidation of collateral, since it was advancing 100 cents on the dollar to LBI intraday.

In consultation with the Federal Reserve, JPMorgan decided in early 2008 to begin mitigating this risk by taking haircuts on its intraday advances to broker-dealer clients, including Lehman. JPMorgan determined that it would be appropriate to take, at a minimum, the same haircuts during the day that the triparty repo investors took overnight. However, in order to allow its clients time to adjust to this change, JPMorgan implemented the haircuts gradually. On March 17, 2008 — shortly after the near-collapse of Bear Stearns — JPMorgan began by increasing the margin it required from Lehman by 20 percent of the haircut that the triparty investors had been requiring, with an expectation that it would ramp up to 100 percent by the end of June.

Increasing margin requirements, however, still did not protect JPMorgan fully from the risks it faced in extending tens of billions of dollars of credit to broker-dealers each morning as part of the unwind. JPMorgan, unlike any single triparty investor, took on a broker-dealer's *entire* triparty repo book each day. This meant it would face far greater risks in a liquidation scenario. Furthermore, JPMorgan had no assurance that investors would return to fund the broker-dealer in the evening, such that the broker-dealer would be provided with the cash necessary to repay JPMorgan's intraday advances. Moreover, the haircuts negotiated between investors and the broker-dealers did not, in many cases, fully reflect the liquidation risk for the increasingly large amount of structured, difficult-to-value securities that were being financed through the triparty repo program.

In addition, throughout the spring and summer of 2008, JPMorgan participated as a member of the Counterparty Risk Management Policy Group III ("CRMPGIII"), an industry-led group of large bank, broker-dealer and investor firms, formed to discuss best practices and structural risks in the market. CRMPGIII specifically addressed the issues inherent in the triparty repo marketplace and articulated a series of best practices to be adopted by broker-dealers, investors, and agent banks — including practices relating to clearing bank intraday margin. JPMorgan discussed these best practices with each of its broker-dealer clients, including Lehman, and strongly recommended to its clients the importance of conforming to the recommendations. These recommended best practices were discussed with the Federal Reserve Bank of New York and other regulators.

Around June 2008, JPMorgan held high-level meetings with its large broker-dealer clients to discuss these risks. For Lehman, such a meeting was held on June 2, 2008. JPMorgan explained the unique risks it faced and pointed to an approximately $6 billion dollar margin shortfall. In response, Lehman executives agreed to pledge additional collateral. Meanwhile, JPMorgan agreed at Lehman's request to begin taking only 40 percent of investor margin by the beginning of July, and not to reach 100 percent until mid-August.

In mid-June 2008, Lehman pledged various structured securities (not cash) — which it valued at approximately $6 billion — in response to JPMorgan's request for additional margin. Because LBI's corporate parent, Lehman Brothers Holdings Inc. ("LBHI"), was the source of these additional securities, LBHI entered into appropriate documentation in late August 2008 to grant JPMorgan a security interest in the collateral.

By late August and early September 2008, Lehman's deteriorating financial condition was becoming increasingly apparent. It became widely recognized by market participants that Lehman was encountering large losses and would face serious problems over the coming weeks absent a significant transaction. In addition, it came to light that many of the securities Lehman had pledged to JPMorgan in June were illiquid, structured debt instruments that appeared to have been assigned overstated values. Nevertheless, JPMorgan was determined to remain supportive of Lehman. It continued to unwind the triparty repo book each morning and otherwise act on a business-as-usual basis.

But JPMorgan's exposure to Lehman was growing. This included exposure in areas unrelated to triparty repo clearing. For example, JPMorgan faced Lehman entities as a counterparty to derivatives transactions, and in each instance where JPMorgan held a position that was "in the money," it incurred the risk of a Lehman default. This included not only derivatives transactions for JPMorgan's own account, but also derivatives transactions between JPMorgan and Lehman entered into for their respective prime brokerage customers, for which JPMorgan shouldered the credit exposure in the event of a Lehman default. Furthermore, JPMorgan continued to accept "novations" in favor of Lehman's counterparties to derivatives transactions: when a counterparty held an "in the money" position but did not want to take on the attendant Lehman exposure, it could request a novation, and JPMorgan, at its sole discretion, would step into the counterparty's shoes and take on the derivative contract and the Lehman exposure itself.

JPMorgan and Lehman understood that Lehman's credibility in the markets could collapse instantly if JPMorgan declined to take on this additional exposure for prime brokerage customers and novations. JPMorgan therefore searched for a way to protect itself without triggering a run on Lehman. After taking all factors into account — including its current derivatives exposure, its potential derivatives exposure in the event Lehman defaulted and the several days it would take for JPMorgan to close-out its open derivatives transactions, the expectation that novations would continue to rise, and its continuing triparty repo and clearance and settlement-related exposures —JPMorgan determined that it could continue to face Lehman in the market if it had $5 billion in additional collateral.

A primary impetus for the decision to request additional collateral was JPMorgan's growing derivatives exposure. The $5 billion figure was far from sufficient to cover all of JPMorgan's potential exposures to Lehman — including triparty repo and clearance and settlement-related exposures — but JPMorgan believed that it was an amount that Lehman reasonably could provide. When JPMorgan conveyed its request to Lehman on September 9, 2008, Lehman executives agreed to pledge additional collateral, and delivered approximately $3.6 billion worth of collateral to JPMorgan over the next few days. Lehman did not indicate that JPMorgan's request was putting undue pressure on Lehman.

As part of JPMorgan's attempt to obtain appropriate protection for the entirety of its exposure to Lehman, on the morning of September 10, LBHI executed new documentation granting JPMorgan a security interest in the new collateral to cover all obligations of all Lehman entities to JPMorgan. This protection allowed JPMorgan to continue making tens of billions of dollars in advances to Lehman, to continue trading with Lehman on its own behalf and for prime brokerage customers, and to accept novations.

JPMorgan meanwhile continued to evaluate its margin position with respect to Lehman. Its daily margin requirements for triparty repo clearance were rising as Lehman was increasing the amount of illiquid securities in its triparty repo book. During the second week of September 2008, JPMorgan analysts conducted a broad review of Lehman's collateral securities. This review indicated that some of the largest pieces of collateral pledged to JPMorgan were illiquid, could not reasonably be valued and were supported largely by Lehman's own credit. This was inappropriate collateral — essentially, claims against Lehman pledged to secure other claims against Lehman. When the true nature of Lehman's collateral came to light on September 11, 2008, it became apparent that JPMorgan was holding a substantial amount of inappropriate collateral, and that it would need additional collateral if it were to continue supporting Lehman. JPMorgan decided that $5 billion in cash was an appropriate request, even though its potential collateral shortfall was greater, as it was a number that JPMorgan believed Lehman could handle.

On the evening of September 11, 2008, JPMorgan representatives made a series of phone calls informing Lehman that JPMorgan wanted to continue to be supportive of Lehman through the extension of credit and other services, but that $5 billion was needed for JPMorgan to continue to support Lehman in as stabilizing a way as possible. JPMorgan explained that it preferred to have Lehman post cash collateral rather than reducing lines of credit or ceasing trading, which would be more visible to the market. Lehman agreed to honor this request. Later that night, JPMorgan sent Lehman a letter stating that, if Lehman did not post the collateral by the open of business the next day, JPMorgan would exercise its right to decline to extend credit to Lehman. On the morning of September 12, 2008, JPMorgan unwound Lehman's triparty repo book, and Lehman delivered $5 billion of cash collateral during the morning and early afternoon. JPMorgan continued to extend credit to Lehman throughout that critical period and thus never had to assess its options concerning further extensions of credit in the face of a failed collateral request.

Despite JPMorgan's constant efforts to support Lehman and not do anything to frighten the market, a run on the bank eventually ensued for reasons unrelated to JPMorgan. Throughout early September, investors raised their haircuts substantially. By September 12, hedge funds and other major customers were withdrawing their assets from Lehman and some of the largest investors pulled back entirely, refusing to provide Lehman with the overnight financing it desperately needed to keep operating.

During the weekend of September 13 and 14, 2008, I and other senior JPMorgan executives — along with representatives from other financial institutions — participated in discussions at the Federal Reserve Bank of New York concerning the financial crisis generally, and Lehman's difficulties in particular. Government representatives made it clear to everyone present that the government would not provide financial assistance to save Lehman, and that discussions should focus on either a strategic transaction for Lehman or a funding package provided by a consortium of banks. After a potential deal with Barclays Capital fell through due to regulatory issues in the United Kingdom, LBHI filed for bankruptcy in the early morning hours of September 15, 2008.

Throughout all of this, JPMorgan did not cut and run but stood by our client. As other parties withdrew from Lehman, JPMorgan continued to make enormous — discretionary — extensions of credit to the ailing bank, and it continued to trade with Lehman and perform novations. JPMorgan never turned its back on its client, even as others did.

Even *after* LBHI filed for bankruptcy on September 15, 2008, JPMorgan continued, at the urging of LBHI and the Federal Reserve Bank of New York, to extend many tens of billions of dollars of credit to LBI on a daily basis, without imposing any additional collateral requirements. JPMorgan's willingness to continue making clearing advances to LBI during those tumultuous days, when it had no obligation to do so, allowed LBI to keep operating and made possible the sale of LBI's business and assets to Barclays Capital, as well as the loss-free transfer of more than 100,000 customer accounts.

As a result of JPMorgan's willingness to extend credit to Lehman in reliance on the collateral it had been provided, JPMorgan ended up with nearly $30 billion in claims against Lehman's bankruptcy estate. The overwhelming majority of those claims — more than $25 billion — arose out of clearing advances made to LBI *after* LBHI's bankruptcy filing. In addition, more than $3 billion of JPMorgan's claims arose from its exposure under derivative agreements, many of which JPMorgan entered into — or assumed through novations — as part of JPMorgan's efforts to support Lehman in increasingly distressed markets.

I appreciate this opportunity to share my views, and I look forward to your questions.

In: The Lehman Brothers Bankruptcy: Analyses
Editors: Gary E. Walker and Lindel D. Clarke
ISBN: 978-1-62081-730-8

Chapter 7

STATEMENT OF TIMOTHY F. GEITHNER. HEARING ON "PUBLIC POLICY ISSUES RAISED BY THE REPORT OF THE LEHMAN BANKRUPTCY EXAMINER"*

Chairman Frank, Ranking Member Bachus, Members of the Committee, thank you for the opportunity to testify before you today.

The failure of Lehman Brothers in September 2008 was a key inflection point during the most critical phase of the recent financial crisis. Lehman's bankruptcy accelerated a classic "run" on our financial system—a phenomenon not witnessed in this country since the 1930s. In the face of this run, the U.S. government, together with governments from around the world, had no choice but to intervene aggressively, on an unprecedented scale, to prevent an economic catastrophe.

The Lehman episode was not just a disaster for Lehman. It was a disaster for our country. And like any calamity, it should be subjected to careful, independent scrutiny. Whenever an airline tragedy occurs, our National Transportation Safety Board conducts a detailed examination of the causes of the accident. Financial disasters should receive similar examinations.

The Valukas Report is a great example of such an inquiry. The authors of that report have done an important service not only to the Lehman bankruptcy proceedings, but also to current and future students of the recent financial crisis.

As this Committee knows, detailed, independent inquiries are a part of what makes our system strong and resilient. Today's hearings are an important part of this process. I welcome the opportunity to participate.

While the causes of the financial crisis extend far beyond any single firm, Lehman Brothers illustrates many of the failures that brought our financial system to the edge of the abyss. The financial reforms proposed by the Administration, and passed by this Committee, are designed to address these failures in a comprehensive fashion.

No regulatory regime will be able to prevent major financial firms from reaching the point of insolvency. But a well-designed regulatory framework must put in place shock absorbers to contain the damage caused by a major firm's default. And it must provide the

* This is an edited, reformatted and augmented version of the remarks given on April 20, 2010 before the House Financial Services Committee.

government with tools to manage the orderly dismantling and liquidation of firms that mismanage themselves into insolvency.

Lehman Brothers: A Case Study in Our System's Failures

Lehman caused Lehman's insolvency. But in many ways, Lehman Brothers serves as an iconic example of what went wrong with our financial system in the years leading up to the crisis. These deficiencies were not limited to Lehman. Rather, they were widespread and far-reaching problems in the basic structure of our financial system. I want to begin by briefly reviewing several of these critical failures.

The Shadow Banking System

Lehman Brothers operated with very high levels of leverage, and it financed itself to a large extent through the issuance of short-term debt. These factors, combined with a high-risk business model, made Lehman vulnerable to collapse.

Of course, leverage and maturity transformation (the use of short-term liabilities to finance longer-duration assets) are inherent in banking. But unlike regulated banking institutions, Lehman conducted its activities largely free from the important prudential constraints that come with banking regulation. In this regard, Lehman Brothers was part of a broader pattern.

In the run-up to the recent crisis, we witnessed a period of explosive growth in leverage and maturity transformation *outside* the perimeter of prudential banking regulation. This parallel, lightly regulated system has come to be known as the "shadow banking system." Large dealer firms like Lehman were a key part of this system—but they were just one part. At its peak, the shadow banking system financed about $8 trillion in assets with short-term obligations, making it almost as large as the real banking system.

The rapid growth of this system was fueled by light regulation and weak or nonexistent capital requirements. It was also driven by cheap funding from large institutional investors, such as money market mutual funds and securities lenders, which furnished a ready supply of short-term financing.

Financing long-term, risky assets with short-term debt was a reliable formula for rapid growth and robust earnings during the boom. But these activities were vulnerable to fragility and rapid deleveraging when conditions deteriorated, as they inevitably did.

The emergence of shadow banking represented a failure of regulation to keep pace with developments in the financial sector. As much as any other factor, this fundamental regulatory failure set the stage for the crisis.

Market Structures: Tri-Party Repo and Money Market Mutual Funds

Like other dealer firms, Lehman Brothers relied heavily on a critical funding market called the repurchase agreement, or "repo," market. This market proved to be a major source of liquidity risk and instability in the crisis—for Lehman as well as other firms. This portion of the shadow banking system merits particular attention.

Repos are essentially loans that financial institutions use to finance securities inventories— typically on an overnight basis. Repos are collateralized by assets on dealers' balance sheets, in the same way that a mortgage is secured by a home.

One particularly large and important segment of the repo market is called "tri-party" repo. In this $2 trillion market, repo lenders (usually money market mutual funds) extend loans overnight to dealers. During the trading day, credit is provided by big banks that act as repo "clearing banks." Through this process, individual dealer firms typically borrow hundreds of billions of dollars each day.

While tri-party repo has been effective in providing liquidity to securities markets during normal times, under stress conditions these arrangements proved to be a source of liquidity risk for important parts of the financial sector. During the recent crisis, there was significant uncertainty in the markets about whether money funds would maintain their investments and whether repo clearing banks might refuse to provide intraday credit. Uncertainty in this area contributed to "flight" risk in the tri-party repo market.

These structural issues were exacerbated by tri-party lenders' concerns around collateral quality. Traditionally, tri-party repo funding had been limited to the safest collateral classes, such as Treasury and agency securities. During the credit boom, however, tri-party repo lenders began to fund riskier collateral—most notably, various forms of complex structured mortgage products. Tri-party repo lenders extended this credit without requiring sufficient haircuts to reflect the risk of the underlying collateral. Not surprisingly, when the value of this lower-quality collateral became uncertain, tri-party lenders became less willing to continue funding.

As a consequence of these issues, the tri-party repo market was a critical source of liquidity strain on dealer firms during the financial crisis. And money market mutual funds, which provide a large portion of tri-party repo funding, made these liquidity problems even more acute. Money funds were themselves shown to be sources of instability during market stress. In a chaotic and uncertain financial environment, savers who parked cash in money funds became concerned that those assets might not have been as safe as they had anticipated. These concerns intensified after Lehman's bankruptcy, when one large money fund "broke the buck," meaning that its net asset value fell below $1 per share. The money fund industry experienced a modern-day bank run in September 2008. This run accelerated dramatically following Lehman's collapse.

Aggressive policy action was required to stabilize the money funds, including a temporary government guarantee of this $3 trillion industry. Although this program was successful and resulted in positive returns to taxpayers through guarantee fees, the money fund guarantee exposed taxpayers to substantial risks.

Tri-party repo and money funds are prominent examples of market structures and practices that were not robust enough to withstand a major disruption.

Derivatives

Lehman was a major participant in the over-the-counter (OTC) derivatives markets. As of August 2008, Lehman held over 900,000 derivatives positions worldwide. The market turmoil following Lehman's bankruptcy was in part attributable to uncertainty surrounding the exposure of Lehman's derivatives counterparties.

In this regard, Lehman's bankruptcy highlights another flaw in our financial infrastructure: the opacity and complexity of the OTC derivatives markets. These products grew exponentially in the run-up to the crisis. The notional amount of outstanding credit default swaps grew from about $2 trillion in 2002 to over $60 trillion at year-end 2007. Because these trades are conducted on a bilateral basis, the market has very little visibility into the magnitude of derivatives exposures between firms.

Before the crisis, regulatory efforts were underway to reduce the risks in this system. The New York Fed played a leading role in improving the OTC derivatives markets infrastructure from 2005 to 2008. Huge backlogs of unconfirmed trades were eliminated. A central repository for credit derivatives trades was established. And, in 2008, the notional amount of aggregate credit default swaps was reduced substantially through regulatory portfolio compression requirements, which caused dealers to collapse superfluous positions. These initiatives were necessary predicates to further reform in the OTC derivatives markets, including central clearing. As a result of these initiatives, the market uncertainty surrounding derivatives exposures in the crisis was substantially less than it might otherwise have been.

Despite this progress, the basic infrastructure of the OTC derivatives markets makes them a dangerous transmission vehicle for instability during periods of market turmoil. When a major derivatives market participant fails, uncertainty around derivatives exposures undermines confidence in other institutions. OTC derivatives markets, in their current form, significantly increase the risk of financial contagion.

Breakdown in Basic Checks and Balances

Lehman's plunge into high-risk businesses in the years before its bankruptcy has become a familiar story. During this period of aggressive growth, Lehman developed significant exposures to risky subprime lending, commercial real estate, structured products, and high-risk lending for leveraged buyouts. Importantly, the Valukas Report indicates that Lehman repeatedly breached its own risk concentration limits in pursuit of higher earnings.

These types of risk management failures were widespread in the financial sector. Sound risk management practices were in many cases disregarded in favor of concentrated, directional bets. AIG, Bear Stearns, and Lehman Brothers, not to mention scores of mortgage lenders, all allowed fundamental breakdowns in risk management.

Our financial system relies on a set of complementary institutional controls to prevent such unsound practices from emerging. Boards of directors, ratings agencies, and audit and disclosure functions are essential checks and balances against risk management failures.

These mechanisms provide an important level of redundancy in oversight. When effective, they identify material business risks and act as independent referees on firms' internal risk management processes. Major risk management failures require multiple failures to take place within this system of checks and balances.

Before and during the crisis, weaknesses in these checks and balances were prevalent. Boards of directors failed to exercise critical judgment and address critical weaknesses in risk management. Ratings agencies failed to do an adequate job of assessing the risks in structured credit products and disclosing their ratings methodologies. Auditors failed to identify practices that may have crossed the line from an accounting perspective. And the existing accounting and disclosure regime did not adequately apprise investors of material risks in a timely fashion.

Pervasive Opportunities for Regulatory and Accounting Arbitrage

Lehman provides a stark example of how gaps in our system have allowed financial firms to maneuver their operations to "optimize" regulatory and accounting treatment.

Our regulatory system has given firms too much leeway to structure their activities for favorable tax, accounting, and regulatory treatment. For internationally active firms, differences between U.S. and foreign tax, accounting, and capital regimes have prompted firms to structure their activities to minimize these constraints.

Our system in many cases allowed risks to migrate to where regulation was weakest. As the SEC has acknowledged, its voluntary oversight regime allowed Lehman and other investment banks to operate with too much leverage and risk.

Accounting arbitrage has also been widespread. The Valukas Report describes how Lehman appears to have moved certain assets off-balance sheet through repo transactions executed in its London broker-dealer subsidiary. According to the Report, these transactions were designed to reduce the firm's reported leverage at quarter-end.

Importantly, regulatory and accounting arbitrage makes institutions far more complex than they need to be. Complexity poses serious challenges to an effective audit and disclosure regime. Readers of the financial reports of major financial institutions know that they are highly opaque and difficult to understand. Indeed, disclosure documents of complex financial firms are often indecipherable even to experienced analysts.

Without transparency and comparability, market discipline cannot operate effectively. The system we have is not tenable in this regard. Financial reporting must be simpler and easier to understand, and must facilitate meaningful comparisons across institutions.

Of course, none of our government's financial supervisors did an adequate job. But the most dangerous practices that precipitated the crisis were heavily concentrated in the most lightly regulated parts of the financial industry. Regulatory arbitrage is not a formula for financial stability.

Flawed Compensation Practices

Compensation structures at Lehman allowed top executives to realize substantial gains without suffering the downside if their business decisions proved unwise. Lehman's top executives received substantial cash compensation during the boom. And they were able to cash out significant amounts from stock compensation they received in the years prior to the crisis.

This phenomenon was not isolated to Lehman. At many financial firms, compensation structures were misaligned with the time horizons of risk: executives were rewarded for short-term performance, with little attention to the risk of future losses. These practices did not incentivize prudent risk-management and long-term value creation. Instead, they encouraged high-risk activities that were designed to achieve short-term profitability.

As I described earlier, our system has checks and balances that are meant to limit such practices. But, in many cases, these checks and balances did not work. Professionals whose jobs were to monitor and constrain risk-taking were generally paid substantially less than those who made investment decisions. Compensation committees gave little attention to the risk-taking implications of pay-setting decisions. And directors charged with making those decisions lacked the sophisticated, independent advice they needed to assess critically the complex relationship between compensation and risk-taking.

No Tools to Wind down Large Financial Firms

Lehman's bankruptcy in September 2008 helped to turn an intensifying global financial crisis into a classic financial panic. Fearing further defaults, investors declined to renew funding to all types of financial institutions. Money fund investors redeemed their shares and redeployed funds from the private sector to Treasury securities, driving yields into negative territory. Credit markets froze, and corporate America found itself unable to access short-term credit through the commercial paper markets. Without forceful government intervention, the financial system would have collapsed.

These circumstances demonstrated a critical shortcoming in our system. In that moment of historic stress, the government lacked any means to wind-down and liquidate a complex, interconnected financial firm in an orderly way.

After the near-failure of Bear Stearns, it was apparent to informed observers that Lehman Brothers was the weakest of the remaining independent investment banking firms. And we knew that a disorderly bankruptcy of Lehman Brothers, if it occurred, would have damaging consequences for the financial system. With the limited powers that we had, we worked diligently to avoid an outcome that would destabilize the financial system and damage the broader economy. But our tools were insufficient.

The stability of the U.S. financial system cannot be left vulnerable to the reckless choices of individual firms. Lehman's disorderly bankruptcy was profoundly disruptive. It magnified the dimensions of the financial crisis, requiring a greater commitment of government resources than might otherwise have been required. Without better tools to wind down firms in an orderly manner, we are left with no good options.

Actions Taken by the FRBNY

Lehman Brothers was symptomatic of many of the deep structural flaws in our financial system. These flaws did not emerge overnight. Rather, they were a product of developments in the financial system that unfolded over the course of many years.

I was President of the Federal Reserve Bank of New York at the time of Lehman's bankruptcy filing and during the period leading up to it.

As an independent investment bank, Lehman was supervised not by the Federal Reserve, but by the SEC. The Federal Reserve had no regulatory authority over the firm—no authority over its capital, no authority over its liquidity, and no oversight over its audit and accounting control functions. The Federal Reserve was not engaged in supervision of Lehman Brothers.

It did not have the legal authority to do so. These roles and responsibilities remained with the SEC. As I mentioned earlier, the failure to subject all large, interconnected financial firms to robust oversight was a major flaw in our system.

Although the New York Fed was not Lehman's supervisor, it did establish an onsite presence at Lehman in March 2008, after the fall of Bear Stearns.

On the day of the Bear Stearns sale in March 2008, the Federal Reserve announced the creation of the Primary Dealer Credit Facility ("PDCF")—a collateralized lending facility to provide liquidity to primary dealers. The creation of the PDCF meant that the Federal Reserve was a potential lender to the major dealer firms. To manage the risks associated with this facility, the New York Fed immediately installed a small number of analysts at each of the major independent dealer firms, including Lehman Brothers.

After creating the PDCF monitoring program, the Federal Reserve entered into a Memorandum of Understanding ("MOU") with the SEC, which was formalized in July. The MOU was designed to facilitate information-sharing and cooperation. It established a clear division of responsibilities between the SEC and the Federal Reserve. It explicitly affirmed the SEC's role as the supervisor of the independent investment banks.

The PDCF monitoring program did *not* establish the full panoply of supervisory oversight powers that the Federal Reserve exercises with respect to bank holding companies. That regime entails large examination teams, with oversight of the firm's audit and control functions.

In accordance with the MOU, the Federal Reserve worked closely with SEC on a number of important initiatives after the near-failure of Bear Stearns in March. The SEC and the Federal Reserve jointly worked to encourage improvements in the capital and liquidity positions of the investment banks. Simultaneously, the SEC and the Federal Reserve cooperated on a range of other priorities, including taking steps to address risks associated with the derivatives and repo markets.

With respect to Lehman Brothers, between March and September, the New York Fed worked closely with Treasury and the SEC to encourage the firm to raise capital, reduce balance sheet risk, find a strategic buyer, and take other actions to survive the storm. Lehman was unsuccessful in these efforts. The global financial crisis had escalated significantly by the fall of 2008, limiting the available options to stabilize the firm.

The Federal Reserve's powers were limited: it could lend on a short-term basis against good collateral, but it could not safely put a failing investment bank out of existence.

In the absence of a willing buyer, the U.S. government did not have the authority to take the steps that would have been necessary to prevent Lehman's disorderly failure. Lehman lacked sufficient high-quality collateral to permit the Federal Reserve to extend a loan large enough to prevent the firm from defaulting. Given the magnitude of the firm's liquidity issues, stabilizing Lehman would have required a buyer that was willing to guarantee its trading obligations during the period between the signing and closing of the acquisition transaction. No such buyer materialized.

Some have asked why Lehman went bankrupt, while AIG received extraordinary assistance that prevented default. The answer is that AIG presented a very different case. AIG had enough high-quality collateral to permit the Federal Reserve to extend a loan sufficient to stabilize the firm—largely the profitable insurance businesses that were relatively insulated from the firm's losses on complex financial transactions.

In the end, in the absence of a willing buyer, bankruptcy was the only option for Lehman Brothers. The government had neither the authority nor the tools to prevent Lehman's failure from imperiling the financial system.

FINANCIAL REFORM

Lehman Brothers illustrates many of the key deficiencies of our current regulatory regime—a regime that simply is not equipped to effectively monitor, constrain or respond to risks in our financial system.

The Administration's reform proposals—which are broadly consistent with the reform bill that passed the House in December and the bill currently working its way through the Senate—have been crafted to address precisely these failures.

If these reforms become law, we will be far better situated to avoid the abuses that led to the crisis. In particular:

- *Any* major financial firm whose failure could pose a risk to the financial system will be subject to robust, comprehensive supervision, with clear regulatory accountability. An insurance company like AIG that operates with massive derivatives exposure, or an investment bank like Lehman Brothers, will not be able to escape robust consolidated supervision by virtue of its corporate form. These regulatory loopholes will be closed, and opting out will not be an option.
- Major financial firms will be subject to *more stringent* prudential requirements than other financial firms—higher capital, higher liquidity, and more exacting oversight. These higher requirements will reflect the fact that major firms pose greater risks to the financial system. So not only would firms like Lehman, Bear Stearns, and AIG be subject to consolidated supervision, but they also would be subject to substantially higher standards than other firms, due to their size and interconnectedness.
- Better disclosure and transparency will reduce opportunities for accounting arbitrage. We have committed to improving accounting standards and moving forward with international accounting convergence. At the Pittsburgh summit last year, the G-20 leaders called on international accounting bodies to redouble their efforts to achieve a single set of high quality, global accounting standards. These initiatives are currently underway, and they will greatly improve the transparency and comparability of financial statements.
- Regulators are taking action to address the unstable aspects of the repo and money fund industries. Under the auspices of the Federal Reserve, an industry-led task force has been working to develop enhancements to the policies, procedures and systems supporting the tri-party repo market. This initiative is designed to ensure that the structure of the tri-party repo market will not amplify systemic risk during future periods of market stress. And the SEC recently enacted new rules to strengthen liquidity and disclosure in the money fund industry. More work remains to be done in this area, and the President's Working Group on Financial Markets is preparing a report setting forth options to address systemic risk and to reduce the susceptibility of money funds to runs.

- Reform will bring comprehensive oversight and transparency to the OTC derivatives markets. These markets have proved to be a major source of uncertainty and risk during periods of financial disruption. The proposed reforms will bring the bulk of these trades into central clearing arrangements, ensuring full transparency and reducing the degree to which financial contagion can spread due to real or perceived counterparty credit exposures. All dealers and major market participants will be subject to tough prudential standards, including margin and capital requirements. And the SEC and CFTC will have full enforcement authority to set position limits and address fraud, manipulation, and abuse. These reforms will make the system far more resistant to the types of disruption we saw when Lehman failed.
- Important standards will be put in place regarding disclosure and accountability for executive compensation. In particular, companies will be required to hold an annual, non-binding shareholder vote to approve executive compensation. And compensation committees will be given the independence and tools they need to drive a harder bargain over executive pay. These reforms will help to ensure that compensation practices are aligned with the long-term interests of shareholders. They will complement other initiatives relating to compensation in the United States and abroad, including the compensation standards agreed upon by the G-20 for financial institutions around the world; new SEC disclosure rules that will give shareholders critical information on the relationship between pay practices and risk-taking; and recent Federal Reserve guidance on compensation principles that will be incorporated into the supervisory process.
- Finally, we will have a resolution regime that will give the government the necessary tools to safely put failing financial institutions out of existence. The pending bills would establish a bankruptcy-like regime for large financial institutions that mismanage themselves into failure. Under the proposed resolution authority, major financial firms facing insolvency will be dismantled, sold, or liquidated in an orderly fashion. Culpable management will be replaced, equity will be extinguished, and creditors will be exposed to losses. Any costs incurred through this wind-down process will be recouped from large financial institutions—not covered by taxpayers. Resolution authority was the critical tool we needed to deal with Lehman, Bear, and AIG. We must have it when the next big financial firm gets into trouble.

Conclusion

There are few better examples of why we need comprehensive financial reform than Lehman Brothers. No financial regulatory system will ever be perfect. Financial firms will always overreach and get into trouble. But it is clear that good financial regulation can mean the difference between a fundamentally sound and resilient financial system, and one that is built on an unstable foundation.

The path we choose will have significant implications for the future of our economy. Like the President, I am confident that our country will once again choose to tackle these tough problems and enact meaningful reform.

Thank you.

In: The Lehman Brothers Bankruptcy: Analyses
Editors: Gary E. Walker and Lindel D. Clarke
ISBN: 978-1-62081-730-8

Chapter 8

STATEMENT OF FEDERAL RESERVE CHAIRMAN BEN S. BERNANKE. HEARING ON "PUBLIC POLICY ISSUES RAISED BY THE REPORT OF THE LEHMAN BANKRUPTCY EXAMINER"*

Chairman Frank, Ranking Member Bachus, and other members of the Committee, I appreciate the opportunity to testify about the failure of Lehman Brothers and the lessons of that failure. In these opening remarks I will address several key issues relating to that episode.

The Federal Reserve was not Lehman's supervisor. Lehman was exempt from supervision by the Federal Reserve because the company did not own a commercial bank and because it was allowed by federal law to own a federally insured savings association without becoming subject to Federal Reserve supervision. The core subsidiaries of Lehman were securities broker-dealers under the supervisory jurisdiction of the Securities and Exchange Commission (SEC), which also supervised the Lehman parent company under the SEC's Consolidated Supervised Entity (CSE) program. Importantly, the CSE program was voluntary, established by the SEC in agreement with the supervised firms, without the benefits of statutory authorization.

Although the Federal Reserve had no supervisory responsibilities or authorities with respect to Lehman, it began monitoring the financial condition of Lehman and the other primary dealers during the period of financial stress that led to the sale of Bear Stearns to JPMorgan Chase.[1] In March 2008, responding to the escalating pressures on primary dealers, the Federal Reserve used its statutory emergency lending powers to establish the Primary Dealer Credit Facility and the Term Securities Lending Facility as sources of backstop liquidity for those firms. To monitor the ability of borrowing firms to repay, the Federal Reserve, in its role as creditor, required all participants in these programs, including Lehman, to provide financial information about their companies on an ongoing basis. Two Federal Reserve employees were placed onsite at Lehman to monitor the firm's liquidity position and its financial condition generally. Beyond gathering information, however, these employees had no authority to regulate Lehman's disclosures, capital, risk management, or other business activities.

* This is an edited, reformatted and augmented version of the remarks given on April 20, 2010 before the House Financial Services Committee.

During this period, Federal Reserve employees were in regular contact with their counterparts at the SEC, and in July 2008, then-Chairman Cox and I negotiated an agreement that formalized procedures for information-sharing between our two agencies. Cooperation between the Federal Reserve and the SEC was generally quite good, especially considering the stress and turmoil of the period. In particular, the Federal Reserve, with the SEC's participation, developed and conducted several stress tests of the liquidity position of Lehman and the other major primary dealers during the spring and summer of 2008. The results of these stress tests were presented jointly by the Federal Reserve and the SEC to the managements of Lehman and the other firms. Lehman's results showed significant deficiencies in available liquidity, which the management was strongly urged to correct.

The Federal Reserve was not aware that Lehman was using so-called Repo 105 transactions to manage its balance sheet. Indeed, according to the bankruptcy examiner, Lehman staff did not report these transactions even to the company's board. However, knowledge of Lehman's accounting for these transactions would not have materially altered the Federal Reserve's view of the condition of the firm; the information we obtained suggested that the capital and liquidity of the firm were seriously deficient, a view that we conveyed to the company and that I believe was shared by the SEC and the Treasury Department.

Lehman did succeed at raising about $6 billion in capital in June 2008, took steps to improve its liquidity position in July, and was attempting to raise additional capital in the weeks leading up to its failure. However, its efforts proved inadequate. During August and early September 2008, increasingly panicky conditions in markets put Lehman and other financial firms under severe pressure. In an attempt to devise a private-sector solution for Lehman's plight, the Federal Reserve, Treasury, and SEC brought together leaders of the major financial firms in a series of meetings at the Federal Reserve Bank of New York during the weekend of September 13-15. Despite the best efforts of all involved, a solution could not be crafted, nor could an acquisition by another company be arranged. With no other option available, Lehman declared bankruptcy.

The Federal Reserve fully understood that the failure of Lehman would shake the financial system and the economy. However, the only tool available to the Federal Reserve to address the situation was its ability to provide short-term liquidity against adequate collateral; and, as I noted, Lehman already had access to our emergency credit facilities. It was clear, though, that Lehman needed both substantial capital and an open-ended guarantee of its obligations to open for business on Monday, September 15.

At that time, neither the Federal Reserve nor any other agency had the authority to provide capital or an unsecured guarantee, and thus no means of preventing Lehman's failure existed.

The Lehman failure provides at least two important lessons. First, we must eliminate the gaps in our financial regulatory framework that allow large, complex, interconnected firms like Lehman to operate without robust consolidated supervision.

In September 2008, no government agency had sufficient authority to compel Lehman to operate in a safe and sound manner and in a way that did not pose dangers to the broader financial system.

Second, to avoid having to choose in the future between bailing out a failing, systemically critical firm or allowing its disorderly bankruptcy, we need a new resolution regime, analogous to that already established for failing banks. Such a regime would both protect our economy and improve market discipline by ensuring that the failing firm's shareholders and creditors take losses and its management is replaced.

Thank you. I would be glad to respond to your questions.

End Note

[1] Primary dealers are broker-dealers that trade in U.S. government securities with the Federal Reserve Bank of New York.

In: The Lehman Brothers Bankruptcy: Analyses
Editors: Gary E. Walker and Lindel D. Clarke
ISBN: 978-1-62081-730-8

Chapter 9

TESTIMONY OF SEC CHAIRMAN MARY L. SHAPIRO. HEARING ON "PUBLIC POLICY ISSUES RAISED BY THE REPORT OF THE LEHMAN BANKRUPTCY EXAMINER"*

INTRODUCTION

Chairman Frank, Ranking Member Bachus, members of the Committee, I appreciate the opportunity to testify regarding the failure of Lehman Brothers and the Lehman Brothers Examiner's Report (Examiner's Report). I should say at the outset that this testimony is on my own behalf as Chairman of the SEC, and does not necessarily represent the views of the Commission or individual Commissioners.

When I became Chairman of the SEC in late January 2009, the agency and financial markets were still reeling from the events of the fall of 2008. Since that time, the SEC has worked tirelessly to review its policies, improve its operations and address the legal and regulatory gaps that came to light during the crisis.

The Lehman failure, both individually and within the context of the broader financial crisis, sheds light on many interconnected and mutually reinforcing causes that contributed to the failure of many major financial institutions, both bank and non-bank, including:

- Irresponsible lending practices, which were facilitated by a securitization process that originally was viewed as a risk reduction mechanism;
- Excessive reliance on credit ratings by investors;
- A wide-spread view that markets were almost always self-correcting and an inadequate appreciation of the risks of deregulation that, in some areas, resulted in weaker standards and regulatory gaps;
- The proliferation of complex financial products, including derivatives, with illiquidity and other risk characteristics that were not fully transparent or understood;

* This is an edited, reformatted and augmented version of the remarks given on April 20, 2010 before the House Financial Services Committee.

- Perverse incentives and asymmetric compensation arrangements that encouraged excessive risk-taking;
- Insufficient risk management and risk oversight by companies involved in marketing and purchasing complex financial products;
- A siloed financial regulatory framework that lacked the ability to monitor and reduce risks flowing across regulated entities and markets; and
- The lack of an adequate statutory framework for the oversight of large investment bank holding companies on a consolidated basis.

My testimony will describe the SEC structure for the supervision of investment banks and their holding companies, the failure of Lehman, the lessons learned from the Consolidated Supervised Entity program, and the legislative and regulatory initiatives necessary to address the supervision and resolution of systemic entities in the future.

THE CONSOLIDATED SUPERVISED ENTITY PROGRAM

Beginning in 2004[1] through September 2008, the SEC was recognized as the consolidated supervisor for the five large independent investment banks – including Lehman Brothers – under its Consolidated Supervised Entity (CSE) program. The CSE program was created, in part, as a way for U.S. global investment banks that lacked a consolidated holding company supervisor to voluntarily submit to consolidated regulation by the SEC.[2] The SEC had no statutory authority to regulate these holding companies, and thus prior to the CSE program they were not subject to any consolidated supervision or capital requirements.

The CSE program was viewed as an effort to fill a significant gap in the U.S. regulatory structure that was left when the Gramm-Leach-Bliley Act failed to require investment bank holding companies to be regulated at the holding company level and to improve the Commission's oversight of broker-dealers. In retrospect, the program created classic regulatory arbitrage – a system in which a regulated entity was permitted to select its regulator. The arbitrage was facilitated by a prevailing regulatory consensus at the time of the program's inception that focused on meeting regulatory objectives while being careful not to undermine the competitiveness of American financial institutions and capital markets vis-à-vis their overseas, more lightly regulated, counterparts.

In addition, the program was implemented at a time when many believed that the inherently self-correcting nature of markets would prevent institutions from taking on excessive risk, including in the origination or trading of exotic financial instruments.

Under the CSE regime, the holding company was required to provide the Commission with information concerning its activities and risk exposures on a consolidated basis; submit its non-regulated affiliates to SEC examinations; and compute on a monthly basis, risk-based consolidated holding company capital in general accordance with the Basel Capital Accord, an internationally recognized method for computing regulatory capital at the holding company level. In connection with the establishment of the CSE program, the largest U.S. broker-dealer subsidiaries of these entities were permitted to utilize an alternate net capital (ANC) computation.[3] Other large broker-dealers, whose holding companies were subject to consolidated supervision by banking authorities, also were permitted to use this ANC approach.[4]

Under the CSE program, the SEC undertook for the first time the consolidated oversight of the five largest U.S. investment banks, whose operations were global in scope and extended well beyond the types of products and business lines typically found in a registered broker-dealer. Participation by the CSE firms in this regime was voluntary, and the consolidated oversight of these holding companies was more prudential in nature than the SEC's traditional rule-based approach for broker-dealer regulation. In brief, this program reflected a profoundly different approach to oversight and supervision for the Commission. Properly executing the program called for a correspondingly significant expansion in human, financial, managerial, technological and other resources devoted to the oversight and examination of CSE holding companies and their subsidiaries.

The SEC believed at the time that it was stepping in to address an existing gap in the oversight of these entities. Once, the agency took on that responsibility, however, it had to follow through effectively. Notwithstanding the hard work of its staff, in hindsight it is clear that the program lacked sufficient resources and staffing, was under-managed, and at least in certain respects lacked a clear vision as to its scope and mandate.

During 2008, the CSE institutions failed, were acquired, or converted to bank holding companies which enabled them to access government support. The CSE program was discontinued in September 2008 by former Chairman Christopher Cox.

The Failure of Lehman Brothers

Events Leading Up to the Failure of Lehman

In retrospect, the seeds of Lehman's failure were sown well before 2008. Key risk-taking activities that eventually contributed to Lehman's collapse began when the firm embarked in 2006 on an aggressive growth strategy. As part of this strategy, Lehman invested its own capital in assets such as subprime and Alt-A residential mortgages and mortgage-backed securities, commercial real estate, and leveraged lending commitments. After the subprime mortgage crisis emerged, Lehman scaled back exposures in this area, but continued its growth strategy and increased its exposures to leveraged finance and to commercial real estate before liquidity dried up in these markets beginning in August 2007.

During this time, Lehman reported its risk-taking activities under the CSE program. The program's oversight of Lehman's risk-taking focused on whether Lehman had an appropriate system of controls designed to ensure that the risk tolerance of Lehman's management and Board was effectively communicated to Lehman staff and that the risks assumed by the firm were appropriately captured and communicated to senior management. The CSE program also was focused on whether the firm had sufficient capital, under then-current standards, and liquidity, to support these activities. Clearly, the firm and the SEC did not anticipate the extent of the coming market dislocation and the issues that the dislocation would create for the firm.

The near collapse of Bear Stearns in March 2008, which was averted only through a government assisted sale to JPMorgan Chase, resulted in a heightened focus on Lehman. Of the four remaining CSE holding companies then supervised by the SEC, Lehman was considered to have the business model closest to Bear Stearns in that it was heavily dependent on fixed income securitization revenues. In March, however, Lehman reported a first quarter profit and a $34 billion liquidity pool.

In April 2008, Lehman issued approximately $4 billion in preferred securities. In June 2008, Lehman posted its first quarterly loss as a public company. Lehman attributed this $2.8 billion loss primarily to write-downs on residential and commercial mortgage securities and hedges related to these securities. Even though the firm reported that its liquidity pool had grown to $45 billion, it still had significant amounts of illiquid assets, consisting primarily of commercial and residential loans and securities.

Throughout the summer, Lehman embarked on various strategies to raise capital and to reduce the size of its exposure to mortgage-related and other illiquid assets. In June 2008, Lehman issued $4 billion in common stock and $2 billion in mandatory convertible debt. Management sought to raise additional capital through direct equity investments in the firm and by selling a stake in its investment management division. They also sought to spin off the bulk of the firm's commercial real estate assets. By the end of August, these additional efforts failed and the firm's write-downs continued to grow, while the sale of illiquid assets slowed.

The Immediate Causes of Failure

The immediate cause of Lehman's bankruptcy filing on September 15, 2008 stemmed from a loss of confidence in the firm's continued viability resulting from concerns regarding its significant holdings of illiquid assets and questions regarding the valuation of those assets. The loss of confidence resulted in counterparties and clearing entities demanding increasing amounts of collateral and margin, such that eventually Lehman was unable to obtain routine financing from certain of its lenders and counterparties.

Several key events in early September contributed to this loss of confidence. On September 9, the Korean Development Bank, which had been in talks to acquire a stake in Lehman, announced that it would not be doing so. In addition, although Lehman retained most of its secured funding lines, its clearing banks demanded more collateral as a condition to continuing their clearing relationship.

According to information provided by Lehman to the SEC, Lehman claimed its liquidity pool was $41.5 billion at the beginning of the week of September 8, and ended the week at $1.4 billion. The largest drains on the liquidity pool included an increase in the amount of clearing deposits required by the firm's lenders and a decline in the amount of secured funding provided by the firm's counterparties.

Over the weekend of September 12th – 14th, representatives from the Treasury, the Federal Reserve Bank of New York and the Commission met with management from Lehman and other major financial firms in an effort to address the situation. According to the Examiner's Report, the government's analysis was that it did not have the legal authority to make a direct capital investment in Lehman, and Lehman's assets were insufficient to support a loan large enough to avoid Lehman's collapse.[5] On September 15th, Lehman's U.K. broker-dealer filed for administration and Lehman's holding company filed for bankruptcy.

On September 19, 2008 a district judge in the Southern District of New York entered an order commencing the liquidation of the Lehman broker-dealer under the Securities Investor Protection Act.

The CSE Program's Supervision of Lehman

As noted above, under the CSE regime, Lehman's holding company was required to provide the Commission with information concerning its activities and exposures on a consolidated basis, submit its non-regulated affiliates to SEC examinations, and compute on a monthly basis risk-based consolidated holding company capital in general accordance with the Basel Capital Accord. As with all CSE firms, SEC staff had a core set of monthly meetings with Lehman's market and credit risk groups and regular quarterly meetings with other internal control functions, including treasury, internal audit, and financial controllers. Beyond this core set of meetings, SEC staff had frequent conversations with the Lehman staff as questions and issues arose.

As noted above, supervision of Lehman was increased in March 2008 after Bear Stearns nearly collapsed. SEC staff had more frequent interaction with the firm, either through on-site visits or telephone calls, with a focus on the firm's liquidity and funding. Lehman also began submitting more frequent reports to the SEC, including reports on the liquidity pool on a daily basis. SEC staff monitoring Lehman also began to have more frequent communications with the staff of the Federal Reserve Bank of New York regarding Lehman's financial position.

As others have noted, once the markets turned, and particularly once Bear Stearns averted collapse only through a government-assisted sale, it is not clear that anything the SEC could have done would have prevented Lehman's bankruptcy. It is also clear that the SEC did not do enough as consolidated supervisor to identify certain risks and require additional capital and liquidity commensurate with the risks. As stated previously, the program was in my view insufficiently resourced, staffed, and managed from its inception. At the time the program was terminated in September 2008, it had approximately 21 staff, including 10 monitoring staff. Further, in light of the prudential nature of the program, it was a substantial departure from the agency's traditional approach of establishing clear rules and enforcing compliance with them. The Examiner's Report appears to confirm these and other shortcomings and the need to continue our reforms to breakdown stovepipes and instill a culture of collaboration.

Lehman's Repo 105 Transactions

Lehman funded itself in large part through short term repurchase transactions, borrowing tens of billions of dollars on a daily basis. In a repurchase transaction, or repo, a company sells securities in exchange for cash with a simultaneous agreement for the purchaser to return the same or similar securities for a fixed price at a later date, generally a short period of time. Accounting standards establish guidance for whether a repurchase transaction should be reported as a financing transaction (debt) or a sale based in part on whether the reporting entity has surrendered control over the asset. Typically, repos are accounted for as financings (debt) as control over the assets is not fully surrendered.

The availability of repo funding was highly dependent upon the confidence of counterparties, rating agencies and the market in general. Beginning in late 2007 and throughout 2008, amidst increase concern about Lehman's leverage, Lehman significantly increased their reliance on repurchase agreements that Lehman referred to as "Repo 105s." Unlike typical repo transactions, Lehman treated Repo 105 transactions as sales for accounting purposes. The Examiner's Report concluded that the motive for the transactions was ultimately to reduce its leverage: to temporarily remove tens of billions of dollars in assets from its balance sheet at the end of financial reporting periods and use the cash to pay down liabilities as a means to reduce its reported leverage.[6] Lehman did not disclose that it accounted for its repurchase transactions as sales. Instead, it reported that it accounted for its repo transactions as financings, the common accounting treatment for repurchase transactions.

As discussed in the Examiner's Report, regulators (including Commission staff), rating agencies and the Lehman Board, were unaware of Lehman's use of Repo 105 transactions.[7] For purposes of the CSE program, the Commission did not perform an audit of Lehman's balance sheet. Instead, the Commission depended on the integrity of the balance sheet information provided by Lehman's management which was audited or, in the case of quarterly reports, reviewed, by Lehman's auditors. Lehman did not disclose in its audited financials that it was undertaking repos as sales – on the contrary, Lehman's disclosure would lead one to believe that it accounted for all of its repos as financings and that the repos were properly reported as such on the balance sheet.

The findings of the Examiner's Report raise critical and legitimate questions about the use of these transactions to manage Lehman's balance sheet at the close of financial reporting periods, and also raise questions as to how widespread this practice may be. Last month our Division of Corporation Finance issued letters to various public companies requesting detailed information about their use of repurchase agreements or similar transactions involving the transfer of assets where they have an obligation to repurchase them. Among other things, these letters instruct companies to (1) describe their accounting for these transactions, their business purpose for engaging in them, and their impact upon liquidity; (2) provide detailed information about the financial statement impact of these transactions throughout each quarter; and (3) discuss how that impact differed from that presented at each quarter end. Not only will this information enable us to better evaluate each company's disclosure, it will help us understand whether companies are complying with our current requirements, and whether changes to current requirements should be made. Where we find that companies are engaging in financial transactions that are inconsistent with their publicly reported financial condition, we will take appropriate action.

Concerns Identified in the Examiner's Report

The Examiner's Report also raised concerns about the SEC's oversight of Lehman's liquidity pool. Ensuring adequate liquidity was a key part of the CSE program's stated objectives, but the Examiner's Report identified a number of issues with how this objective was implemented.

Each CSE firm was expected to maintain a liquidity pool consisting of cash or highly liquid and highly rated unencumbered debt instruments. However, the standards regarding the types of assets that could be included in this liquidity pool, and the manner in which those assets could be held, were not set forth in a Commission regulation and were otherwise unclear. In fact, practices varied across CSE firms. Though the CSE program began an inspection in early 2008 to gain a better understanding of liquidity practices across the CSE firms, the inspection was not completed prior to the termination of the CSE program. In my view, consolidated supervision requires detailed and clearly stated criteria for what assets are eligible for inclusion in a liquidity pool, meaningful verification efforts and established procedures for addressing concerns that are identified.

In addition, the CSE program appears to have been insufficiently skeptical about the information provided by the firm regarding its liquidity or other risk indicators. As discussed in the Examiner's Report, it appears that Lehman did not fully report to the Commission significant changes affecting assets in its liquidity pool in the period leading up to Lehman's bankruptcy. Although each firm is fully responsible for providing accurate information to its regulators, in certain instances it appears there was insufficient follow-up on issues that should have raised potential concerns.

The Examiner's Report concludes that the SEC did not aggressively restrain Lehman's appetite for taking on increasing risk between 2005 and 2008.[8] The requirement of having sound internal risk management controls was a key element of the CSE regime. However, in practice, the firm apparently treated risk limits not as requirements, but as softer guidelines or thresholds that would trigger necessary internal management approvals when exceeded. The philosophy of the CSE program and its management was that regulators should avoid substituting their views for the business judgment of the firm's management and its Board, as long as the firm continued to satisfy applicable capital requirements and was following its internal controls and escalation processes around increasing risk limits.

While it may be true that ultimate responsibility for the management of financial institutions rest with their management and boards of directors, it is necessary that regulators of large interconnected financial institutions demand more of a firm's management. In the Lehman case, management should have been challenged more forcefully with respect to the types of risks they were taking and, where necessary, had meaningful requirements or limitations imposed.

Finally, the Examiner's Report expresses concerns about a lack of information sharing among the federal regulators involved in Lehman. Effective information sharing by regulators is critical to fulfilling our regulatory obligations, and it is something that the American public has every right to expect. Cooperation and coordination with other financial institution regulators is essential. I expect SEC staff to work closely with our colleagues in other agencies. In addition, I am demanding full information sharing within the SEC – without silos that undermine our effectiveness.

Incorporating Lessons Learned from the CSE Program

The CSE program was terminated in September 2008, and the SEC is no longer the consolidated supervisor of these firms.[9] However, the SEC is taking steps to incorporate the lessons learned from the CSE experience into its ongoing role as primary functional regulator of broker-dealers. Lessons learned include the following.

Capital Adequacy Rules Were Flawed and Assumptions Regarding Liquidity Risk Proved Overly Optimistic

The applicable Basel capital adequacy standards depended heavily on the models developed by the financial institutions themselves. All models depend on assumptions. Assumptions about such matters as correlations, volatility, and market behavior developed during the years before the financial crisis were not necessarily applicable for the market conditions leading up to the crisis, nor during the crisis itself.

The capital adequacy rules did not sufficiently consider the possibility or impact of modeling failures or the limits of such models. Indeed, regulators worldwide are reconsidering how to address such issues in the context of strengthening the Basel regime. Going forward, risk managers and regulators must recognize the inherent limitations of these (and any) models and assumptions – and regularly challenge models and their underlying assumptions to consider more fully low probability, extreme events.

While capital adequacy is important, it was the related, but distinct, matter of liquidity that proved especially troublesome with respect to CSE holding companies. Prior to the crisis, the SEC recognized that liquidity and liquidity risk management were critically important for investment banks because of their reliance on private sources of short-term funding.

To address these liquidity concerns, the SEC imposed two requirements. First, a CSE holding company was expected to maintain funding procedures designed to ensure that it had sufficient liquidity to withstand the complete loss of all short term sources of unsecured funding for at least one year. In addition, with respect to secured funding, these procedures incorporated a stress test that estimated what a prudent lender would lend on an asset under stressed market conditions (a haircut). Second, each CSE holding company was expected to maintain a substantial "liquidity pool" that was composed of unencumbered highly liquid and creditworthy assets that could be used by the holding company or moved to any subsidiary experiencing financial stress.

The SEC assumed that these institutions, even in stressed environments, would continue to be able to finance their high-quality assets in the secured funding markets (albeit perhaps on less favorable terms than normal). In times of stress, if the business were sound, there might be a number of possible outcomes. For example, the firm might simply suffer a loss in capital or profitability, receive new investment injections, or be acquired by another firm. If not, the sale of high quality assets would at least slow the path to bankruptcy or allow for self-liquidation.

As we now know, these assumptions proved much too optimistic. Some assets that were considered liquid prior to the crisis proved not to be so under duress, hampering their ability to be financed in the repo markets. Moreover, during the height of the crisis, it was very difficult for some firms to obtain secured funding even when using assets that had been considered highly liquid.

Thus, the financial institutions, the Basel regime, and the CSE regulatory approach did not sufficiently recognize the willingness of counterparties to simply stop doing business with well-capitalized institutions or to refuse to lend to CSE holding companies even against high-quality collateral. Runs could sometimes be stopped only with significant government intervention, such as through institutions agreeing to become bank holding companies and obtaining access to government liquidity facilities or through other forms of support.

Consolidated Supervision is Necessary but Not a Panacea

Although large interconnected institutions should be supervised on a consolidated basis, policymakers should remain aware of the limits of such oversight and regulation. This is particularly the case for institutions with many subsidiaries engaging in different, often unregulated, businesses in multiple countries.

Before the crisis, there were many different types of large interconnected institutions subject to consolidated supervision by different regulators. During the crisis, many consolidated supervisors, including the SEC, saw large interconnected, supervised entities fail, merge, or seek government liquidity or direct assistance.

Systemic Risk Management Requires Meaningful Functional Regulation, Active Enforcement & Transparent Markets

While a consolidated regulator of large interconnected firms is an essential component to identifying and addressing systemic risk, a number of other tools must also be employed. These include more effective capital requirements, strong enforcement, functional regulation, and transparent markets that enable investors and other counterparties to better understand the risks associated with particular investment decisions. Given the complexity of modern financial institutions, it is essential to have strong, consistent functional regulation of individual types of institutions, along with a broader view of the risks building within the financial system.

Steps the SEC is taking to incorporate lessons learned from the CSE experience into its ongoing role as primary functional regulator of broker-dealers are as follows:

- ***Improvements to Broker-Dealer Reporting and Monitoring.*** With respect to the SEC's ongoing monitoring of certain large broker-dealers, the staff has developed enhanced reporting requirements for the firms, including information regarding balance sheet composition to monitor for the build-up of positions in particular asset classes. In addition, the SEC's 17-h Risk Assessment Program, under which it monitors for potential risks posed to broker-dealers by their affiliates, is in the process of being improved and upgraded.
- ***Improved Coordination.*** There must be full information sharing within the SEC. I have directed senior staff across all divisions to establish dedicated teams – including staff from the Division of Trading and Markets, Division of Risk, Strategy, and Financial Innovation, Division of Investment Management, and the Office of Compliance, Inspections and Oversight – with responsibility for key financial institutions for which the Commission is the primary functional regulator. We also will be seeking additional opportunities to coordinate more effectively with our fellow regulators.

  In addition, we have created and staffed a new division – the Division of Risk, Strategy, and Financial Innovation (Risk Fin) – to develop and expand our institutional expertise. Risk Fin will re-focus the agency's attention on and response to new products, trading practices, and risks. Already, this new division has attracted renowned experts in the financial, economic, and legal implications of the financial innovations being crafted on Wall Street.

- ***Improved Examination, Oversight and Enforcement.*** The SEC's Office of Compliance Inspections and Oversight and our Division of Trading and Markets will be working together with Risk Fin to review and improve our broker-dealer oversight and examination program, initially starting with our ANC firms. This collaboration will address key supervision functions, including risk assessment, exam planning, information gathering and analysis, policy-making, interpretive guidance, monitoring, and reporting. A key theme will be to act in a more coordinated and integrated manner, improving information sharing on a Commission-wide basis and better realizing the potential synergies among our examination, supervision and rule-making functions. Another objective is to better enhance and deploy our expertise, particularly in connection with the planning and analysis of our supervision and examination programs. These programs must be aggressive in their execution, and possible violations of the securities laws and regulations will be vigorously investigated and enforced.
- ***Further Improvements to Rules and Requirements.*** Effective January 2010, the SEC staff instructed the ANC firms to take standardized net capital charges on certain less liquid mortgage and other asset-backed securities positions rather than using financial models to calculate net capital requirements. In addition to increasing the capital required to be held for these positions, this approach will reduce reliance on value-at-risk models.

  The SEC also is reviewing other ways to further enhance and strengthen our financial responsibility requirements for broker-dealers. With respect to ANC firms in particular, we are taking a fresh look at our rules with a view to determining whether the entire ANC approach should be substantially modified.

  With respect to all broker-dealers, some steps the staff is reviewing include: (1) raising minimum net capital requirements for broker-dealers; (2) enhancing the requirements for treating securities as liquid for purposes of the Commission's net capital rule; (3) limiting circumstances when clearing deposits would be allowable for net capital purposes; (4) narrowing the types of unsecured receivables that would be allowable for net capital purposes; and (5) imposing certain explicit leverage-based requirements, such as requiring broker-dealers to provide "early warning" notice to regulators if their leverage exceeds certain levels.

REGULATORY REFORM

The failure of Lehman demonstrates the need for important legislative changes in supervisory and resolution structures for large financial entities that can have a systemic impact on the financial system. The bills passed in the House and being considered in the Senate, although different in many details, are designed to address key issues raised by the financial crisis.

Regulation of Systemic Risk

The financial crisis demonstrated the need to watch for, warn about, and eliminate conditions that could cause a sudden shock and lead to a market seizure or cascade of failures that put the entire financial system at risk. While traditional financial oversight and regulation can help prevent systemic risks from developing, it is clear that this regulatory structure failed to identify and address systemic risks that were developing over recent years. The current structure was hampered by regulatory gaps that permitted regulatory arbitrage and failed to ensure adequate transparency. This contributed to the excessive risk-taking by market participants, insufficient oversight by regulators, and uninformed decisions by investors that were key to the crisis.

Given the shortcomings of the current regulatory structure, I believe there is a need to establish a framework for macro-prudential oversight that looks across markets and avoids the silos that exist today. Within that framework, I believe a hybrid approach consisting of a single systemic risk regulator and an empowered council of regulators is most appropriate. Such an approach would provide the best structure to ensure clear accountability for systemic risk, enable a strong, nimble response should adverse circumstances arise, and benefit from the broad and differing perspectives needed to best identify developing risks and minimize unintended consequences. This should be a mechanism for providing a second set of eyes over large interconnected firms and ensuring that standards and investor protections are *raised* so that there is no regulatory benefit to being large and interconnected.

End Too-Big-To Fail

One of most important regulatory arbitrage risks is the potential perception that large interconnected financial institutions are "too-big-to fail" and will therefore benefit from government intervention in times of crisis. This perception can lead market participants to favor large interconnected firms over smaller firms of equivalent creditworthiness, fueling greater risk.

In addition to establishing a strong Systemic Risk Council and higher standards, a key element to ending "too-big-to-fail" is the creation of a credible resolution regime to unwind and liquidate institutions of any size. In times of crisis when a systemically important institution may be teetering on the brink of failure, policymakers currently must immediately choose between two highly unappealing options: (1) providing government assistance to a failing institution (or an acquirer of a failing institution), thereby allowing markets to continue functioning but creating moral hazard; or (2) not providing government assistance but running the risk of market collapses and greater costs in the future. Markets recognize this dilemma and can fuel more systemic risk by "pricing in" the possibility of a government backstop of large interconnected institutions. This can give such institutions an advantage over their smaller competitors and make them even larger and more interconnected.

A credible resolution regime can help address these risks by giving policy makers a third option: a controlled unwinding of a large, interconnected institution over time. Structured correctly, such a regime could force market participants to realize the full costs of their decisions and help reduce the "too-big-to-fail" dilemma. Structured poorly, such a regime could strengthen market expectations of government support, thereby fueling "too-big-to-fail" risks.

Insuring Independence and Resources for Market Regulation

Although traditionally independent of the executive branch, the SEC lacks an independent source of funding like most financial regulators. Most financial regulators have been established as independent entities with bipartisan management and dedicated funding sources. Unlike its regulatory counterparts, however, the SEC's funding is subject to the budget and appropriations process. As a result, the SEC has been unable to maintain stable, sufficient long-term funding necessary to conduct long-term planning and lacks the flexibility to apply resources rapidly to developing areas of concern.

Despite the damage done by the financial crisis, trading volume has more than doubled since 2003, the number of investment advisers has grown by roughly 50 percent, and the assets they manage have increased nearly 120 percent, to $46 trillion. The SEC's 3,800 employees oversee approximately 35,000 entities – including 11,500 investment advisers, 7,800 mutual funds, 5,400 broker-dealers, and more than 10,000 public companies – a nearly 10 to 1 ratio that is only growing larger. These numbers do not include the many unregulated entities that our enforcement staff must pursue to protect investors.

By guaranteeing independence, facilitating long-term planning, and closing the resource gap between the agency and the entities it regulates, independent funding will allow the SEC to better protect millions of investors. In addition, independent funding will ensure an SEC that is more effective at identifying and addressing the kinds of risk that dealt a significant blow to the American economy.

An independently funded SEC will be better able to take strong action to prevent future risky activities by the entities under its supervision and to fulfill the important new responsibilities assigned to it under any future legislation.

CONCLUSION

In conclusion, there are many lessons to be learned from both the Lehman failure and the larger financial crisis. The enormity and worldwide scope of the crisis, and the unprecedented government response required to stabilize the system, demands a full and careful evaluation of every aspect of our financial system.

As I have said in previous testimony, we cannot hesitate to admit mistakes, learn from them and make the changes needed to address the identified shortcomings and reduce the likelihood that such crises reoccur.

More vigorous regulation and a new culture and approach are essential, and I look forward to continuing to work with you as you consider ways to strengthen our financial system. Thank you again for the opportunity to discuss these important issues with you today, and I look forward to answering your questions.

End Notes

[1] The SEC was recognized as the consolidated supervisor of Merrill Lynch in 2004. The other investment banks came into the CSE program beginning in 2005.

[2] Exchange Act Rel. 34-49830, 69 Fed Reg 34428, June 21, 2004.

[3] In 2004, the SEC amended its net capital rule to permit certain broker-dealers subject to consolidated supervision to use their internal mathematical models to calculate net capital requirements for the market risks of certain positions and the credit risk for OTC derivatives-related positions rather than the prescribed charges in the net capital rule, subject to specified conditions. These models were thought to more accurately reflect the risks posed by these activities, but were expected to reduce the capital charges by the broker-dealer subsidiaries. Accordingly, the SEC required that these broker-dealers have, at the time of their ANC approval, at least $5 billion in tentative net capital (i.e., "net liquid assets"), and thereafter to provide an early warning notice to the SEC if that capital fell below $5 billion. This level was considered an effective minimum capital requirement.

[4] Currently six broker-dealers utilize the ANC regime and all are subject to consolidated supervision by banking authorities.

[5] *See* Examiner's Report at 11-12.

[6] *See, e.g.*, Examiner's Report at 732-4.

[7] *See id.* at 739.

[8] In addition, the Examiner's Report notes that Lehman management excluded some of Lehman's riskiest assets from its stress testing, thereby substantially limiting the usefulness of these tests. *See* Examiner's Report at 67-9. While Commission staff believed Lehman had other ways of measuring these risks, those procedures plainly were insufficient.

[9] The Gramm-Leach-Bliley Act had created a voluntary program for the oversight of certain investment bank holding companies (i.e., those that did not have a U.S. insured depository institution affiliate). The firms participating in the CSE program did not qualify for that program or did not opt into that program. Only one firm (Lazard Ltd.) has ever opted for this statutory program and remains in the program today.

In: The Lehman Brothers Bankruptcy: Analyses
Editors: Gary E. Walker and Lindel D. Clarke
ISBN: 978-1-62081-730-8

Chapter 10

STATEMENT OF ANTON R. VALUKAS. HEARING ON "PUBLIC POLICY ISSUES RAISED BY THE REPORT OF THE LEHMAN BANKRUPTCY EXAMINER"*

Dear Chairman Frank, Ranking Member Bachus and Members of the Committee:

I appreciate this opportunity to appear before you in connection with my role as the Examiner in the Lehman bankruptcy – the largest bankruptcy proceeding ever filed.

As you know, on February 8, 2010, I filed my Final Report with the Court under seal. On March 11, 2010, a redacted version was publicly released; and on April 14, the entire, unredacted Report was made public. The Report is 2209 pages exclusive of appendices and details my findings – formed from interviews of more than 250 persons and review of approximately 35 million pages of documents.

Your letter dated April 14, 2010, inviting me to appear before the Committee, requests that I address five specific bulleted topics, with a sixth bullet inviting me to comment on other issues I deem relevant to public policy issues raised by my Report. I will address each bullet in the order listed in your letter.

Bullet one: The extent to which corporate governance should be enhanced to appropriately manage firm risk.

We conducted an extensive investigation to learn how Lehman managed, monitored and limited its exposure to risk. Lehman had adequate corporate governance procedures in place. It had quantitative risk models that accurately calculated risk and that accurately warned that Lehman was taking on significant levels of risk in excess of the limits generated by the models. Lehman's procedures included reporting of the limits, and exceedances of the limits, to senior management and the Board.

But we found that Lehman was significantly and persistently in excess of its own risk limits. Lehman management decided to disregard the guidance provided by Lehman's risk management systems. Rather than adjust business decisions to adapt to risk limit excesses, management decided to adjust the risk limits to adapt to business goals.

* This is an edited, reformatted and augmented version of the remarks given on April 20, 2010 before the before the House Financial Services Committee.

We found that the SEC was aware of these excesses and simply acquiesced. With no regulator in place that required Lehman to adhere to its risk limits (I will discuss that issue further in bullet two below), Lehman's risk limits became meaningless.

To be sure, Lehman's corporate governance procedure could have been better. A proper system should have had an independent risk management function that reported directly to senior management, to the Board of Directors, and to the regulators, rather than to a business unit; indeed that is a regulatory requirement (SEC Reg 15c3-4); but in 2006-2007, the Lehman risk function reported to the head of a business line rather than directly to senior management.

Lehman was unique among the investment banks in measuring "risk appetite" – the amount of loss it could expect to incur from market risk, credit risk, and event risk and still return a minimal level of profitability. Lehman had in place a series of risk appetite limits, including a firm-wide limit. Every day, Lehman measured its risk usage and compared the usage to see if it was under or over the risk limit.

Lehman represented to the SEC in writing that its firm-wide risk appetite limit was a "*binding constraint on its risk-taking*" that *"could not be exceeded under any circumstances.*" Lehman repeatedly represented to the SEC that this firm-wide risk appetite limit was a hard limit – a meaningful constraint on Lehman's risk taking. Lehman advised the SEC that the limits were set by senior management and the Board. Excesses of limits were reported to the Board.

So an appropriate governance plan was in place to set risk limits. But management did not observe the limits. For example, Lehman committed to what was its largest single investment – Archstone – in May 2007, with closing to occur later. It was clear prior to the commitment that the Archstone transaction would put Lehman over its then existing risk limits, but the deal was committed anyway. With the inclusion of Archstone, Lehman was clearly in excess of its established risk limits. But in the face of exceeding its risk limits, Lehman did not take steps to reduce risk; rather, it simply raised the risk limits.

Lehman ultimately took writedowns on its investment in Archstone of hundreds of millions of dollars; our retrospective analysis was that the writedowns should have been significantly higher. Archstone was one of the investments that put Lehman on or over the brink; yet it was a transaction that would not have been made had Lehman adhered to its own risk limits.

I ultimately concluded that there were no colorable claims arising from investment decisions such as Archstone. Senior management made the conscious decisions to exceed risk limits and complete the Archstone and other deals because they believed, erroneously, that those deals would be profitable. Likewise the decisions to exceed risk limits were flawed but made in the expectation of profit, not loss.

Archstone was the largest, but not the only instance in which risk management's view was overruled or disregarded. Lehman was in breach of its established risk appetite limits on a persistent basis during the second half of 2007. Lehman ultimately cured the breaches at the end of the year, not by reducing risk, but by raising risk appetite limits again.

To be fair, Lehman made some efforts to reduce some risks during this period, but we found that Lehman did not make a systematic effort to reduce its overall commercial real estate risks, the major factor in the breach, until some time in the spring of 2008.

Lehman also had in place a "single transaction limit" framework to limit the size of individual transactions as a risk control. But in late 2006, Lehman management made the affirmative decision to disregard the single transaction limit because it had cost Lehman significant profit-making opportunities. As a result, Lehman committed to and closed dozens of transactions that were vastly in excess of that business unit's risk limits.

The decision not to enforce these limits had consequences for Lehman in the summer of 2007 when certain Lehman executives became concerned whether Lehman would be able to fund all of its outstanding commitments. At that time, a senior Lehman officer, Ian Lowitt, observed: "In case we ever forget; this is why one has concentration limits and overall portfolio limits. Markets do seize up."

By 2008, Lehman had in place a stress testing program, designed to assess whether Lehman could survive a series of both hypothetical and historical stress scenarios. But Lehman did not include many of its riskiest assets in its stress testing, such as commercial real estate. Without including these investments, the stress testing was – at best – meaningless, because a large proportion – perhaps the majority – of Lehman's risk lay with those business lines. And at worst the stress testing was affirmatively misleading, because it provided false comfort. Because the stress testing was not meaningful, Lehman's management and Board were deprived of information that would have more accurately described Lehman's true risk picture and that might have led to more decisive action to reduce risk.

Lehman had in place a system for reporting risk issues and breaches of limits to its Board. The reports to the Board were not always timely or in adequate detail. But in sum, Lehman had in place an appropriate set of procedures to track and set limits to control risk, procedures for management review of the limits and compliance with the limits, and procedures for Board reporting and oversight. Lehman had the procedures; it simply chose to ignore them when it reached established limits. And with no effective external regulation, there was no one to require that Lehman stay within limits. Which brings me to the second bullet:

Bullet two: The role of the SEC and other agencies in oversight, examination and enforcement.

By at least 2007, various agencies of the US government were concerned – at the highest levels – with the prospects for Lehman's survival. Former Treasury Secretary Paulson, Fed Chairman Bernanke, then President of the Federal Reserve Bank of New York (FRBNY) Geithner, and Former SEC Chairman Cox each told us that they were concerned about Lehman's future and the effect of Lehman's possible demise on the US economy. That concern intensified after Bear Stearns' near collapse in March 2008. Indeed, on June 13, 2008 - three months before Lehman's bankruptcy - Donald L. Kohn, Vice Chairman of the Federal Reserve, sent an email to Chairman Bernanke stating that "the question is when and how [Lehman] go[es] out of business not whether." The concern at the top was reflected in the personal role each of the individuals assumed in staying abreast of Lehman's situation.

After the near-collapse of Bear Stearns in March 2008, the SEC and FRBNY placed embedded teams at Lehman to gather information and monitor Lehman's condition. Then-FRBNY President Geithner spoke regularly with Lehman's CEO, Richard Fuld and advised him that Lehman needed to raise more capital and/or form a strategic alliance with an entity with a stronger balance sheet.

Secretary Paulson spoke to Mr. Fuld regularly and repeatedly urged that Lehman raise capital, find a strategic partner, or sell Lehman. Beginning in March 2008, Chairman Cox had direct calls with Mr. Fuld every few weeks. Chairman Bernanke spoke infrequently to Mr. Fuld but frequently with Geithner and Paulson about Lehman. Chairman Bernanke observed that Secretary Paulson was frustrated by Mr. Fuld's "more inertial behavior" to raise capital or find a strategic partner. The Fed was trying to pressure Lehman to be more aggressive, but was conscious of its "appropriate role" as a lender, not a regulator, given that the SEC was the regulator.

So the agencies were concerned. They gathered information. They monitored. *But no agency regulated.*

The Fed and Treasury took pains to tell us that the SEC was Lehman's regulator, and that they therefore deferred to the SEC. For its part, the FRBNY viewed its role as a potential lender, not as a regulator. Secretary Geithner viewed the SEC, not the FRBNY, as Lehman's primary regulator; he told us that the FRBNY had "no knowledge, reach or capacity to affect [Lehman's] behavior." Secretary Geithner stated that the FRBNY had authority to obtain information from Lehman solely from the FRBNY's status as a "rather late, reluctant creditor" to Lehman through the Fed's discount window.

But former SEC Chairman Cox took equal pains to say, during our interview with him on January 8, 2010, that the SEC's statutory jurisdiction was limited to Lehman's broker-dealer subsidiary and that it was not the regulator of Lehman itself.

Despite Chairman Cox's statement, we believe it is clear that the SEC was Lehman's primary regulator. In 2005, the European Union ("EU") announced that it would regulate global financial institutions unless they were regulated by an equivalent domestic agency. In response, all of the major investment banks – Lehman, Bear Stearns, Goldman Sachs, Morgan Stanley and Merrill Lynch – voluntarily submitted to regulation under the SEC's Consolidated Supervised Entity ("CSE") program. Lehman was free to withdraw, but if it had done so, it would have become subject to EU supervision; so the SEC thus had *de facto* supervisory authority; the SEC's General Counsel's office has acknowledged that it had that authority, stating that "CSE staff thus had broad authority in its supervision of Lehman Brothers."

The SEC Rule governing the CSE program, 69 Fed. Reg. 34.428, mandates that, in order to participate in the CSE program, the broker-dealer must submit a written undertaking by the ultimate holding company - LBHI - that "[a]cknowledge[s] that the [SEC] may implement *additional supervisory conditions* if the ultimate holding company fails to comply in a material manner with any provision of its undertaking" which requires the holding company to provide the SEC with information about the company's capital and other specified financial, operational and risk management information on a monthly, quarterly and annual basis, as well as to "implement and maintain a consolidated internal risk management control system . . . ." The SEC rule expressly contemplates SEC regulatory authority over the holding company.

Perhaps most significant, in February 2008 testimony to the Senate Banking Committee, Chairman Cox acknowledged that, through the CSE Program, the SEC had authority to "monitor for, and act quickly in response to, financial or operational weakness in a CSE holding company or its unregulated affiliates that might place regulated entities . . . or the broader financial system, at risk."

We believe it clear, then, that the SEC was in fact Lehman's primary regulator. The SEC told us that were constantly monitoring Lehman's risk and liquidity. But there was little if any actual regulation; we observed no instance in which the SEC did anything, in Chairman Cox's words, to "act quickly in response to financial or operational weaknesses" at Lehman.

The SEC made a few recommendations or directions here and there, but in general it simply collected data; it did not direct action, it did not regulate.

It is one thing for Lehman to have exercised the business judgment, although in retrospect clearly bad judgment, to forge ahead and take on excessive risk. But it was quite another for the supposed regulator – a regulator who had been told by Lehman that its risk controls were binding and not meant to be exceeded under any circumstances – to stand by idly and simply acquiesce to management's decision. The SEC's mission – clearly stated on its own website – is "to protect investors, maintain fair, orderly, and efficient markets, and facilitate capital formation." The SEC's role was not to simply absorb and acquiesce to Lehman's decisions; the SEC's role was to supervise and regulate to protect investors and the markets.

I will briefly address three critical areas, which are described in complete detail in my Report, in which the SEC had actual knowledge – or could have, with minimal effort, obtained that knowledge – of significant issues that, if they had been the subject of regulation, might have altered the outcome.

The SEC *knew* that Lehman was reporting sums in its reported liquidity pool that the SEC did not believe were in fact liquid; the SEC *knew* that Lehman was exceeding its risk control limits; and the SEC *should have known* that Lehman was manipulating its balance sheet to make its leverage appear better than it was. Yet even in the face of actual knowledge of critical shortcomings, and after Bear Stearns' near collapse in March 2008 following a liquidity crisis, the SEC did not take decisive action.

Liquidity. The SEC and the FRBNY each told us that Lehman's liquidity was of critical importance. But Lehman included in its reported liquidity pool assets that both the SEC and the FRBNY concluded, when they were advised of the facts, were not proper components of liquidity because they were not readily monetizable.

Lehman publicly disclosed its liquidity pool – the amount supposedly available to Lehman to satisfy its short-term obligations – because liquidity was essential to maintain the confidence of Lehman's trading partners. On June 9, 2008 - just three months before declaring bankruptcy - Lehman announced its liquidity pool was at $45 billion, its "largest ever."

On September 10, 2008 - five days before it filed for bankruptcy - Lehman publicly announced that its liquidity pool was holding steady at approximately $41 billion. By Friday, September 12, however, Lehman had less than $2 billion of assets that could readily be turned into cash; it literally did not have sufficient cash to open for business on Monday, and it filed for bankruptcy protection on September 15.

We know in retrospect that Lehman's report of a $41 billion liquidity pool on September 10 was off by tens of billions of dollars. In the course of my investigation, we discovered an internal Lehman document that lists Lehman's actual liquidity during Lehman's final week, categorizing the assets as "High," Mid" and "Low" "Ability to Monetize." On September 9, the day before the announcement of the $41 billion pool, Lehman had $40.6 billion of assets in its supposed pool. But the internal document shows that only $24.7 billion of that amount was in the "High" category; there was $0.9 billion in "Mid" category; and $15 billion of the $41 billion liquidity pool was in fact not liquid at all, because those amounts were pledged to the clearing banks. On September 10, after the announcement of a $41 billion pool, the "High" ability to monetize assets plummeted from $24.7 to 9.4 billion; on September 11 the amount fell further to $7 billion; and by September 12 it was a mere $1.4 billion.

The SEC did not learn all of these precise facts until September 12 or later. But months earlier, it *had* learned critical information that put it on notice that Lehman's liquidity was not as was portrayed to the investing public. But the SEC did not act on its knowledge, it simply acquiesced.

In June 2008, one of Lehman's clearing banks, Citibank, required that Lehman post $2 billion as a "comfort deposit" as a condition for Citi's continued willingness to clear Lehman's trades. Lehman was technically free to withdraw the deposit, but it could not do so as a practical matter without shutting down or disrupting the business it ran through Citi. Later in June, Lehman posted $5 billion of collateral to JPMorgan, Lehman's main clearing bank, in response to an earlier demand by JPMorgan. Lehman continued to count virtually all of these deposits in its reported liquidity pool – nearly $7 billion of a reported $40 billion, 17.5% of the total.

The SEC had actual knowledge, in June 2008, of the Citi deposit. The SEC believed that it was not proper to include such deposits in a reported liquidity pool. The FRBNY, when it ultimately learned about the deposit months later, likewise agreed that it was improper to include such deposits in a liquidity pool. But while the SEC disapproved of Lehman's inclusion of that amount in its liquidity pool, it took no action to require that Lehman not do so. The SEC did not direct that Lehman publicly disclose the facts so that no one was misled about Lehman's liquidity. And, remarkably, the SEC did not ask the logical question "Are there other deposits like this one?" so they did not learn – until September 12 – that virtually all of the $5 billion JPMorgan deposit was also included in the reported liquidity pool, as well as more than $9 billion Lehman posted to JPMorgan after September 8.

On September 12, 2008, the significance of Lehman's collateral postings became clear to the SEC's Michael Hsu. Mr. Hsu connected the dots in an email that day that "lehman's liquidity pool is almost totally locked up with clearing banks to cover intraiday [sic] credit []. This is a really big problem." But even then, with Lehman shares being actively traded, the SEC did not require Lehman to make any announcements about its severely depleted liquidity.

Risk. The SEC knew that Lehman was in repeated and persistent breach of its own risk limits, yet the SEC simply acquiesced; it took no action either to get Lehman back into control or to require that Lehman publicly disclose the full extent of its risk-taking.

When Lehman applied for and was granted CSE status, it advised the SEC that it had a robust procedure to calculate and set risk limits as a *"binding constraint on its risk-taking"* that *"could not be exceeded under any circumstances."*

The SEC received monthly information about Lehman's risk limits and risk usage from Lehman. In October 2007, the CSE staff learned that Lehman was more than 20% over its recently increased risk appetite limit amount. But the SEC simply acquiesced; it did nothing with that information other than to ask whether the limit breaches had been properly escalated within Lehman. It did not direct compliance with risk limits. It did not direct public disclosure that Lehman failed to stay within its limits.

Lehman's CSE application also advised the SEC that Lehman was "in the process of developing single transaction limits," but that the businesses were "currently operating as if the limits [were] in place." But by July 2007, Lehman had committed to approximately 30 deals that exceeded its then existing limit. The SEC simply acquiesced; it did nothing to require adherence to single transaction limits; it did not require public disclosure of management's decision not to apply those limits.

Under the CSE Program, Lehman was required to develop and maintain a market-based stress testing program, under which the firm's portfolio would be tested against a series of both hypothetical and historical stress scenarios. Lehman did test, but it did not include many of its riskiest assets – such as commercial real estate – in the testing models. For example, the SEC knew that Lehman's internal stress test excluded untraded positions, including commercial real estate. The SEC simply acquiesced; it did nothing to require adjustment to the tests. When Lehman did experimental testing in 2008 with those excluded assets added into the tests, the results were stunning: The tests that were shared with the SEC showed potential losses in all cases of less than $4 billion; but with the excluded assets factored in, the losses soared to $9.4 billion in one instance, $13.4 billion in another.

Balance Sheet Manipulation. I will address this point in a bit more detail below as an independent bullet point, but it is pertinent here. My Report details Lehman's use of an accounting device known as Repo 105 – a device which was described in contemporaneous e-mails from Lehman executives as a "gimmick" and a "drug we r on" whose only purpose was to "manage" the balance sheet – to temporarily move $50 billion of assets of balance sheet at quarter end reporting periods. The effect of these transactions was to allow Lehman to report significantly lower leverage numbers at a time when the rating agencies and business parties viewed leverage as a critical metric.

The SEC did not know about the practice. But it is difficult to understand why not. In the post-Enron world, it would be logical, if not obvious, to ask public companies to explain their off-balance sheet transactions. I saw nothing in my investigation to suggest that the SEC asked even the most fundamental questions that might have uncovered this practice early on, before Lehman escalated it to a $50 billion issue.

I must emphasize, as I attempted to set out in my Report, that Lehman's failure was the result of many factors; there is no single cause or actor. I do not view my appearance today as an occasion to assign blame but rather as an opportunity to offer insights that might enhance the government's ability to protect the nation's financial infrastructure from another Lehman.

But it is my conclusion that the SEC did not effectively regulate. The SEC even had the benefit of its own Inspector General's draft report regarding Bear Stearns during the summer before Lehman failed – a report that highlighted, in the context of Bear, the SEC's failures to effectively regulate Bear's risk, leverage, capital and liquidity. And still the SEC failed to act with respect to Lehman.

Recently, current SEC Chairman Mary Schapiro came to Chicago with her senior staff to meet with me and my partners to discuss the Report. We sincerely appreciate the SEC's efforts to follow up on issues raised by the Report. I did not suggest to her, and I am not here today to suggest, any specifics for what regulations there should be or what agency should enforce those regulations. But as someone who has spent considerable time investigating the facts which preceded Lehman's failure, I have views on what was not done – there was a void that I believe merits additional attention and action, by this Committee or by others.

Bullet three: The relationship and means of communication between the SEC, FRBNY and other agencies.

Like most Americans, I was disturbed to learn after 9/11 that various intelligence agencies did not always share information with one another. I thought we learned something from that, but apparently not.

Lehman's collapse was not unanticipated. After Bear Stearns -- a firm whose business model was nearly identical to Lehman's -- almost collapsed, the SEC and the FRBNY assigned dedicated teams to Lehman to monitor its affairs in real time. One would expect that both agencies would work together to avert Lehman's failure. And for the most part, they did. But there were serious lapses.

Both the SEC and the FRBNY focused much of their attention on Lehman's liquidity, but neither agency directed Lehman to take any action. Both agencies had access to daily liquidity reports from Lehman soon after Bear Stearns' near collapse in March 2008. And both agencies monitored Lehman on site beginning in March 2008. On occasion, the SEC deferred to the FRBNY to develop stress test parameters to determine Lehman's vulnerability to a bank run. But we found little evidence that the two agencies pooled their resources as a team to maximize their ability to regulate Lehman. For example, after Lehman failed several stress tests in May and June 2008, neither the SEC nor the FRBNY directed Lehman to take corrective action to strengthen its liquidity position.

Significantly, the SEC and the FRBNY failed to share information about Lehman's liquidity and Lehman's inclusion of encumbered collateral in its liquidity pool. The SEC knew in June 2008 about the $2 billion Citi deposit and that it was included by Lehman in its reported liquidity pool. It did not share that information with the FRBNY, which did not learn those facts until late August 2008. Additionally, the SEC prepared liquidity analyses of the CSE firms, including Lehman, but the SEC affirmatively declined to share these with the FRBNY because, they explained to us, the analyses were in draft form and never finalized.

The FRBNY knew by at least July 2008 about the $5 billion JPMorgan collateral pledge which had been made in June 2008. The FRBNY did not pass on that information to the SEC. By August 20, 2008, the FRBNY realized that Lehman was including virtually all of the $5 billion collateral pledge to JPMorgan in Lehman's reported liquidity pool, but - again - the FRBNY did not share this with the SEC.

So as of August 20, the combined knowledge of the government was that at least $7 billion of Lehman's supposed liquidity – a significant portion of the total – was not liquid because it was pledged. But there was no combined knowledge because the SEC and FRBNY had not shared their individual knowledge.

The FRBNY knew about agreements that Lehman executed with its clearing banks on August 26 and September 9, 2008 that significantly increased the clearing banks' rights with respect to Lehman collateral. It did not share that information with the SEC. In sum, the FRBNY did not *volunteer* information regarding the CSEs. Instead, the FRBNY only shared information specifically *requested* by the SEC.

The failure to share was not a top down decision. At the top, Chairman Bernanke and Chairman Cox were personally involved in the negotiation and execution of a Memorandum of Understanding between the Fed and the SEC that provided for the exchange of information. The failure was at a staff level, but it was a genuine failure.

The FRBNY and Fed witnesses we spoke to, from Chairman Bernanke and Secretary Geithner down to their staffs, indicated to us that they had some question with the competence of the SEC personnel who were supposedly regulating Lehman. These comments were not a reflection on the competence of particular individuals, but rather on the culture of the SEC. As Chairman Bernanke put it, with due deference to the lawyers he was speaking to, the SEC has a lawyer, enforcement mentality rather than a banker, regulator point of view. The SEC is competent to enforce rules, but it may lack the experience and skill sets possessed by bank regulators to evaluate financial risks of particular loans and other investments.

The agency with the skill sets to regulate a financial institution like Lehman – the Fed – did not have the authority; and the agency with the authority – the SEC – may not have had the skills. And the two agencies were unable to smooth out the gaps because they failed to have full and open sharing of information.

Bullet four: The appropriateness of accounting practices such as Repo 105.

I devote 320 pages of my Report to Lehman's Repo 105 practices, detailing Lehman's use of an accounting technicality to temporarily remove significant amounts of assets off balance sheet for no apparent reason other than to artificially and deceptively reduce Lehman's reported net leverage and, therefore, the market perception of Lehman's viability.

I express no view on whether, as a technical matter of GAAP accounting, it is permissible to treat transactions as sales which are by all other measures financings. But I have a definite view that it is *not* appropriate to engage in significant amounts of such transactions without disclosure.

Lehman did not disclose that it used $50 billion of these transactions. To the contrary, it affirmatively and erroneously stated in its public filings that it used repo transactions solely as financings. The effect of these transaction was to reduce its net leverage by nearly two full points – when Lehman itself defined a material transaction as one which affected net leverage by one tenth of one point. The failure to disclose the facts was not appropriate.

Bullet five: The quality of Lehman's Management Discussion and Analysis Disclosures.

I found that there are colorable claims that the Management Discussion and Analysis ("MD&A") sections of Lehman's Form 10-K for 2007 and Form 10-Q filings in 2008 were misleading.

Lehman emphasized to the investing public that it had worked to lower its net leverage ratio, and stated in its MD&A that net leverage is "more meaningful" than a simple leverage ratio. But Lehman did not disclose that it had only temporarily reduced its net leverage ratio through Repo 105 transactions. Consequently, Lehman's statement that the net leverage ratio was a "more meaningful" measurement of leverage was rendered misleading because that ratio – as reported by Lehman – was not an accurate indicator of Lehman's actual leverage, and in fact, understated Lehman's leverage significantly. In light of the market's focus on the leverage of investment banks in late 2007 and 2008, I found that sufficient evidence exists for a judge or jury to find that Lehman's reported net leverage ratio was materially misleading during that period.

An MD&A should include an "analysis" of known material trends, events, demands, commitments, and uncertainties – not simply a restatement of financial statement information. For example, an MD&A should provide information about the *quality* of, and potential variability of, a company's earnings and cash flow so that investors can ascertain the likelihood that past performance is indicative of future performance. Regulation S-K requires a registrant to discuss known trends involving its capital resources, *specifically including off-balance sheet financing arrangements*. The same regulation specifies that a registrant should discuss, among other things, the "nature and business purpose to the registrant of such off-balance sheet arrangements" and "[t]he importance to the registrant of such off-balance sheet arrangements in respect of its liquidity, capital resources, market risk support, credit risk support or other benefits." My report details statements, in both interviews and in contemporaneous e-mails, by senior Lehman employees that the Repo 105 transactions had no business purpose at all, but did have a marked effect on Lehman's reported net leverage ratio.

SEC guidance also states that an MD&A should describe "unusual events and transactions" to help identify apparent trends. Lehman did not disclose the unusual nature of the Repo 105 transactions or the trend of the temporary reduction of Lehman's reported net leverage ratio at the end of reporting periods.

Lehman's obligation to repurchase $50 billion of Repo 105 transactions should have been disclosed in its MD&A. That obligation was a known event that was reasonably likely to occur and would have had a material effect on the company's financial condition or results of operations. In addition, in the Liquidity and Capital Resources section of Lehman's MD&A's, Lehman should have included a discussion of the timing and/or amounts of the cash flow created by the repayment of the Repo 105 cash borrowing in the first seven to ten days after the end of the reporting period.

Bullet six: Other relevant issues.

Because neither the SEC nor any other agency directed Lehman to correct its misleading and incomplete public statements, the public did not know there were holes in the reported liquidity pool, nor did it know that Lehman's risk controls were being ignored, or that reported leverage numbers were artificially deflated. Billions of Lehman shares traded on misinformation.

Lehman officers emphasized to us that they freely and fully provided information to various government agencies. I found no evidence to suggest that Lehman withheld any information requested by any agency. But it is my conclusion that the government simply acquiesced to the information it was given; it took no regulatory action, it did not ask hard questions.

It is difficult to speculate on what might have happened in the past had the SEC or the Fed or the Treasury taken more decisive action. We cannot say with certainty what might have worked, but we do know what did not work. If Lehman had been directed to follow its risk controls, it presumably would have taken on less risk. If Lehman had been required to disclose its true liquidity when its pool was first depleted with the $2 billion Citi deposit in June 2008, when the depletion was not terribly material, it presumably could not have continued to count increasingly large amounts of encumbered assets as liquidity as it was required over the summer to pledge more assets with its clearing banks.

I have to state the obvious. There is no bright line action that can be said in retrospect "had the government done this, Lehman would not have failed." It is far from clear that the most engaged regulator could have saved Lehman from its fate. But what is clear is that had the government acted sooner on what it did or should have known, there would have been more opportunities for a soft landing. The markets might have been spared the turmoil of Lehman's abrupt failure.

What is clear is that the regulators were not fully engaged and did not direct Lehman to alter the conduct we know in retrospect led Lehman to ruin. Someone must be in charge. And the agency in charge must have the will to act.

In: The Lehman Brothers Bankruptcy: Analyses
Editors: Gary E. Walker and Lindel D. Clarke
ISBN: 978-1-62081-730-8

Chapter 11

STATEMENT OF RICHARD S. FULD JR. HEARING ON "PUBLIC POLICY ISSUES RAISED BY THE REPORT OF THE LEHMAN BANKRUPTCY EXAMINER"*

Mr. Chairman, Ranking Member Bachus, and Members of the House Committee on Financial Services, you have invited me here today to address a number of public policy issues raised by the Lehman Brothers bankruptcy report filed by the Examiner.

Since September of 2008, I have given much thought to the financial crisis and the perfect storm of events that forced Lehman into bankruptcy. Everyone's focus is now on how to prevent another crisis. The key is how regulation and governance should be deployed going forward to better protect the financial markets and the entire system.

The idea of a "super regulator" that monitors the financial markets for systemic risk, I believe, is a good one. To be successful in today's challenging environment, this new regulator should have actual experience and a true understanding of the business of financial institutions, the capital markets and risk management and must be given the resources sufficient to accomplish its important mission.

My view is that the new regulator also should have access, on a real-time basis, to all information and data regarding transactions, assets and liabilities, as well as current and future commitments. In addition, we should put in place established and effective methods of communication between the regulator and the firms being regulated, all of whom should be guided by clear standards for capital requirements, liquidity and other risk management metrics.

The job of the new regulator can only be done, in my opinion, with the creation and utilization of a master mark-to-market capability that determines valuations and capital haircuts on all assets, commitments, loans and structures.

In short, to have a fair and orderly market, I believe we need a single set of transparent rules for all of the participants.

You have asked specifically about the role of the SEC and the Federal Reserve Bank of New York. Beginning in March of 2008, the SEC and the Fed conducted regular, at times daily, oversight of Lehman. SEC and Fed officials were physically present in our offices

---

* This is an edited, reformatted and augmented version of the remarks given on April 20, 2010 before the House Financial Services Committee.

monitoring our daily activities. The SEC and the Fed saw what we saw, in real time, as they reviewed our liquidity, funding, capital, risk management and mark-to-market processes. The SEC and the Fed were privy to everything as it was happening. I am not aware that any data was ever withheld from them, or that either of them ever asked for any information that was not promptly provided.

After an extended investigation into Lehman's bankruptcy, the Examiner recently published a lengthy report stating his views. Despite popular and press misconceptions about Lehman's valuations of mortgage and real estate assets, liquidity, and risk management, the Examiner found no breach of duty by anyone at Lehman with respect to any of these.

Speaking of asset valuations, the world still is being told that Lehman had a huge capital hole. It did not. The Examiner concluded that Lehman's valuations were reasonable, with a net immaterial variation of between $500 million and $2.0 billion. Using the Examiner's analysis, as of August 31, 2008 Lehman therefore had a remaining equity base of at least $26 billion. That conclusion is totally inconsistent with the capital hole arguments that were used by many to undermine Lehman's bid for support on that fateful weekend of September 12, 2008.

The Examiner did take issue, though, with Lehman's "Repo 105" sale transactions.

As to that, I believe that the Examiner's report distorted the relevant facts, and the press, in turn, distorted the Examiner's report. The result is that Lehman and its people have been unfairly vilified.

Let me start by saying that I have absolutely no recollection whatsoever of hearing anything about Repo 105 transactions while I was CEO of Lehman. Nor do I have any recollection of seeing documents that related to Repo 105 transactions. The first time I recall ever hearing the term "Repo 105" was a year after the bankruptcy filing, in connection with questions raised by the Examiner.

My knowledge, therefore, about Lehman's Repo 105 transactions, and what I will say about them today, is based upon my understanding of what I have recently learned.

As CEO, I oversaw a global organization of more than 28,000 people with hundreds of business lines and products and with operations in more than forty countries spread over five continents. My responsibility as the CEO was to create an infrastructure of people, systems and processes, all designed to ensure that the firm's business was properly conducted in compliance with the applicable standards, rules and regulations.

There has been a lot of misinformation about Repo 105. Among the worst were the completely erroneous reports on the front pages of major newspapers claiming that Lehman used Repo 105 transactions to remove toxic assets from its balance sheet. That simply was not true. According to the Examiner, virtually all of the Repo 105 transactions involved highly liquid investment grade securities, most of them government securities. Some of the newspapers that got it wrong were fair-minded enough to print a correction.

Another piece of misinformation was that Repo 105 transactions were used to hide Lehman's assets. That also was not true. Repo 105 transactions were sales, as mandated by the accounting rule, FAS 140.

Another misperception was that the Repo 105 transactions contributed to Lehman's bankruptcy. That was not true either. Lehman was forced into bankruptcy amid one of the most turbulent periods in our economic history, which culminated in a catastrophic crisis of confidence and a run on the bank. That crisis almost brought down a large number of other financial institutions, but those institutions were saved because of government support in the form of additional capital and fundamental changes to the rules and regulations governing banks and investment banks.

The Examiner himself acknowledged that the Repo 105 transactions were not inherently improper and that Lehman vetted those transactions with its outside auditor. He also does not dispute that Lehman appropriately accounted for those transactions as required by Generally Accepted Accounting Principles.

I have recently learned that, in 2000, the Financial Accounting Standards Board published detailed accounting rules for transactions of this very type, described them and dictated how they should be accounted for. In 2001, Lehman adopted a written accounting policy for Repo 105 transactions that incorporated those accounting rules. E&Y, the firm's independent outside auditor, reviewed that policy and supported the firm's approach and application of the relevant rule, FAS 140.

As I now understand it, because Lehman's Repo 105 transactions met the FAS 140 requirements, that accounting rule *mandated* that those transactions be accounted for as a sale. That was exactly what I believe Lehman did. Lehman should not be criticized for complying with the applicable accounting standards.

In other words, those transactions were modeled on FAS 140. The accounting authorities wrote the rule that expressly provided for those transactions and how they should be accounted for. To the best of my knowledge, Lehman followed those rules and requirements.

My job as the CEO was also to put in place a robust process to ensure that Lehman complied with all of its obligations to make accurate public disclosures. I had hundreds of people in the internal audit, finance, risk management and legal functions to ensure that we did, in fact, comply with all of our obligations.

Part of that process was E&Y's role in auditing our financial statements and reviewing our quarterly and annual SEC filings. Each year, E&Y issued formal opinions that Lehman's audited financial statements were fairly presented in accordance with GAAP, and they were.

We also had in place a rigorous certification process that was carried out in advance of every annual and quarterly SEC filing. That bottom-up process involved hundreds of people who had first-hand knowledge of the firm's day-to-day business and the responsibility to review for accuracy and compliance the firm's SEC disclosures before they were filed.

Before we made any annual or quarterly filing, the key people who were involved in this process signed certifications confirming that, to their knowledge, the filing did not contain any untrue statement of a material fact or any material omission and that it fairly presented Lehman's financial position.

Our certification process culminated, every quarter, with a mandatory, all-hands, in-person meeting, which was chaired by Lehman's Chief Legal Officer. In addition to me, that meeting was attended by the firm's President, Chief Financial Officer, Financial Controller, Executive Committee members, business heads, the principal internal audit, finance and risk managers, legal counsel and our outside auditors.

After we had reviewed the draft annual or quarterly filing in detail, the Chief Legal Officer and I would each ask everyone present to speak up if there was anything in the document that caused them concern, or if anything had been omitted that they thought should be included. Attendees were also told that they should speak separately with the Chief Legal Officer if they had an issue that they did not want to raise at the meeting. To my knowledge, no one ever, at any of those meetings, raised any issue about Repo 105 transactions.

I relied on this certification process because it showed that those with granular knowledge believed the SEC filings were complete and accurate. I never signed an SEC filing unless it was first approved by the Chief Legal Officer.

Mr. Chairman, I thank you for allowing me to speak on these issues and I will be pleased to answer any questions this Committee may have.

In: The Lehman Brothers Bankruptcy: Analyses
Editors: Gary E. Walker and Lindel D. Clarke
ISBN: 978-1-62081-730-8

Chapter 12

STATEMENT OF THOMAS H. CRUIKSHANK. HEARING ON "PUBLIC POLICY ISSUES RAISED BY THE REPORT OF THE LEHMAN BANKRUPTCY EXAMINER"*

I would like to thank the House Financial Services Committee for inviting me to appear at today's hearing on public policy issues raised by the Lehman Bankruptcy Examiner's Report. No one can deny that the bankruptcy of Lehman Brothers has had a disastrous impact – on the company, its employees, its investors, and even on our country and its economy. As a director of the firm, Lehman's collapse weighs on me personally each and every day. It is vital that we learn from Lehman's history so we do not repeat it. In this spirit, I applaud the Committee for holding these hearings today.

MY BACKGROUND

I joined Lehman Brothers Holdings Inc. ("Lehman") as a director in 1996, and have served on the Board for approximately 14 years. I have been a member of the Audit Committee of the Board since the beginning of my tenure and chairman of that Committee since 2003. I have also served on the Board's Nominating and Corporate Governance Committee.

After graduating from Rice University with a degree in Business Administration and Economics, I began my career at the accounting firm Arthur Andersen. While working, I also attended law school. I left Arthur Andersen in 1955 to serve as an officer in the Navy at the end of the Korean War. After completing my service, I rejoined Arthur Andersen for a few years until I decided to try my hand at practicing law at Vinson & Elkins. Looking for another new challenge, in 1969 I joined Halliburton. I spent the next 25 years working in a number of roles, including Chief Financial Officer, President, Chief Executive Officer and Chairman. I finally retired from Halliburton after the end of 1995.

During my career, I have had the honor of serving on a number of boards of directors, including those of Goodyear, the Williams Companies, Seagull Energy, and Central and

* This is an edited, reformatted and augmented version of the remarks given on April 20, 2010 before the House Financial Services Committee.

Southwest, in addition to serving as the chairman of both National Junior Achievement and Up with People (an international education organization that addresses the need for young adults and leaders to develop global perspectives, intercultural understanding and knowledge of worldwide social issues). I joined Lehman's Board because I had been very impressed by the firm's work for Halliburton when I was CEO, and because I was interested in its aspiration to build a world-class investment banking enterprise based on the "One Firm" model. During my time on Lehman's Board, I saw the company grow from a modest niche player, specializing in corporate finance and trading, into a global powerhouse that was the fourth largest investment bank in America.

Over the years, I attended dozens upon dozens of Board and Committee meetings. I also got to know a number of incredibly talented and dedicated employees (not to mention my fellow directors for whom I have an enormous amount of admiration). I developed a great respect for and strong attachment to Lehman. All of this made it so much harder to see the company collapse during the early morning hours of September 15, 2008. Indeed, that Monday was the darkest day of my professional career.

Lehman's Fall

I, along with my fellow directors, know all too well that Lehman's fall has had drastic consequences. Thousands of employees lost their jobs and much, if not all, of their savings. Investors, including me and my fellow directors, collectively lost billions of dollars. Notably, consistent with the Board's view of proper compensation practices, Lehman's employees owned approximately one quarter of the company's common shares.

Lehman's bankruptcy has had a ripple effect on America's economy – the Dow Jones index plunged 500 points on the day of the bankruptcy, and, just weeks later, Congress stepped in and passed a $700 billion rescue program for the economy (now commonly known as TARP). The collapse of Lehman, a company to which I have been devoted for nearly fifteen years, troubles me very deeply and will always continue to do so.

The Examiner's Report

Given the staggering impact that Lehman's bankruptcy has had not only on the company, but our country, it is critical that we explore the reasons behind the firm's failure so that we can learn from it and do our best to make sure something like this does not happen again. I want to thank Anton Valukas, Lehman's Bankruptcy Examiner, for all the hard work that went into producing his report. It is important to study, analyze, assess, debate and learn from it. Indeed, the Examiner, his attorneys, and his accountants spent tens of thousands of hours investigating and chronicling their understanding of Lehman and the events leading up to its bankruptcy – reviewing millions of pages of documents and interviewing more than 250 witnesses. The resulting 2200 page report (before even counting its 34 separate appendices) is a testament to the complexity of the myriad issues that Lehman faced over its last two years.

Looking back, I am sure that there are things Lehman could have done differently. But, as has often been pointed out, hindsight is twenty-twenty. And what may seem crystal clear today in 2010 was much less so back in 2007 and 2008. As you may recall, in the spring of 2007, Benjamin Bernanke, the Chairman of the Federal Reserve, advised that "the effect of the troubles in the subprime sector on the broader housing market [would] likely be limited," and that there should not be "significant spillovers from the subprime market to the rest of the economy or to the financial system."[1] Indeed, even after Bear Stearns nearly collapsed in March 2008, then Treasury Secretary Henry Paulson stated that the "worst [was] likely behind us,"[2] and that "[t]his [was] a very manageable situation . . . ."[3] If only they, and many other leaders in the financial world, had been right.

Still, even in retrospect, the Examiner found that there are absolutely no colorable claims against the independent directors in connection with our work on behalf of the company. The Examiner carefully reviewed the facts and circumstances regarding, among other things, Lehman's: (1) risk-taking and risk-management activities; (2) efforts to raise capital, attract strategic investors, and spin off its commercial real estate assets; (3) purported use and disclosure of "Repo 105" transactions; and (4) disclosure of its liquidity pool. His conclusion, that there are no claims against the outside directors for breaching their duties,[4] comports with my own belief and the belief of my fellow directors that we did our absolute best in exercising our business judgment to try and help navigate Lehman through what was the greatest financial tsunami since the Great Depression.

The Role of Lehman's Board of Directors

Going forward, as Congress continues to consider corporate governance issues, it is important to remember the role of a board of directors. It is not to manage, or micromanage, a corporation. That is the province of the company's officers and senior management who devote their careers to the corporation – 60, 80, 100 hours a week, 52 weeks a year. A board of directors, on the other hand, brings its collective wisdom, experience, and outside perspective to bear in "thoughtfully appointing officers, establishing or approving goals and plans and monitoring [a company's] performance."[5] And that is exactly what we, as Lehman's outside directors, worked extremely hard to do.[6]

Since the beginning of 2007 through Lehman's bankruptcy filing in September 2008, our Board and its committees convened on more than 80 occasions in that less than 21 month span. I still remember one week in July 2008, when we were examining and analyzing the company's strategic options, meeting every day for six days in a row.

At just about every Board meeting, we received detailed reports from management on Lehman's financial performance and other important issues. These reports were made by various groups and individuals at Lehman and included, where appropriate, consultation with outside experts. We reviewed numerous metrics including the firm's balance sheet, leverage, average risk appetite usage, long term capital, as well as comparative competitive information such as ten-year debt spreads and long-term debt credit ratings. We also looked into the firm's monthly financial results and the key initiatives in each division, including fixed income, equities, banking, investment management and principal investments.

Moreover, management regularly made presentations to the Board and its committees on key topics. Such presentations included updates on:

- Lehman's Subprime Mortgage Origination Business (March 20, 2007);
- Lehman's Liquidity, Leveraged Loan Commitments and Mortgage Positions (September 11, 2007);
- Lehman's ABS CDO Exposure (November 8, 2007);
- Lehman's 2008 Financial Plan Summary (January 29, 2008);
- Liquidity and the Market (March 25, 2008);
- Lehman's Commercial Real Estate (March 25, 2008);
- Lehman's Risk Management (April 15, 2008);
- Lehman's Fixed Income Division (May 7, 2008);
- Concerns Raised Regarding Balance Sheet and Legal Entity Controls (July 22, 2008);
- Lehman's Strategic Alternatives (July 22, 2008);
- Risk Issues Facing Lehman (June 19, 2008 and August 13, 2008); and
- Lehman's Valuations (July 22, 2008).

Board meetings were an active and dynamic affair. Board members probed management, asked numerous questions and demanded and received detailed, cogent answers. In my entire career, I have never seen officers and employees who were more responsive to answering questions from its Board members. I still recall, after seeing Lehman's second quarter 2008 results, asking management for a full presentation on the company's valuations. In response, at the July Audit Committee meeting, two members of senior management presented a 23-page report, which provided an in-depth discussion and analysis of Lehman's valuation adjustments, mark downs, processes and procedures.

RISK MANAGEMENT

One issue that management spent a great deal of time discussing with the Board was risk. Risk-related issues were addressed by the full Board at nearly every regularly scheduled meeting. They were analyzed at the meetings of the Finance and Risk Committee. And risk issues were also addressed by other committees as well – such as the Audit Committee. Thus, as the Examiner himself noted, Lehman's Board "plainly implemented a sufficient reporting system and controls."[7]

As directors, we took great comfort from management's reports regarding Lehman's extensive risk management system, which was widely regarded as being among the best in the business. Indeed, management described in detail how risk management was at the heart of the culture of the firm; how the firm's CEO, President and entire Executive Committee took an active leadership role in key risk decisions and oversight; and how the Risk Committee, which included members of the Executive Committee and heads of key trading businesses, met weekly to discuss such topics as risk appetite, counterparty risks, market risks, and event risks. In addition, we were told about how Lehman made decisions on large risk exposures by committee; how frequently those decisions included the full Executive Committee of the firm; and how there were more than 20 different committees that served as a check on Lehman's risk taking activities. Management also informed the Board that Lehman's internal control environment had multiple overlapping and reinforcing elements.

And, the Board was further reassured by the size, structure and expertise of Lehman's Global Risk Management Group, which employed industry-leading quantitative approaches to risk management and qualitative approaches to risk evaluation. This group, which had approximately 250 employees, plus more than 200 technologists (two thirds of whom had advanced degrees), was organizationally independent of the business, but had risk managers placed in the business units they covered so that they were a part of what was happening real time, day-to-day. The Board took additional comfort from management's reports regarding Lehman's extensive Valuation and Control group, which consisted of a technical staff well-versed in the products they covered.

Reliance on Professionals

In performing its oversight role, Lehman's Board of Directors – like boards at companies across the country – relied upon the expertise of a variety of professionals, both inside and outside the firm. For example, the Audit Committee worked closely with Lehman's Corporate Audit Group, which employed more than 140 people and allocated its resources to address key risks across the firm, including financial, compliance, and operational risks.

We also retained Ernst & Young ("E&Y"), one of the most highly-regarded accounting firms in the world, as the company's auditors. E&Y performed reviews on a quarterly basis by applying analytical review procedures and making inquiries of persons responsible for financial and accounting matters. They further conducted a robust annual audit of the firm's financial statements. E&Y regularly attended Audit Committee meetings, met in private sessions with the Audit Committee members and certified Lehman's financial disclosures. While E&Y regularly had substantive discussions with the Audit Committee about Lehman's audited financial statements, at no time in 2007 or 2008 did E&Y raise any red flags regarding Lehman's risk management, valuation, or the firm's certified filings.

In addition to E&Y, in early 2007, Lehman retained another world-renowned accounting firm – PricewaterhouseCoopers – to support the more quantitative aspects of risk testing by evaluating the completeness of the supporting documentation for the firm's risk models, assessing the adequacy of the methodology and testing to ensure that the models were implemented appropriately. Lehman also worked intimately with one of the most well-respected law firms in the nation, which advised it on public disclosure issues.

Interaction with Government Regulators

As a Board of Directors, we had confidence in what we understood to be Lehman's close working relationship with government regulators. Even before the financial crisis, Lehman voluntarily subjected itself to the scrutiny of the Securities and Exchange Commission ("SEC") as a part of that agency's consolidated supervised entity ("CSE") program. The purpose of this program was to give global investment banks a way to submit voluntarily to regulation that was not required by law. Under the CSE program, which provided the SEC with new and far greater transparency into Lehman's financial information, not only did Lehman meet with regulators from the SEC on at least a quarterly basis, but Lehman's

Corporate Audit group also implemented systems to verify the operating effectiveness of controls supporting Lehman's capital calculation and other CSE activities and adopted a testing framework to meet the SEC's expectations. The Board understood that the SEC's CSE reviews covered corporate governance, functional risk management activities, business specific products, and capital calculation and reporting. And, we were told by management that the SEC considered Lehman a model member of the CSE program.

In addition, as the financial crisis deepened, both the SEC and the Federal Reserve Bank of New York ("FRBNY") worked intimately with Lehman to monitor and assess the firm's liquidity. The weekend after Bear Stearns's near collapse, Lehman, together with the SEC and the FRBNY, collaborated to identify all refinancing risk. By that time, both the FRBNY and SEC had installed teams of monitors at Lehman's offices. Thereafter, management maintained a constant dialogue with the SEC and the FRBNY regarding liquidity issues.

Lehman's Efforts to Respond to the Worsening Financial Crisis

Notwithstanding the start of what became the subprime crisis, Lehman's year-end 2007 financial results reached record levels.[8] Still, in 2007 and 2008, the firm took numerous steps to adjust to the worsening economic climate. For example, by August of 2007, Lehman had shut down its subprime mortgage lending unit. The firm reduced its mortgage and asset-backed securities exposure by many billions of dollars between the fourth quarter of 2007 and third quarter of 2008. Indeed, during this period, both residential mortgage exposure and commercial real estate exposure were substantially reduced.[9] We also discussed what had appeared to have gone wrong at Bear Stearns, how Lehman was different, and what we should nonetheless do to strengthen Lehman in light of Bear Stearns's collapse. In response, through the spring of 2008, Lehman raised more than $15 billion in new capital.

Throughout 2008, Lehman also explored and pursued a number of strategic alternatives in an effort to strengthen the firm as the financial crisis deepened. Such initiatives included selling some or all of its highly lucrative investment management division, spinning off commercial real estate assets into a new company, lowering costs, reducing its dividend, decreasing leverage, and searching for strategic partners and for buyers of the entire business. While times remained troubling, a number of Lehman's efforts appeared to pay off. The Board was told how Lehman's liquidity had, between the second quarter of 2007 and the second quarter of 2008, nearly doubled to a record high.

Repo 105

The Examiner's Report has raised questions about certain transactions now known as "Repo 105." While the Examiner does not claim that Lehman's accounting for these transactions was wrong, his report suggests that these transactions should have been better disclosed.

As the Examiner has concluded, this Repo 105 issue was never brought to the attention of the Board by anyone.[10] During 2007 and 2008, the Audit Committee discussed a broad array of financial matters with E&Y on an average of once a month. In order to ensure that the Audit Committee obtained unfettered information from our respected independent auditors, we routinely met with E&Y outside the presence of any management representatives as part of our regular process. If they had any question whatsoever about Lehman's accounting or disclosure regarding Repo 105's or any other issue, I believe that E&Y would have promptly raised the issue with the Audit Committee and I would have expected them to do so. They did not.

Still, I think it is clear that Repo 105 is not the reason Lehman failed. According to the Examiner's Report, without the use of Repo 105, Lehman's net leverage was still substantially reduced from the fourth quarter of 2007 to the second quarter of 2008.[11] And, as I have now learned, Repo 105 generally involved highly liquid government bonds that constituted a small percentage of Lehman's balance sheet.

Lehman's Bankruptcy

So, if Repo 105 was not the culprit, why did Lehman collapse into bankruptcy? I am not so presumptuous as to say that I know the definitive answer to this question. I believe that there were many factors that contributed to this failure – including, among other things, the firm's real estate exposure (which was exacerbated by the rules for applying mark-to-market accounting), the numerous short-sellers who were capitalizing on and fueling rumors about Lehman's troubles, the tightening of the short-term credit market, and perhaps most of all, a loss of confidence in Lehman in the financial world that led to a run on the bank. Since Lehman, like all investment banks, relied on a sizable amount of short-term refinancing for its survival, loss of confidence and a market-wide panic was a fatal combination.

That said, I was dismayed when, on the evening of Sunday, September 14, 2008, the Chairman of the SEC and the general counsel of the FRBNY essentially told the Board that Lehman needed to file for bankruptcy before the Asian markets opened. I do not purport to be an expert on what would have been best for our national economy, nor do I generally have a view on bailouts and the like as policy matters. Nonetheless, to this day I wonder whether more could have been done to save Lehman and stabilize the financial system. While there may be good reasons that I do not comprehend, I still do not understand why the government did not help finance a sale of Lehman to Barclays (which was on the verge of buying our company), like it did to facilitate JP Morgan's purchase of Bear Stearns. I still do not know why, the same day Lehman was told to file for bankruptcy, the Fed expanded access to its Primary Dealer Credit Facility for other major investment banks. Nor do I understand why the government did not expedite Lehman's conversion to a bank holding company, as was done for Goldman Sachs and Morgan Stanley within a week of Lehman's bankruptcy, granting those investment banks long-term access to the Fed's discount window. I still do not know why Lehman was allowed to fail after the government had saved Fannie Mae and Freddie Mac by injecting billions of dollars into them. And, I remain at a loss as to why AIG was given a $85 billion bailout on September 16, 2008, when Lehman was given nothing. There may be good and reasonable reasons for all of these distinctions, but as a director of Lehman I do not know them.

The drastic impact of Lehman's bankruptcy on the wider economy was swift and severe. The Dow Jones dropped more than 500 points the day Lehman declared bankruptcy – at the time the largest single-day drop by points since the days following the terrorist attacks on September 11, 2001. The commercial paper market dried up. And relentless pressure was put on other major financial institutions who themselves teetered on the edge of ruin. As a result, the government stepped in with the TARP program. While we cannot rewrite history, had the government acted to stabilize Lehman so that it could have been sold or unwound, it is quite possible our country's financial crisis would not have been nearly as severe and widespread.

MY FELLOW DIRECTORS

Before concluding my remarks, I would like to take a moment to recognize and thank my fellow Board members for their hard work and dedication to Lehman. Lehman had a practice of selecting directors who had a history of successfully managing major companies and who had the wisdom, experience, talent and mettle to provide oversight and guidance to management and the corporation. My fellow directors have held CEO positions at such esteemed companies as I.B.M., the U.S. Export-Import Bank, Vodafone, Sotheby's, Celanese, Telemundo, U.S. Bancorp, and a large brokerage firm. The Lehman directors have also sat on various other boards of well run, successful companies. One director, a former executive committee member and chief economist at Salomon Brothers, is a world-renowned luminary in the field of economics. And yet another was a Rear Admiral in the United States Navy, the first woman to command a U.S. naval station, and the head of the American Red Cross. They truly are a remarkable group of people and it has been an honor and a privilege to serve alongside them.

My thanks to Chairman Frank, Ranking Member Bachus, and the rest of the House Financial Services Committee for the opportunity to speak with you today. While I may not have the knowledge and expertise of my fellow panelists appearing before this Committee, I am happy to address any questions you may have.

End Notes

[1] Ben Bernanke, Chairman, Fed. Reserve, Speech at Federal Reserve Bank of Chicago's 43rd Annual Conference on Bank Structure and Competition (May 17, 2007).

[2] Michael M. Phillips & Damian Paletta, *Paulson Sees Credit Crisis Waning*, Wall Street Journal (May 7, 2008), available at, http://online.wsj.com/article/SB121011652297872261.html (last visited Apr. 19, 2010).

[3] "Paulson braces public for months of tough times," Associated Press Online (July 21, 2008).

[4] *See, e.g.,* Report of Anton R. Valukas, Examiner ("Examiner's Report"), at 188-95, 611, 992, 1479-80, Case No. 08-13555 (JMP) (Bankr. S.D.N.Y. Mar. 11, 2010) [Docket No. 7531].

[5] R. Franklin Balotti & Jesse A. Finkelstein, *Balotti and Finkelstein's Delaware Law of Corporations and Business Organizations*, DELCBO 4.10, 2006 WL 2450219, *1 (2009) (internal citations omitted).

[6] Courts have recognized that "[b]usiness decision-makers must operate in the real world, with imperfect information, limited resources, and an uncertain future," and that imposing "liability on directors for making a 'wrong' business decision," would be bad public policy and "cripple their ability to earn returns for investors by taking business risks." *In re Citigroup Inc. Shareholder Derivative Litig.*, 964 A.2d 106, 126 (Del. Ch. 2009).

[7] Examiner's Report at 194.

[8] Press Release, *Lehman Brothers Reports Record Net Revenues, Net Income and Earnings Per Share for Fiscal 2007* (Dec. 13, 2007).

[9] Press Release, *Lehman Brothers Announces Preliminary Third Quarter Results and Strategic Restructuring* (Sept. 10, 2008) (Attachments II - V).

[10] Examiner's Report at 945.

[11] Examiner's Report at 748.

In: The Lehman Brothers Bankruptcy: Analyses
Editors: Gary E. Walker and Lindel D. Clarke
ISBN: 978-1-62081-730-8

Chapter 13

STATEMENT OF WILLIAM K. BLACK. HEARING ON "PUBLIC POLICY ISSUES RAISED BY THE REPORT OF THE LEHMAN BANKRUPTCY EXAMINER"*

Chairman Frank, Ranking Member Bachus, and Members of the Committee:

Thank you for your invitation to discuss public policy issues arising from Lehman's failure. I will address the six issues you asked that I comment on in your letter of invitation.

1. The extent to which corporate governance should be enhanced to appropriately manage firm risk. Please share your views regarding the communication, knowledge and understanding among risk managers, Boards of Directors and senior management.
2. The role of the SEC as Lehman's primary regulator in oversight, examination and enforcement in advance of Lehman's bankruptcy filing, and the role of the other government agencies, including the Federal Reserve Bank of New York (FRBNY), that were monitoring Lehman during the crisis.
3. The relationship and means of communication, especially formal and informal information sharing, between the SEC and FRBNY as Lehman's financial condition deteriorated as well as between Lehman, the SEC, the Treasury Department, the Board of Governors Federal Reserve, and the FRBNY.
4. Please reflect on the appropriateness of accounting practices such as Repo 105 or 108 and the adequacy of the disclosure of such accounting practices.
5. The quality of Lehman's Management Discussion and Analysis disclosures in its public filings for the 2007 reporting periods.
6. Other issues that you deem relevant to the public policy issues raised by the Lehman Report.

I begin with a short description of my background that is relevant to your questions. My primary appointment is in economics. I have a joint appointment in law. I am a white-collar criminologist. My research specialization is financial fraud by elites and financial regulation.

* This is an edited, reformatted and augmented version of the remarks given on April 20, 2010 before the House Financial Services Committee.

I was a senior regulator during the S&L debacle (and had the honor of testifying many times before this Committee). As a regulator, I was:

- The Litigation Director of the Federal Home Loan Bank Board (Bank Board). We had independent litigation authority – we were not represented by the Justice Department.
- The Deputy Director of the Federal Savings and Loan Insurance Corporation (FSLIC)
- The staff leader of the reregulation of the S&L industry in 1984-1987
- The Senior Vice President and General Counsel of the Federal Home Loan Bank of San Francisco (FHLBSF)
- The Senior Deputy Chief Counsel for Enforcement and Litigation (West Region) of the Office of Thrift Supervision (OTS)
- The Deputy Staff Director of the National Commission on Financial Institution Reform, Recovery and Enforcement (NCFIRRE)

Several aspects of this background may be of particular use to the Committee.

1. The Bank Board was both a safety and soundness regulator and a securities regulator for publicly traded savings & loan holding companies. We were vigorous in bringing actions against those that abused the accounting rules.
2. I worked extensively, and cooperatively, with many other regulatory agencies.
3. The Federal Home Loan Banks (before the passage of FIRREA in 1989), were similar to the Federal Reserve Banks. The FHLBs had boards of directors dominated by industry members and had both a lending function and a regulatory function. We used the information gained through, and the leverage inherent in, the FHLBSF's lending activities to aid our, and our sister agencies', supervisory effectiveness.
4. We always made extensive referrals to the SEC, the FBI, and the Department of Justice when we found evidence of unsafe and unsound practices or violations of law. I was one of the officials charged with making sure that these referrals became far more effective. One result was that the government obtained over 1000 priority felony convictions of S&L insiders and those that aided and abetted their frauds.
5. In late 1983, the agency recognized that the S&L crisis, which began as an interest rate risk crisis was entering a new phase in which elite frauds were the dominant problem. The agency realized that the frauds would defeat any regulatory approach based on standard operating procedures (SOP). Instead, the agency went to an emergency footing in which, for example, it took over 20 percent of the entire national examination force and sent it to the region (Dallas) where the frauds posed the greatest danger to the public.
6. Bank Board Chairman Gray, over the intense opposition of the administration, the industry, Speaker Wright, a majority of the Members of the House, the "Keating Five", and the financial press, proceeded to reregulate the industry. The administration was so outraged that OMB threatened to file a criminal referral against Chairman Gray – on the grounds that he was closing too many insolvent S&Ls. Because I was the staff leader of this reregulation, Speaker Wright tried to get me fired by Gray's successor, Chairman Wall. (The Speaker succeeded in getting

> Wall to fire our top supervisor in Texas.) Charles Keating was so threatened by reregulation that he directed his chief political fixer that his "Highest Priority" was to "Get Black ... Kill him Dead." Keating hired private detectives twice to investigate me and filed a $400 million *Bivens* action against me and other regulators in our personal capacity. But we stayed the course.

The Members of the Committee know that the practices I have just described contrast sharply with the manner in which the federal officials behaved with regard to Lehman, as documented in the Valukas Report. The Senate Banking investigation of WaMu and the Treasury IG investigation of its regulators reveal equally distressing disregard for the public interest and the regulators' oaths of office.

1. The extent to which corporate governance should be enhanced to appropriately manage firm risk. Please share your views regarding the communication, knowledge and understanding among risk managers, Boards of Directors and senior management.

The Report documents at least three major deficiencies in Lehman's corporate governance that need to be addressed globally. First, it points out that Lehman, and many other Delaware corporations, have eliminated the fiduciary duty of "care." This statutory change is the product of a naïve "law and economics" theory of corporate law that I addressed in an article (Black 2003). Judge Easterbrook and Professor Fischel are the leading proponent of the theory. They view managers as so pure that "a rule against fraud is not an essential or even necessarily an important ingredient of securities markets" (1991: 283). Alan Greenspan has admitted that he had a similar view and that events have falsified this naïve account. It is insane to withdraw accountability for negligence. Doing so encourages negligence. Congress should mandate that corporate officers and directors be subject to the fiduciary duties of care and loyalty. They will still, of course, have the very substantial protection of the business judgment rule.

Second, there same individual should not serve as the CEO and Chair of the Board of Directors of a large corporation. The imperial CEO is a consistent problem in this and prior crises.

Third, Lehman ignored its stated risk "limits" and simply increased its limits retroactively to accommodate its violations of its risk limits. In plain English, that means it had no meaningful limits. Systemically dangerous institutions (SDIs) (aka "too big to fail") should be required to have, and comply with, prudent risk limits.

I have a different view than Mr. Valukas about the overall state of Lehman's corporate governance. First, Lehman's nominal corporate governance structure was a sham. Lehman was deliberately out of control with regard to "risk" in its dominant operation – making "liar's loans." Lehman did not "manage" the risk of making liar's loans. It engaged in massive, fraudulent transactions that were "sure things" (Akerlof & Romer 1993). The Valukas Report bears witness to the consequences of these transactions. The Report provides further evidence of the accuracy of Akerlof's and Romer's famous article – "Looting: Bankruptcy for Profit." George Akerlof is a Nobel Laureate in Economics (2001) and Paul Romer is a Professor of Economics at Stanford, so their work is an important component of modern economic understanding of the elite frauds that can cause economic crises. The "looting" that Akerlof & Romer identified is a "sure thing" in both directions – firms that loot through accounting scams will report superb (fictional) income in the short-term and catastrophic losses in the long-term. (The title of my book reflects the same concept – *The Best Way to Rob a Bank is to Own One*.)

Akerlof & Romer's insights were based in part on research by S&L regulators. Their insights have been confirmed by white-collar criminologists. Lehman was a "control fraud." That is a criminology term that refers to situation in which the persons controlling a seemingly legitimate entity use it as a "weapon" (Wheeler & Rothman 1982) of fraud (Black 2005). Financial control frauds' "weapon of choice" for looting is accounting.

Lehman's principal source of (fictional) income and real losses was making (and selling) what the trade accurately called "liar's loans" through its subsidiary, Aurora. (The bland euphemism for liar's loans was "Alt-A.") Liar's loans are "criminogenic" (they create epidemics of mortgage fraud) because they create strong incentives to provide false information on loan applications. The FBI began warning publicly about the epidemic of mortgage fraud in 2004 (CNN). Liar's loans also produce intense "adverse selection" – even the borrowers who are not fraudulent will tend to be the least creditworthy. The combination of these two perverse incentives means that liar's loans, in economics jargon, have a deeply "negative expected value" to the lender. In English, that means that the average dollar lent on a liar's loan creates a loss ranging from 50 – 85 cents.

> The value of Lehman's Alt-A mortgage holdings fell 60 percent during the past six months to $5.9 billion, the firm reported last week.[1]

Gambling against the casino creates a negative expected value, but making liar's loans creates inevitable, catastrophic losses.

That loss, however, may not be recognized for many years – particularly if the liar's loans become so large that they help hyper-inflate a financial bubble. In the near-term, making massive amounts of liar's losses loans creates a mathematical guarantee of producing record (albeit fictional) accounting income. (As long as the bubble inflates, the liar's loans can be refinanced – creating additional fictional income and delaying (but increasing) the eventual loss. The industry saying for this during the S&L debacle was: "a rolling loan gathers no loss."

Lehman's underlying problem that doomed it was that it was insolvent because it made so many bad loans and investments. It hid its insolvency through the traditional means – it refused to recognize its losses honestly. It could not resolve its liquidity crisis because it was insolvent and its primary source of fictional accounting income collapsed with the collapse of the secondary market in nonprime loans. If Lehman sold its assets to get cash it would have to recognize these massive losses and report that it was insolvent. Investors knew that Lehman was grossly inflating its asset values, so they were generally unwilling buy stock in Lehman or acquire it.

There is no way to "manage" the "risk" of making massive amounts of liar's loans. Lehman was the world leader in making liar's loans. As the name makes clear, Lehman's top managers knew that their principal source of income was making fraudulent loans. It was necessary, therefore, that Lehman not document that its liar's loans were frequently fraudulent. Lehman, instead, classified its massively fraudulent liar's loans as "prime" loans. Its disclosures did not identify how many of the "prime" loans it held were actually liar's loans. As I will discuss in more detail in response to your final question, Lehman personnel that pointed out the fraudulent liar's loans were attacked, even fired, by Lehman's management. Honest managers, of course, would be delighted if employees identified frauds.

That same pattern of conscious managerial indifference to pervasive mortgage and accounting fraud was the norm at other nonprime mortgage participants that have been investigated. I refer to it as the financial "don't ask; don't tell" policy. Here is a classic example from Standard & Poors. The context is that the professional credit rating specialist has asked his boss for a copy of the "tapes" which contain the nonprime loan files that are the "underlying" backing a collateralized debt obligation (CDO). The professional plans to review a sample of the lender's loan files so that he can evaluate their credit quality. Here is the response he receives (the punctuation is from the original).

> Any request for loan level tapes is TOTALLY UNREASONABLE!!! Most investors don't have it and can't provide it. [W]e MUST produce a credit estimate. It is your responsibility to provide those credit estimates and your responsibility to devise some method for doing so.[2]

Making liar's loans is not risky – it is suicidal. That is why every significant lender specializing in liar's loans failed. The pervasive fraud cannot be admitted – for Lehman's entire business model was premised on massive sales of liar's loans to others. If Lehman admitted that its liar's loans were often fraudulent it could not sell them – cutting off one of its largest sources of income. Worse, it would be stuck with a portfolio full of fraudulent loans and have to recognize (or hide through further accounting fraud) that it was insolvent. Worse still, if it admitted its liar's loans were often fraudulent it would risk having to repay past purchasers of its liar's loans and risk SEC suits and criminal prosecutions. This is why "risk management" is always a sham at firms holding liar's loans. Risk management is premised on honest operations, honest data, and honest managers. Honesty is fatal to entities making, or purchasing, large amounts of liar's loans.

Second, the right "tone at the top" is essential to effective corporate governance. Lehman's managers too often created an unethical tone. The Valukus Report contains an example of this problem. When SVP Lee blew the whistle on accounting abuses, as he was required to do under Lehman's employee policies, management responded by firing him.

Lehman is alleged to have treated another whistleblower in a similar fashion.

> The HR lady pulled Michael Walker into a room and told him he was fired. The reason: Talking to the FBI. It was a violation of the company's privacy policy. "I was stunned," Walker told me. "I couldn't believe it. But that's what she said." Walker, a "high-risk specialist," was then walked out of the building as if he were the risk. His job at Aurora Loan Services LLC, Littleton, Colo., ended on Sept. 4, 2008.
>
> Aurora was a subsidiary of Lehman Brothers, the big, failing Wall Street investment bank that didn't get a bailout. A week after Walker was fired, Lehman filed history's biggest bankruptcy.
>
> His job was to uncover mortgage fraud. But he claims he was fired for doing it. In a lawsuit recently filed in Denver District Court, he claims Lehman's mortgage subsidiary wanted to remain profitably unaware of fraud.
>
> Aurora made its loans through independent mortgage brokers, who often didn't have to meet any criteria to be brokers, not even criminal background checks in some cases. Inevitably, some percentage of the mortgage applications they took would be laced with fraud. But like everyone else, they got paid by loan volume, not by loan quality.

> Consequently, Walker and his fraud-seeking colleagues were always busy. "They just absolutely flooded us with work," he said. "There was no way we could possibly keep up with it. And that's what they wanted.
>
> "They were putting the loans into an investment trust," he explained. "When they became aware of fraud, they had to buy those loans back out of the trust. So it ended up costing them money."
>
> What were the chances that Bob's Fly-By-Night Mortgage Co. Would be able to return the funds it got from Aurora? What were the chances that the losses could be recovered through foreclosure? Better to let it ride.
>
> But Walker couldn't play this game. A "Suspicious Activity Report" that he filed in 2006 led to interviews with the FBI and the IRS in 2008, and then ultimately to his bizarre dismissal.[3]

Walker endangered the fraud scheme that lay at the heart of Lehman's (fictional) profitability because he violated the "don't ask; don't tell" rule and brought the FBI to Aurora's offices. Control fraud turns everything that is normally good about private markets perverse. It creates a "Gresham's dynamic" in which bad ethics drives good ethics from the marketplace.

The Walker case is stunning, but it is important to step back and see the contours of the forest. Any firm that specializes in making liar's loans that it purchases from others (who are paid on the basis of volume and conducted no meaningful underwriting prior to lending) and sells to others without any meaningful underwriting will have a pervasive corrupt tone.

Lehman's senior managers consciously chose to take the unethical path because they viewed it as extraordinarily profitable.

> Mr. Hibbert was a vice-president at Lehman Brothers and he'd been sent to meet First Alliance founder Brian Chisick to see if Lehman could form some kind of relationship with the mortgage lender.
>
> "This is a weird place," he wrote later in an internal memo. While he noted the company's "efficient use of their tools to create their own niche," he also pointed out that "there is something really unethical about the type of business in which [First Alliance] is engaged."
>
> Mr. Chisick had become one of the biggest players in subprime loans. First Alliance's annual revenue had doubled in four years to nearly $60-million (U.S.) and its profit had increased threefold to $30-million.
>
> In his detailed report, he described the marketing operation as a "work of art" and marvelled at the profit margin, cash flow, collection practices and growth prospects of First Alliance.
>
> But Mr. Hibbert also had some concerns. The company targeted too many elderly customers; he had seen several 30-year loans given to people in their 70s. "It is a sweat shop," he wrote. "High pressure sales for people who are in a weak state." First Alliance is "the used car salesperson of [subprime] lending. It is a requirement to leave your ethics at the door. … So far there has been little official intervention into this market sector, but if one firm was to be singled out for governmental action, this may be it."
>
> Despite the warning, Lehman officials recommended a $100-million loan facility for First Alliance. Mr. Chisick turned it down, but he agreed to take a $25-million line of credit and hire Lehman to work with Prudential on several securitizations.
>
> First Alliance was now set. It went public a year later on Nasdaq at $17 a share, with Mr. Chisick keeping 75-per-cent control. The stock hit $27 by year end and peaked at $36.25 shortly afterward. Mr. Chisick opened two dozen offices across the U.S., and

made other expansion plans. By 1997, First Alliance was on track to arrange more than $500-million worth of loans, up from $324-million a year earlier.

At this juncture, various state Attorneys General began to sue First Alliance for consumer fraud. Prudential terminated its ties with the lender.

> But Lehman jumped at the opportunity to move in. Senior vice-president Frank Gihool asked Mr. Hibbert to pull together a review of First Alliance for Lehman's credit risk management team. Mr. Hibbert once again marvelled at the company's operations and financial outlook. But he also said the lawsuits posed a serious problem. The allegation about deceptive practices "is now more than a legal one, it has become political, with public relations headaches to come," he wrote.
>
> Nonetheless, on Feb. 11, 1999, Lehman approved a $150-million line of credit, and became the company's sole manager of asset-backed securities offerings. The bottom line for Lehman was made clear in another internal report: The firm expected to earn at least $4.5-million in fees.
>
> But within a year, the weight of the lawsuits crippled First Alliance. On March 23, 2000, the company filed for bankruptcy protection. Mr. Chisick managed to walk away with more than $100-million in total compensation and stock sales over four years. Lehman, owed $77-million, collected the full amount, plus interest.
>
> First Alliance eventually settled the lawsuits filed by the state attorneys, agreeing to pay $60-million. In the California class-action case, a jury found Lehman partially responsible for First Alliance's conduct and ordered the firm to pay roughly $5-million.

Lehman acquired Aurora to be its liar's loan specialist. Aurora, which was inherently in the business of buying and selling often fraudulent loans, set its ethical tone at subterranean levels.

> Mark Golan was getting frustrated as he met with a group of auditors from Lehman Brothers.
>
> It was spring, 2006, and Mr. Golan was a manager at Colorado-based Aurora Loan Service LLC, which specialized in "Alt A" loans, considered a step above subprime lending. Aurora had become one of the largest players in that market, originating $25-billion worth of loans in 2006. It was also the biggest supplier of loans to Lehman for securitization.
>
> Lehman had acquired a stake in Aurora in 1998 and had taken control in 2003. By May, 2006, some people inside Lehman were becoming worried about Aurora's lending practices. The mortgage industry was facing scrutiny about billions of dollars worth of Alt-A mortgages, also known as "liar loans"– because they were given to people with little or no documentation. In some cases, borrowers demonstrated nothing more than "pride of ownership" to get a mortgage.
>
> That spring, according to court filings, a group of internal Lehman auditors analyzed some Aurora loans and discovered that up to half contained material misrepresentations. But the mortgage market was growing too fast and Lehman's appetite for loans was insatiable. Mr. Golan stormed out of the meeting, allegedly yelling at the lead auditor: "Your people find too much fraud."

Lehman senior management, however, responded to problems of fraud and unethical behaviour by cranking up the volume of liar's loans by Aurora and BNC Mortgage (which specialized in subprime loans).

> Lehman had become the only vertically integrated player in the industry, doing everything from making loans to securitizing them for sale to investors.
>
> Lehman was a dominant player on all sides of the business. Through its subsidiaries – Aurora, BNC Mortgage LLC and Finance America – it was one of the 10 largest mortgage lenders in the U.S. The subsidiaries fed nearly all their loans to Lehman, making it one of the largest issuers of mortgage-backed securities. In 2007, Lehman securitized more than $100-billion worth of residential mortgages.
>
> These demands posed a much larger problem: contagion. Because these CDOs were thinly traded, many of them did not yet reflect the loss in value implied by their crumbling mortgage holdings. If
>
> Bear Stearns or its lenders began auctioning these CDOs off, and nobody wanted to buy them, prices would plummet, requiring all banks with mortgage exposure to begin adjusting their books with massive writedowns.
>
> Lehman, despite its huge mortgage exposure, appeared less scathed than some. Mr. Fuld was awarded $35-million in total compensation at the end of the year.

http://www.theglobeandmail.com/report-on-business/article703526.ece

Volume of liar's loans and subprime was everything – as long as Lehman could sell the liar's loans to other parties. Volume created immense real losses, but it also maximized Mr. Fuld's compensation.

> Aurora was originating more than $3 billion a month of such loans in the first half of 2007.
>
> Lehman's real estate businesses helped sales in the capital markets unit jump 56 percent from 2004 to 2006, faster than from investment banking or asset management, the company said in a filing. Lehman reported record earnings in 2005, 2006 and 2007.

http://www.bloomberg.com/apps/news?pid=newsarchive&sid=aVZKah.at5fY
September 15, 2008

2. The role of the SEC as Lehman's primary regulator in oversight, examination and enforcement in advance of Lehman's bankruptcy filing, and the role of the other government agencies, including the Federal Reserve Bank of New York (FRBNY), that were monitoring Lehman during the crisis.

The Consolidated Supervised Entities (CSE) program never made the SEC a real "primary regulator." The SEC is incapable, as constituted, staffed, and led to be a primary regulator of anything – and that includes the rating agencies. "Safety and soundness" regulation is a completely different concept than a "disclosure" regime. The SEC's expertise, which it has allowed to rust away for a decade, is in enforcing disclosure requirements. The SEC did not have the mindset, rules, or appropriate personnel to make the CSE program a success even if the agency had been a "junk yard dog." Given the fact that the SEC was self-neutered by its leadership during the period Lehman was in crisis in 2001-2008, there was no chance that it would succeed. Its only hope was to form an effective partnership with the Fed. The Fed had unique authority under the Home Ownership and Equity Protection Act of 1994 (HOEPA) to regulate all mortgage lenders and had unprecedented practical leverage during the crisis because of its ability to lend and convert investment banks to commercial bank holding companies. The Fed is supposed to be an experienced "safety and soundness" regulator (though I will express doubts that it is effective). An SEC/Fed partnership would at least have some chance. The Valukas report reveals that the FRBNY staff at Lehman recognized that the SEC staff at Lehman's offices were not capable of understanding its financial condition.

One approach that other nations use is to combine the securities and financial regulation functions in a single Financial Services Agency (FSA).

3. The relationship and means of communication, especially formal and informal information sharing, between the SEC and FRBNY as Lehman's financial condition deteriorated as well as between Lehman, the SEC, the Treasury Department, the Board of Governors Federal Reserve, and the FRBNY.

It was a painful, as a former regulator, to read the Valukas report's discussion of the FRBNY staff's open disdain for working cooperatively with the SEC to protect the public. The Valukas report exposes the sick relationship between the country's main regulatory bodies and the systemically dangerous institutions (SDIs) they are supposed to be policing. The FRBNY, led by President Geithner, had a clear statutory mission -- promote the safety and soundness of the banking system and compliance with the law – stood by while Lehman deceived the public through a scheme that FRBNY officials likened to a "three card monte routine" (p. 1470).

> The FRBNY discounted the value of Lehman's pool to account for these collateral transfers. However, the FRBNY did not request that Lehman exclude this collateral from its reported liquidity pool. In the words of one of the FRBNY's on-site monitors: "how Lehman reports its liquidity is between Lehman, the SEC, and the world" (p. 1472).

Translation: The FRBNY knew that Lehman was engaged in fraud designed to overstate its liquidity and, therefore, was unwilling to loan as much money to Lehman. The FRBNY did not, however, inform the SEC, the public, or the OTS (which regulated an S&L that Lehman owned) of the fraud. The Fed official doesn't even make a pretense that the Fed believes it is supposed to protect the public. The FRBNY remained willing to lend to a fraudulent systemically dangerous institution (SDI). This is an egregious violation of the public trust, and the regulatory perpetrators must be held accountable. The Fed wanted to maintain a fiction that toxic mortgage product were simply misunderstood assets, so it allowed Lehman to keep dealing the three card monte scam. We now know from Valukas and from former Treasury Secretary Paulson that the Treasury and the Fed knew that Lehman was massively overstating its on-book asset values: "According to Paulson, Lehman had liquidity problems and no hard assets against which to lend" (p. 1530). We know from Valukas' interview of Geithner (p. 1502):

> The challenge for the Government, and for troubled firms like Lehman, was to reduce risk exposure, and the act of reducing risk by selling assets could result in "collateral damage" by demonstrating weakness and exposing "air" in the marks.

Or, in plain English, the Fed didn't want Lehman and other SDIs to sell their toxic assets because the sales prices would reveal that the values Lehman (and all the other SDIs) placed on their toxic assets (the "marks") were inflated with worthless hot air. Lehman claimed its toxic assets were worth "par" (no losses) (p. 1159), but Citicorp called them "bottom of the barrel" and "junk" (p. 1218). JPMorgan concluded: "the emperor had no clothes" (p. 1140). The FRBNY acted shamefully in covering up Lehman's inflated asset values and liquidity. It constructed three, progressively weaker, stress tests – Lehman failed even the weakest test. The FRBNY then allowed Lehman to administer its own stress test. Surprise, it passed.

The Fed's defense of its disgraceful refusal to protect the public is meritless. It argues that it was not there in its regulatory capacity and that it sent only a few staffers that laced the capacity or the leverage to accomplish any supervisory goals. This is either a deliberate obfuscation or a confession of a core failure. As Senior Vice President and General Counsel of the FHLBSF I was always a regulator – even when I was providing involved in credit-side activities. As a lender, the FHLBSF often learned material information about the institutions we regulated because we engaged in effective underwriting of asset quality. My predecessor famously used the leverage of the FHLBSF as lender of last resort for the largest S&L in America, which was in a liquidity crisis, to force out the fraudulent CEO controlling the institution and to enter into a broad array of steps that greatly reduced the institution's risk exposure and frauds. At its peak, we had roughly 50 FHLBSF credit personnel resident at the S&L. The fact that the FRBNY, which had far more resources than the FHLBSF, chose to send only a token crew to be on-site at a potential global catastrophe is a demonstration of failure, not a valid excuse for their failure to act to protect the public. The FRBNY has vastly greater leverage than the FHLBSF ever had and in the context of the Lehman crisis it had the leverage to force any change it believed was necessary, including an immediate conversion of Lehman to a bank holding company and a commercial bank.

The Fed has inherent problems even in safety & soundness regulation due to its structure. First, the regional FRBs have boards of directors dominated by the industry. Congress already made the policy decision, in removing all regulatory functions from the FHLBs in the 1989 FIRREA legislation, that this is an unacceptable conflict of interest.

Second, supervision is, at best, a tertiary activity at the Fed and regional banks. Monetary policy gets all the emphasis, the credit windows come second, and economic research and safety & soundness regulation vie for a distant third place. (Consumer regulation is a bastard step child at the Fed and most agencies.)

Third, the Fed is far too close to the systemically dangerous institutions. The SDIs are in an ideal position to exploit opportunities for regulatory "capture."

Fourth, the Fed is dominated by neo-classical economists that have no theory of, experience with, or interest in the complex financial frauds that are the dominant cause of our recurring, intensifying financial crises. Bernanke appointed an economist, Patrick Parkinson, with no examination or supervision experience to head all Fed examination and supervision.

Fifth, the Fed is addicted to opaqueness and its senior ranks believe the bankers when they claim that the people must never be allowed to learn the truth about asset losses. One of the conflicts of interest that a banking regulator must never succumb to is the temptation to encourage or allow the regulated entity to lie about its financial condition for the purported purpose of preventing a run on the bank. Geithner, unfortunately, embraced that temptation and stated it openly to the Bankruptcy Examiner. It is very easy, psychologically, to believe that you are letting a bank lie to the public for a noble reason – protecting the public. The bankers always tell the regulators that the world will end if the banks tell the truth – but that is a lie. Regulators' greatest asset is their integrity. I was one of the four FHLBSF regulators that met with the "Keating Five." To this day, I have no idea what political affiliations, if any, my three colleagues hold. We simply insisted on honest disclosures and we always made a referral to our agency to alert the SEC (and the FBI) to any efforts we found to use accounting to deceive the investors or the regulators.

4. Please reflect on the appropriateness of accounting practices such as Repo 105 or 108 and the adequacy of the disclosure of such accounting practices.

The reason accounting approaches are used to attempt to achieve GAAP treatments that are contrary to the true economic substance of the transaction is to deceive. There are no social benefits to such deception and there are enormous harms. At law, the element that distinguishes fraud from other forms of larceny is deceit. Fraudsters get the victim to trust them – then betray that trust in order to cheat them. This is why fraud is the most effective acid for destroying trust. We need trust in most areas of life, including economics and finance. When bankers no longer trust bankers, markets fail rather than "clear." This can cause global contagion. The economic substance, in every case, of Lehman's Repo transactions was a loan, not a true sale. The sole purpose of entering into the transactions was to attempt to achieve an accounting treatment directly contrary to the true nature of the transaction for the purpose of deceiving investors and regulators. If these transactions are not frauds, then accounting and accountancy have ceased to have any value or integrity. It is time for accountants, business people, and regulators to demand an end to the deliberate use of accounting to deceive.

5. The quality of Lehman's Management Discussion and Analysis disclosures in its public filings for the 2007 reporting periods.

Wholly inadequate and deceptive, but may I respectfully suggest that the question needs to be broadened to prior years. Lehman, for example, lumped fraudulent liar's loans in with prime loans and called them all "prime." This is a disgrace and an attempt to deceive. Even after multiple warnings, including the FBI in 2004, about the "epidemic" of mortgage fraud and even after the rare serious internal review was made of Aurora's liar's loan portfolio was made and revealed endemic fraud, Lehman made no meaningful disclosure of the fraud or the fatal consequences of selling fraudulent loans to other parties as a business strategy.

6. Other issues that you deem relevant to the public policy issues raised by the Lehman Report.

Lehman was an international leader in making "Alt a" loans. The trade called alt a loans "liar's loans" for the very good reason that they are liar's loans. The failure of the SEC and Fed to deal effectively with something the trade openly called fraudulent is astonishing. Wherever we have looked we find a staggering incidence of fraud in liar's loans (often 90%). Any lender that made large amounts of liar's loans was guaranteed in the short-term (and the intermediate term given the bubble that liar's loans and subprime caused to hyper-inflate) to report record (albeit fictional) profits. The bubble leads to "refis", which mask the true loss for several years. (They can even lead to "cash out" refis through a second or third liar's loan that makes the borrower deeply underwater on his mortgage but provides him with lots of cash).

We have known for centuries that underwriting home loans is essential to avoid "adverse selection." We have known for centuries that adverse selection (1) is "criminogenic" -- it can produce widespread fraud and (2) has a "negative expected value." To put that in English, it means that, on average, you lose money by making liar's loans. That loss is inherent -- it can be masked for a time by a rapidly inflating bubble (in which case, the loss grows greatly) and it may be passed to others -- but it is inescapeable that someone will bear that loss (successful hedging, for example, simply shifts the loss to another victim). Both "principals" to the "alt a" loan generally suffer severe losses. The borrower is put into a home he cannot afford at a true market value that is significantly smaller than his mortgage. The lender (or whoever bears the loss when the loan defaults) loses. We need not have any sympathy for the fraudulent borrower, but it turns out that the fraudulent loan applications and appraisals were commonly prepared by the lender personnel or their agents. The unfaithful agents gain -- and their gains are large. The SEC's failure to take action against such blatant misrepresentations to shareholders was egregious.) Those purported profits led to very large bonuses (and stock appreciation) for Lehman's senior officers. Given Lehman's origination and sale of enormous amounts of liar's loans, I believe that the data would show that it was largely the fraudulent origination and sale of liar's loans (and mortgage paper backed by such loans) that made Lehman's officers exceptionally wealthy in 2003-2006.

Industry observers began to use the term “epidemic” to describe mortgage fraud as early as 2003. The FBI warned in Congressional testimony in 2004 of an “epidemic” of mortgage fraud. In 2005, observers released a report documenting widesrpead inflated appraisals. No honest secured lender would cause, or permit, widespread inflated appraisals, yet studies of appraisers demonstrate that the intimidation (and reprisals where intimidation failed) of appraisers grew sharply and became endemic after these warnings. The SEC took (1) no effective regulatory action against the securities firms it regulated that originated, sold, and purchased liar's loan product and (2) no effective action against firms that failed to disclose (1) the acute risk of failure that comes from originating, selling, or purchasing liar's loans or (2) the losses from making or purchasing liar’s loans. (It may seem strange to talk of “risk” or “losses” from selling liar's loans, but such sales were typically made with “reps & warranties” and with “put” options where the purchaser had a right to demand that the seller repurchase bad loans. Contrary to the common refrain, the contracts were typically drawn to require that the sellers of nonprime mortgages retain some “skin in the game.”)

The Fed deserves special criticism for its failure to respond to these warnings by taking any effective action to stop liar's loans. The Fed had unique authority under HOEPA to ban liar’s loans, which would have prevented the bubble from hyper-inflating and contained the rapdily growing epidemic of mortgage fraud. Most liar's loans were made by lenders that were not federally insured or regulated, so only the Fed had the power to crack down on all liar's loans. The Fed refused to use its authority under HOEPA (until mid-2008) -- a full year after the secondary market in nonprime loans collapsed. Seven years late and $2.5 trillion short (roughly the amount of nonprime loans).

Criminologists refer to entities that spread fraud epidemics as “vectors” (continuing the public health metaphor, the anopheles mosquito is a “vector” that spreads malaria and can create epidemics). Lehman was one of the largest vectors that spread the fraud epidemic. We must not focus only on what bad assets it held in portfolio at a particular time. If Lehman, for example, had sold more of its “alt a” loans earlier its losses would, of course, have been reduced but system losses on liar’s loans would be unchanged. If Lehman had sold large amounts of "alt a" loans at an earlier date to Fannie and Freddie, for example, it might have caused them to collapse at an earlier date with even greater losses. This might have set off an even worse global crisis. The Fed, due to its unique HOEPA authority, and the SEC, because it has jurisdiction over every publicly traded company, were the only entities that could have shut down the vectors spreading the fraud epidemic. This should have been there most important priority. They had ample warnings of the epidemic of liar's loans and the fact that it was spreading rapidly. Lehman, Citi, WaMu, Indymac, and Bear Stearns were on everyone's list of the worst vectors, yet the Fed and the SEC took no effective action until after virtually every major originator of liar's loans had failed. It would be as if the Public Health Service waited to start killing mosquitoes until 2.5 million Americans had died of malaria over the course of a decade.

It is critical to understand that making liar's loans required multiple frauds by multiple parties. Because liar's loans create an intensely criminogenic environment, they produce fraud epidemics. Because liar's loans also create severe adverse selection, they inherently have a negative expected value. It's easy to put that in English. When Aurora (Lehman's firm that specialized in making liar's loans) made a $400,000 liar's loans they created annual (fictional) accounting income of perhaps $50,000. They also created a real loss of $200,000 - $300,000. If Lehman sold the $400,000 liar's loan to another company for $410,000, Lehman created a (real -- but likely fraudulent) gain of $10,000. This, however, simply increased the purchaser's eventual loss to $210,000 - $310,000. Whatever entity purchased the liar's loan (directly or via a CDO) owned an asset with massive real losses (50% - 85%). Assume a realistic hypothetical. Fannie purchases $60 billion in liar's loan paper from Lehman. The liar's loans are really worth $20 billion, so Fannie has just suffered a real $40 billion loss. Ask yourself: will Fannie's senior officers recognize this loss? If they do, Fannie will report that it is massively unprofitable and insolvent. The senior officers will not get their bonuses and will almost certainly be fired. Not a hard decision for Fannie's senior leadership.

Similarly, the typical Fannie purchase requires "reps and warranties" from the seller that the assets it is selling conform to higher underwriting and credit quality standards. (See Mr. Bowen's (Citi) testimony before FCIC.) Will Lehman senior managers disclose to Fannie's senior managers that the liar's loans do not conform? If they do, the deal likely dies. The typical Fannie purchase allows Fannie to "put" bad loans back to the seller. Will Fannie senior managers, once it is "pregnant" with a portfolio filled with scores of billions of dollars of nonprime loans, choose to "put" $60 billion in liar's loan paper to Lehman in, say, June 2008? If Fannie's senior managers do so they (1) will cause Lehman to collapse and (2) will violate the key "don't ask, don't tell" rule that governed nonprime mortgages. If Fannie exercises the "put" it will be announcing to the world that (1) fraud is pervasive in liar's loans, (2) Lehman sold fraudulent liar's loans to a large number of financial firms at grossly inflated prices -- and those firms have not recognized their losses, and (3) Fannie (and presumably Freddie and other investment bankers and end purchasers) are all likely to start exercising their "put" options on liar's loan paper issues by entities other than Lehman. The (previously grossly inflated) price of liar's loans will promptly collapse to the real value (which is only 15 - 50 cents on the dollar). Among the entities that will have to report that they are massively insolvent are Fannie and Freddie. Which is to say, Fannie was not about to exercise its put on any really large block of liar's loans.

Yes, Lehman went down in a liquidity crisis, but that crisis was caused overwhelmingly by its bad assets (leverage, of course, magnifies gains and losses in asset values). Lehman's fundamental problem was that it was insolvent and unprofitable. The operations that produced much of its fictional income produced these real losses. It could not sell enough assets to solve its liquidity problems because its assets were so bad that it would have to recognize fatal levels of losses on such sales. It could not sell enough equity (which also gives cash) to deal with its liquidity problems because everyone knew it was in desperate shape and had to (honest) means of making sufficient earnings to dig itself out of the hole. It could not find an acquirer for the same reason. Potential equity investors and acquirers could see by late 2008 that the music had stopped. House prices began to decline in late 2006. Most uninsured nonprime speciality lenders collapsed in 2007 or early 2008. The secondary market in nonprime paper collapsed in March 2007 (and there were no signs it would be recreated). Fitch (finally) went public in November 2006 with its study of CDOs backed by nonprime mortgages which found evidence of fraud in nearly every loan. Recall the repeated private efforts to create an industry fund to purchase (and hold at their inflated prices) nonprime paper -- it raised exactly $0. Bankers no longer trusted other bankers' asset valuations, which shut down a series of markets.

The relevant issue was never: can Lehman be saved? The relevant issue, one that the SEC and the Fed appear never to have even asked, was: how can we stop Lehman from serving as a vector spreading the epidemic of liar's loans? They should have asked themselves that question – and acted -- no later than 2001. We (OTS) acted in 1991 to contain a growing problem in nonprime lending because we understood adverse selection and its role in causing fraud and negative expected value. The Fed and the SEC, therefore, had the duty, the power, the background in economics, and the example of our successful regulatory intervention that prevented an earlier nonprime crisis -- all of which should have made it far easier for them to contain the crisis. Unlike 1991, when we acted to prevent a nonprime crisis, the loans that the current "alt a" lenders made were openly called "liar's loans" by the trade. How difficult was it for the SEC and the Fed to figure out that we should end "liar's loans"? Even it you assume that the SEC and the Fed were so committed to the mantra that regulation is the source of all evil, they have no excuse for their failure to respond effectively in 2004 when the FBI warned them that the "epidemic" of mortgage fraud would cause a crisis if it were not contained. The SEC and the Fed had the unique authority to contain the crisis. They failed to do so.

Mortgage Fraud became Endemic

Roughly 40% of U.S. mortgage lending during 2006 was nonprime, evenly split between subprime (known credit defects) and "alt-a" (purportedly high credit quality, but lacking verification of key underwriting data). "Alt-a" loans, by definition, did not conduct traditional underwriting (Bloomberg 2007; Gimein 2008). Almost half of subprime loans, by 2006, did not conduct traditional underwriting. Nearly 30% of total mortgage lending in 2006 lacked traditional underwriting. A small sample review of nonprime loan files by Fitch (2007), found that underwriting had to be eviscerated to permit the endemic fraud that came to characterize nonprime mortgage lending.

> Fitch's analysts conducted an independent analysis of these files with the benefit of the full origination and servicing files. The result of the analysis was disconcerting at best, as there was the appearance of fraud or misrepresentation in almost every file.

> [F]raud was not only present, but, in most cases, could have been identified with adequate underwriting, quality control and fraud prevention tools prior to the loan funding. Fitch believes that this targeted sampling of files was sufficient to determine that inadequate underwriting controls and, therefore, fraud is a factor in the defaults and losses on recent vintage pools.

MARI, the Mortgage Bankers Association (MBA's) experts on fraud, warned that "low doc" lending caused endemic fraud.

> Stated income and reduced documentation loans … are open invitations to fraudsters. It appears that many members of the industry have little historical appreciation for the havoc created by low-doc/no-doc products that were the rage in the early 1990s. Those loans produced hundreds of millions of dollars in losses for their users.
>
> One of MARI's customers recently reviewed a sample of 100 stated income loans upon which they had IRS Forms 4506. When the stated incomes were compared to the IRS figures, the resulting differences were dramatic. Ninety percent of the stated incomes were exaggerated by 5% or more. More disturbingly, almost 60% of the stated amounts were exaggerated by more than 50%. These results suggest that the stated income loan deserves the nickname used by many in the industry, the "liar's loan."

The same obvious question (which neither Fitch nor MARI asked) arises: why did lenders fail to use well understood underwriting systems that are highly successful in preventing fraud – even when they knew that fraud was endemic and would cause massive losses? The same obvious answer exists – it was in the interests of the controlling officers to optimize short-term accounting income. Turning a blind eye to endemic fraud helped optimize reported income and their executive compensation.

MARI's reference to the "early 1990s" refers to a number of S&Ls that originated or purchased "low doc" loans in the early 1990s. These loans caused "hundreds of millions of dollars in losses." Those losses were contained because the regulators promptly used their supervisory powers to halt the practice when they realized that it was growing and becoming material. We acted because we recognized that not underwriting maximized adverse selection and guaranteed high real losses (after near-term, fictional, profits). We ordered a halt to the practice even while many of the lenders were reporting that the lending was profitable. "Hundreds of millions of dollars in losses" is serious, but if the losses are contained at that level the number of lender failures will be minimal and there will be no risk of a crisis. Unfortunately, our regulatory successors had no "historical appreciation" for successful supervisory policies or the identification of accounting control fraud. They issued ineffective "cautions" to the industry that "low doc" loans could be risky, but refused to order an end to the practice and never considered the possibility that the lenders were control frauds.

Thomas J. Miller, Attorney General of Iowa, testimony at a 2007 Federal Reserve Board hearing shows why fraud losses are enormous:

> Over the last several years, the subprime market has created a race to the bottom in which unethical actors have been handsomely rewarded for their misdeeds and ethical actors have lost market share…. The market incentives rewarded irresponsible lending and made it more difficult for responsible lenders to compete. Strong regulations will create an even playing field in which ethical actors are no longer punished.

> Despite the well documented performance struggles of 2006 vintage loans, originators continued to use products with the same characteristics in 2007.
>
> [M]any originators … invent … non-existent occupations or income sources, or simply inflat[e] income totals to support loan applications.
>
> Importantly, our investigations have found that most stated income fraud occurs at the suggestion and direction of the loan originator, not the consumer.

These risks were "layered" – interacting to produce far greater risk (IMF 2008: 4-5 & n.6). Honest nonprime lenders would have responded by establishing record high general loss reserves in accordance with generally accepted accounting principles (GAAP). Instead, A.M. Best reported in February 2006 that: "the industry's reserves-to-loan ratio has been setting new record lows for the past four years" (A.M. Best 2006: 3). The ratio fell to 1.21 percent as of September 30, 2005 (*Id.*: 4-5). One year later, A.M. Best reported: "loan loss reserves are down to levels not seen since 1985" (roughly one percent) (A.M. Best 2007: 1). A.M. Best went on to point out that these grossly inadequate loss reserves in 1985 led to a decade-long crisis in banking and S&Ls. In 2009, IMF estimated losses on U.S. originated assets of $2.7 trillion (IMF 2009: 35 Table 1.3). Total U.S. bank and S&L general loss reserves in 2006 were under $100 billion, so general loss reserves would have had to be roughly 30 times larger to be adequate. If the lenders had established adequate loss reserves they would have reported that they were deeply unprofitable, which was the economic reality. The banking regulatory agencies, the SEC, and "private market discipline" all failed to require even remotely adequate reserves and minimal honesty in financial reports. The current control frauds used the same optimization techniques as did the S&Ls – but they did it on steroids. The primary epidemic directly created the upstream epidemic and was a necessary, but not sufficient, cause of the upstream epidemic.

If You Don't Investigate, You Won't Find

Criminologists and financial regulators have long warned that the failure to regulate the financial sphere *de facto* decriminalizes control fraud in the industry. The FBI cannot investigate effectively more than a small number of the massive accounting control frauds. Only the regulators can have the expertise, staff, and knowledge to identify on a timely basis the markers of accounting control fraud, to prepare the detailed criminal referrals essential to serve as a roadmap for the FBI, and to "detail" (second) staff to work for the FBI and serve as their "Sherpas" during the investigation.

The agency regulating S&Ls made criminal prosecution a top priority. The result was over 1000 priority felony convictions of senior insiders and their co-conspirators. That is the most successful effort against elite white-collar criminals. The agency also brought over 1000 administrative enforcement actions and hundreds of civil lawsuits against the elite frauds. One result of this was an extensive, public record of fact that fraud was "invariably present" at the "typical large failure" (NCFIRRE 1993). The Enron-era frauds were accounting control frauds and while the effort against them was too late and weaker than the effort against the S&L frauds it involved scores of prosecutions and provided substantial public documentation.

The FBI, however, after a brilliant start in identifying the epidemic of mortgage fraud, went tragically astray and its efforts to contain the epidemic failed. The FBI suffered from a horrific systems capacity problem. It did not have the agents or expertise to deal with the concurrent control fraud epidemics it faced this decade. Its systems capacity problems became crippling when 500 white-collar specialists were transferred to national security investigations in response to the 9/11 attacks and the administration refused to allow the FBI to hire new agents to replace the lost white-collar specialists.

The most crippling limitation on the regulators', FBI's, and DOJ's efforts to contain the epidemic of mortgage fraud and the financial crisis was not understanding of the cause of the epidemic and why it would cause a catastrophic financial crisis. The mortgage banking industry controlled the framing of the issue of mortgage fraud. That industry represents the lenders that caused the epidemic of mortgage fraud. The industry's trade association is the Mortgage Bankers Association (MBA). The MBA followed the obvious strategy of portraying its members as the victims of mortgage fraud. What it never discussed was that the officers that controlled its members were the primary beneficiaries of mortgage fraud. It is the trade association of the "perps." The MBA claimed that all mortgage fraud was divided into two categories – neither of which included accounting control fraud. The FBI, driven by acute systems incapacity, formed a "partnership" with the MBA and adopted the MBA's (facially absurd) two-part classification of mortgage fraud (FBI 2007). The result is that there has not been a single arrest, indictment, or conviction of a senior official of a nonprime lender for accounting fraud.

One of the most dramatic, and unfortunate differences between the S&L debacle and the current crisis is that the financial regulatory agencies gave the FBI no help in this crisis – even after it warned of the epidemic of mortgage fraud. The FBI does not mention the agencies in its list of sources of criminal referrals for mortgage fraud. The data on criminal referrals for mortgage fraud show that regulated financial institutions, which are required to file criminal referrals when they find "suspicious activity" indicating mortgage fraud, typically fail to do so. There is no evidence that the agencies responsible for enforcing the requirement file criminal referrals have taken any action to crack down on the widespread violations.

The crippling mischaracterization of the nature of the mortgage fraud epidemic came from the top, as the *New York Times* reported in late 2008.

> But Attorney General Michael B. Mukasey has rejected calls for the Justice Department to create the type of national task force that it did in 2002 to respond to the collapse of Enron.
>
> Mr. Mukasey said in June that the mortgage crisis was a different "type of phenomena" that was a more localized problem akin to "white-collar street crime."

The nation's top law enforcement official swallowed the MBA's mischaracterization of the mortgage fraud epidemic and economic crisis hook, line, sinker, bobber, rod, reel, and boat they rowed out into the swamp. Because Mukasey refused to investigate the elite frauds he created a self-fulfilling prophecy in which the FBI and DOJ pursued only the "white-collar street crim[inals]" (the small fry) and therefore confirmed that the problem was the small fry. The pursuit of the small fry was certain to fail.

The MBA's success in causing the FBI to ignore the control frauds reminds me of this passage in the original *Star Wars* movie where Obi-Wan uses Jedi powers to pass through an Imperial check point with two wanted droids in plain sight:

Stormtrooper: Let me see your identification.
Obi-Wan : [*with a small wave of his hand*] You don't need to see his identification.
Stormtrooper: We don't need to see his identification.
Obi-Wan : These aren't the droids you're looking for.
Stormtrooper: These aren't the droids we're looking for.
Obi-Wan : He can go about his business.
Stormtrooper: You can go about your business.
Obi-Wan : Move along.
Stormtrooper: Move along... move along.
Luke : I don't understand how we got by those troops. I thought we were dead.
Obi-Wan : The Force can have a strong influence on the weak-minded.

The FBI isn't supposed to be "weak-minded" about elite white-collar criminals. It is not supposed to be misled by "Jedi mind tricks" by the lobbyists for the "perps." It is not supposed to fail to understand the importance of endemic markers of accounting control fraud at every nonprime specialty lender where even a preliminary investigation has been made public.

The FBI, DOJ, banking regulators, SEC, and all the purported sources of "private market discipline" failed to act against (and even praised) the *perverse incentive structures* that the accounting control frauds created to cause the small fry to act fraudulently. Those incentive structures ensured that there were always far more new small fry hatched to replace the relatively few small fry that the DOJ could imprison. Accounting control frauds deliberately produce intensely criminogenic environments to recruit (typically without any need for a formal conspiracy) the fraud allies that optimize accounting fraud. They create the perverse Gresham's dynamic that means that the cheats prosper at the expense of their honest competitors. The result can be that the unethical drive the ethical from the marketplace. Had Mukasey been aware of modern white-collar criminological research he would have been forced to ask why tens of thousands of small fry were able to cause an epidemic of mortgage fraud in an industry that had historically successfully held fraud losses to well under one percent of assets. Ignoring good theory produces bad criminal justice policies.

The Size of the Mortgage Fraud Epidemic Swamps the FBI

The size of the current financial crisis and the incidence of fraud in the current crisis vastly exceed the S&L debacle. The FBI testified that it "increased the number of agents around the country who investigate mortgage fraud cases from 120 Special Agents in FY 2007 to 180 Special Agents in FY 2008…." Its testimony noted that it employed "1000 FBI agents and forensic experts" against the S&L frauds (Pistole 2009). It received over 63,000 criminal referrals for mortgage fraud in the last year for which it has full data (a figure that has risen substantially every year). The FBI, therefore, can investigate only a tiny percentage of criminal referrals for mortgage fraud. The FBI reports that 80% of mortgage fraud losses occur when "industry insiders" are involved in the fraud (FBI 2007).

Only federally insured banks and S&Ls are required to file criminal referrals. Non-insured lenders made 80% of nonprime mortgage loans (subprime and "alt-a"), and the made the worst nonprime loans that most invited fraud. These lenders can make criminal referrals and it would be in the interests of honest lenders to do so, but they rarely do. That means that the first approximation of the true annual incidence of mortgage fraud would be to multiply 63,000 by five (315,000). That extrapolation, however, would only be sound if (A) insured lenders spotted all mortgage fraud and (B) filed criminal referrals when they spotted likely frauds. The FBI believes that insured entities identify mortgage frauds prior to lending in about 20% on "no doc" loans (known in the trade as "liar's loans") (*New York Times,* April 6, 2008). Multiplying 315,000 by five produces a product of over 1.5 million.

The data on referrals show that the typical insured lender rarely files when it finds mortgage fraud. The October 2009 FinCEN report on criminal referrals for mortgage fraud (in jargon, Suspicious Activity Reports (SARs) found:

> In the first half of 2009, approximately 735 financial institutions submitted SARs, or about 50 more filers compared to the same period in 2008. The top 50 filers submitted 93 percent of all [mortgage fraud] SARs, consistent with the same 2008 filing period. However, SARs submitted by the top 10 filers increased from 64 percent to 72 percent.

Only a small percentage of mortgage lenders, 75 in total (roughly 10% of federally-insured mortgage lenders), filed even a single criminal referral for mortgage fraud during a mortgage fraud epidemic. Of the 735 that make at least one filing, fewer than 200 file more than four referrals. A mere ten filers provide the FBI with almost three-quarters of all SARs mortgage fraud filings. We cannot form an appropriate estimate of the degree of under-filing of criminal referrals when insured banks find fraud, but we can infer that the failure to file is pervasive. The logical explanation for the widespread failure of lenders to file criminal referrals when they discover mortgage frauds is that they fear that if they file FBI would come to the lender and discover its complicity in the fraud.

To sum it up, in FY 2007 the FBI has had less than one-eighth of the resources it had to investigate the S&L frauds despite the fact that the current crisis is perhaps 30 times worse than the S&L debacle. It was facing well over a million mortgage frauds annually. It could investigate under 1000 cases per year. If every investigation was successful the FBI would be completely ineffective in preventing or even slowing materially the epidemic of mortgage fraud. Mukasey's strategy of going after the small fry gave the control frauds a free pass and had to fail to deter the small fry. Representative Kaptur's bill to fund the FBI's replacement of the reassigned agents is a necessary step that I hope will gain bipartisan support.

WHAT IF WE HAD LOOKED?

Within the last month, facts have been revealed about four massive nonprime players that show the strong evidence of elite criminality that would have been revealed – in some cases, five years ago – had there been real investigations. In addition to Lehman, there have been recent disclosures on:

WaMu

Members interested in reading the Senate Banking Committee report and the underlying documents can find them through this link:

http://levin.senate.gov/newsroom/release.cfm?id=323765

Citicorp

The full prepared statement of Mr. Richard Bowen, Former Senior Vice President and Business Chief Underwriter of CitiMortgage Inc. before the Financial Crisis Inquiry Commission on April 7, 2020 can be found here:

http://www.fcic.gov/hearings/04-07-2010.php

Mr. Bowen's testimony received far less attention because he testified on the same day as Alan Greenspan and Citi's former top officials. This is unfortunate because he was far more candid about Citi's operations than were its former senior officials. Mr. Bowen disclosed that Citi was also a massive vector, selling roughly $50 billion annually in mostly bad mortgages (primarily to Fannie and Freddie).

> The delegated flow channel purchased approximately $50 billion of prime mortgages annually. These mortgages were not underwriten by us before they were purchased. My Quality Assurance area was responsible for underwriting a small sample of the files post-purchase to ensure credit quality was maintained.
>
> These mortgages were sold to Fannie Mae, Freddie Mac and other investors. Although we did not underwrite these mortgages, Citi did rep and warrant to the investors that the mortgages were underwritten to Citi credit guidelines.
>
> In mid-2006 I discovered that over 60% of these mortgages purchased and sold were defective. Because Citi had given reps and warrants to the investors that the mortgages were not defective, the investors could force Citi to repurchase many billions of dollars of these defective assets. This situation represented a large potential risk to the shareholders of Citigroup. I started issuing warnings in June of 2006 and attempted to get management to address these critical risk issues. These warnings continued through 2007 and went to all levels of the Consumer Lending Group. We continued to purchase and sell to investors even larger volumes of mortgages through 2007. And defective mortgages increased during 2007 to over 80% of production.

Goldman Sachs

The SEC charges that Goldman Sachs should be added to the list of elite financial frauds.

References and Suggested Readings

[1] Akerlof, George A. (1970). "The Market for 'Lemons': Quality Uncertainty and the Market Mechanism". *Quarterly Journal of Economics, 84* (3), pp. 488–500.

[2] Akerlof, G. & Romer P. (1993). Looting: The Economic Underworld of Bankruptcy for Profit, in: Brainard, W., Perry, G. (Eds.), *Brookings Papers on Economic Activity, 2*, 1-73.

[3] A.M. Best. February (2006). "U.S. Banking Trends for 2005 – Signaling End of Peak Industry Cycle." www.ambest.com/banks/reports/ambest-bankingtrends2005.pdf

[4] Becker, G. (1968). "Crime and Punishment: An Economic Approach". *The Journal of Political Economy, 76*, 169-217.

[5] Black, W. (2000). Control Fraud and Control Freaks. In: *Contemporary Issues in Crime and Criminal Justice*, Pontell, H., Shichor, D. (Eds.). Prentice Hall, Saddle River, N.J., 67-80.

[6] Black, W., (2003). Reexamining the Law-and-Economics Theory of Corporate Governance. *Challenge 46*, No. 2 March/April, 22-40.

[7] Black, W., (2005). *The Best Way to Rob a Bank is to Own One: How Corporate Executives and Politicians Looted the S&L Industry.* University of Texas, Austin.

[8] Black, W., Calavita, K. & Pontell, H. (1995). The Savings and Loan Debacle of the 1980s: White-Collar Crime or Risky Business? *Law and Policy*, 23-55.

[9] *BusinessWeek.* May 19, (2003). "Getting Money to Where it Hasn't Gone." http://www.businessweek.com/magazine/content/ 03_20/ b3833125_mz020.htm

[10] Calavita, K., Pontell, H. & Tillman, R. (1997). *Big Money Crime.* University of California Press, Berkeley.

[11] "FBI warns of mortgage fraud 'epidemic': Seeks to head off 'next S&L crisis"'CNN, Sept. 17, 2004.

[12] Cutter, B. November 24, (2009). "Keep Tim Geithner." http://www.new deal20.org/?p=6569

[13] Easterbrook, F. & Fischel, D. (1991). *The Economic Structure of Corporate Law.* Harvard University Press, Cambridge, Mass.

[14] Financial Crimes Enforcement Network (FinCEN). October (2009). "The SAR Activity Review." http://www.fincen.gov/news_room/rp/ files/sar_tti_16.pdf

[15] Gormley, Michael. November 1, (2007). "Cuomo: Appraisers pressured to inflate subprime mortgage values." http://seattletimes.nwsource.com/html/business technology /2003987769_webwamu01.html

[16] Harney, Kenneth R. February 3, (2007). "Appraisers Under Pressure to Inflate Values." http://www.washingtonpost.com/wp-dyn/content/article/ 2007/02/02/AR2007020200712.html

[17] Ip, Greg & Damiam Paletta. "Regulators Scrutinized In Mortgage Meltdown." March 22, 2007. *The Wall Street Journal Online*

[18] MARI. (2007). "Mortgage Fraud: Strengthening Federal and State Mortgage Fraud Prevention Efforts" (2007). Tenth Periodic Case Report to the Mortgage Bankers Association.

[19] Mortgage Bankers Association. October (2007). "Policy Position: The Importance of Accurate Appraisals Performed by Independent Appraisers." http://www.mbaa.org/ Advocacy/IssuePapers/ Independent Appraisers.htm

[20] Morgenson, Gretchen. April 6, (2008). "Fair Game: A Road Not Taken by Lenders." http://www.nytimes.com/2008/04/06/business/06gret.html? scp=2&sq=mortgage+fraud&st=nyt

[21] National Commission on Financial Institution Reform, Recovery and Enforcement (NCFIRRE), (1993). Origins and Causes of the S&L Debacle: A Blueprint for Reform. A Report to the President and Congress of the United States. Government Printing Office, Washington, D.C.

[22] Pierce, J., (2004). *Causes of the S&L Debacle.* Unpublished paper presented at the annual meeting of the Allied Social Sciences Association. On file with author.

[23] Pistole, John. February 11, (2009). *Testimony before the United States Senate Committee on the Judiciary.* "The Need for Increased Fraud Enforcement in the Wake of the Economic Downturn."

[24] Pummer, Chris. April 24, (2007). "Real-Estate Appraisers Feel Pressure to Inflate Home Values." In *Market Watch.*

[25] http://www.realestatejournal.com/buysell/markettrends/20070424-pummer.html

[26] E-mail from Frank Raiter to Richard Gugliada et al., March 20, 2001 http://oversight.house.gov/story.asp?ID=2250

[27] Wheeler, S. & Rothman, M. (1982). The Organization as Weapon in White Collar Crime. *Michigan Law Review* 80, No. 7: 1403-1426.

End Notes

[1] http://www.denverpost.com/headlines/ci_10473057 "Local Lehman arm led in Alt-A loans." **By Greg Griffin *The Denver Post*.** Posted: 09/16/2008 12:30:00 AM MDT

[2] E-mail from Frank Raiter to Richard Gugliada et al., March 20, 2001 http://oversight.house.gov/story.asp?ID=2250

[3] http://www.foxbusiness.com/story/markets/al-lewis-privacy-policy-hides-mortgage-fraud/ (December 31, 2009).

In: The Lehman Brothers Bankruptcy: Analyses
Editors: Gary E. Walker and Lindel D. Clarke
ISBN: 978-1-62081-730-8

Chapter 14

STATEMENT OF MATTHEW LEE. HEARING ON "PUBLIC POLICY ISSUES RAISED BY THE REPORT OF THE LEHMAN BANKRUPTCY EXAMINER"*

Chairman Frank, Ranking Member Bachus, and Members of the Committee:

Thank you for the Committee's invitation to appear here today. As you may know, I was employed by Lehman Brothers for 14 years, ultimately as Senior Vice President, Global Financial Control. In 2008, I identified several accounting and corporate governance issues that caused me considerable and growing concern both from an accounting and a corporate governance perspective. On multiple occasions, I attempted to bring these issues to the attention of Lehman Brothers' executive management, and on one occasion to the attention of Lehman's outside auditors. Within days of first raising issues, I was terminated.

I was born, raised and educated in the United Kingdom, and I am an adopted citizen of the United States. I received a Bachelor of Commerce degree (1981), and a Master of Arts (Honors) degree in Economics (1976), both from the University of Edinburgh, Scotland. In the field of accounting, I am a member of the Institute of Chartered Accountants of Scotland, an Associate of the Institute of Cost and Management Accountants, and a Certified Public Accountant registered in the State of New York.

In 1977, I joined the London office of Arthur Young, McClelland, Moores & Co as an auditor. In 1981, I transferred to the New York office of Arthur Young & Company, which later became Ernst & Young. I specialized in auditing financial services clients and I was eventually promoted to the position of Principal, as a global technical expert in Financing Products, International Securities and Trust Banking. In that capacity, I was asked to identify potential client accounting control issues, bring them to the attention of client management, and to assist our clients in resolving them.

In 1994, Lehman Brothers recruited me to work as the Global Product Controller of its Equity Finance Division. I learned that Lehman had sought me out based on my reputation as an auditor with a keen ability to identify and resolve complex internal accounting control issues. In 2005, I was promoted to Senior Vice President, Global Financial Control, head of consolidated legal entities and consolidated and unconsolidated daily and monthly balance

* This is an edited, reformatted and augmented version of the remarks given on April 20, 2010 before the House Financial Services Committee.

sheets. In that capacity, I oversaw Lehman's global balance sheet production, and supervised approximately 150 employees worldwide. During the last year of my employment, I reported directly to Martin Kelly, Managing Director & Global Financial Controller.

During my fourteen years working at Lehman, I periodically identified problematic issues with Lehman's internal accounting control practices, including the validity of the assets and liabilities represented on Lehman's balance sheets. I typically reported my findings to management orally, and in my experience my concerns were usually addressed and appropriately resolved. Over the course of my employment, I received positive performance evaluations, as well as promotion in title and responsibilities, and I was compensated commensurate with my positions and duties.

During late 2007 and early 2008, several accounting control issues (some longstanding, others new) that I believed were material to Lehman's financial condition, were causing me increasing concern, including Lehman's use of so-called "Repo 105" transactions to temporarily remove debt and assets from its balance sheet, evidently to coincide with public financial reporting dates. These issues were discussed on numerous occasions among my peers, most of whom shared my concerns; these discussions often included my direct supervisor, Martin Kelly. However, I became increasingly concerned that management was not responding to these concerns and that indeed the problems were getting worse.

On May 16, 2008, I sent a letter raising certain of these accounting and balance sheet issues — essentially, those which were most directly within my scope of responsibility -- to the senior financial management of Lehman, which included the Global Financial Controller (Martin Kelly), the Head of Capital Markets Product Control (Gerard Reilly), and the Chief Financial Officer (Erin Callan). Because I felt that these issues created operational risk for Lehman, I also sent the letter to the Chief Risk Officer (Christopher J. O'Meara). Subsequently, I prepared another writing addressing additional accounting-control issues of significant concern existing outside my immediate scope of responsibility, including the "Repo 105" transactions. That communication was sent to Jack Johnson, a Managing Director in Lehman corporate compliance. In both communications, I outlined what I believed to be the critical issues, as was my obligation as an employee of Lehman and consistent with Lehman's Code of Ethics.

Shortly after sending my first letter, I was interviewed by Joseph Polizzotto, Lehman's General Counsel, and Elizabeth Rudofker, Head of Corporate Audit. On May 22, 2008, the day after that interview, I was terminated without warning. Approximately two weeks after my termination, notably *after* I had communicated additional concerns including Repo 105, I was interviewed by Ernst & Young auditors. I later learned that in July 2008, a detailed presentation regarding issues I had raised was made to the Audit Committee of Lehman's Board of Directors, (Examiner's Report at p. 960) but I was not informed of the presentation nor asked to participate. Subsequently, associates of Mr. Valukas, Lehman's bankruptcy examiner, interviewed me. I cooperated fully with each and every one of these inquiries, both internal and external.

Based on what I observed during my employment, I believe that there were serious, material accounting control and corporate governance issues at Lehman. I am here today to answer any questions that the committee may have regarding those issues.

INDEX

C

D

G

H

I

J

K

L

M

N

O

P

Q

R

S

T

U

V

W

Y